AF661602

SHĪ'ĪSM:
Identity, Scholars, Education and Culture

SHĪ'ĪSM
Identity, Scholars, Education and Culture

Syed Najmul Raza Rizvi

With Foreword
Prof. N.R. Farooqi

ANAMIKA PUBLISHERS & DISTRIBUTORS (P) LTD.
4697/3, 21A, Ansari Road, Daryaganj, New Delhi 110 002
Phones: 011-2328 1655, 011-43708938
E-mail: anamikapublishers@yahoo.co.in

First Published 2022
Reprinted 2023
© Syed Najmul Raza Rizvi
ISBN 978-93-91524-70-8

PRINTED IN INDIA

Published by Anamika Publishers & Distributors (P) Ltd., 4697/3, 21A, Ansari Road, Daryaganj, New Delhi 110 002. Typeset by Shivani Compuers, Delhi 110093 and Printed at Vikas Computer & Printers, Tronica City, Ghazāiabad

DEDICATED

TO

MY PARENTS

Bismillah Begum and Abul Hashim

AND

MY WIFE

Yasmin Fatima Rizvi

(Who are no more in this world)

CONTENTS

Acknowledgement

This book is a collection of my revised and new aricles, that were published in separate journals, Proceedings of Indian History Congress and edited books. Few years back, my friend Professor S.Z.H. Jafri (University of Delhi) suggested me to compile these articles and give them a shape of a book. But at that time, all the articles were not enough for a book. Therefore, I revised all the previous articles, added many new aspects and wrote a new article also, so a book can be justified. Finally, the purpose is accomplished. Therefore, I am thankful to him for the idea.

I express my gratitude to my friend and learned scholar Professor N.R. Farooqi, the former Vice-chancellor of Central University of Allahabad and a renowned historian of Medieval India, who, at my request graciously agreed to write the Foreword of this book. Professor Farooqi have good command on the Arabic, Persian and Turkish languages. He did his Doctorate on 'Mughal-Ottoman Relations' from the University of Wisconsin, Madison, United States. His 'Foreword' is significant as it covers many untouched aspects of the book.

In my project, I have benefited from the assistance extended to me by many well-wishers. First of all, I would like to thank Dr. Manisha Choudhary, Assistant Professor, Department of History, Delhi University, Delhi,who provided me many books during the Corona epidemic, to re-check the references and also electronic copies of my previous articles to revise them. It was not possible without her help to complete the project, as I was in Delhi and could not travel to Gorakhpur to access my research materials and personal library. Also, in the list is, Syed Iqbal Murtaza Rizvi (Shārib), my brother-in law, who provided me rare books for writing the first article. Mr. Sharib informed me about many traditions of Lucknow related to Muharram. Therefore, I thank him for his assistance. Thanks goes to Pratap Gopendra Yadav (I.P.S. and author of *Azamgarh: Itihas ke aaine mein*) also, who suggested me to go through the article, entitled "Zila Azamgarh mein Azādārī ki Rawāyat"written by Dr. Alauddin Khan of Shibli P.G. College, Azamgarh. This article proved very informative. I am thankful to Dr. Khan for providing me the copy of his article within few hours of my request.

Members of Shi'a community also took interest in this project and encouraged me in many ways. Syed Alamdar Husayn Rizvi took keen interest in the progress of writing. Mirza Ali Abbas (Khadim Qadā, Gorakhpur) provided me many photographs of Muharram at Gorakhpur. Agha Ali Mohammad and many others also provided me the minute informations about the Muharram of Gorakhpur. I express my gratitude to all of them.

My friends and students were the source of inspiration for this project. They regularly encouraged me to complete the writing and to publish it soon. Among them Dr. Mahendra Pratap (Varanasi), Dr. O.N. Upadhyay (Jaunpur), Dr. Mohammad Arshad (Delhi), Dr. Ram Pratap (Gorakhpur), Dr. Ram Bilas Bharti (Mau) and Dr. Mohd. Arif (Varanasi) are mentionable. Therefore, I heartily thank them.

I received utmost cooperation from my family members also. My eldest son Syed Mehdi Raza and his wife Meraj Fatima took care of all my needs and comfort. My other sons, Syed Mohd. Raza and Syed Abbas Raza Rizvi, my daughter-in-laws--Dr.Tamhid Fatima and Sabiha Kazim and my grand daughter Zainab Raza from United States gave me the moral support to achieve the target. My grandsons Ayaan Mehdi and Ruhaan Mehdi, the new member of the family, provided me a pleasant atmosphere at home to work.

So, I never felt tired or bored. Therefore, I give all my blessings to them.

At the end, I would like to remember my revered teachers, Professor (Late) Radhe Shyam and Professor (Late) Hari Shankar Srivastava. They both made me capable of writing and contributing to the subject. On this occasion, I would also like to remember my colleague, late Professor Poonam Pant, who was the co-author with me in one article entitled, "Nauroz". Peace be upon her soul.

Syed Najmul Raza Rizvi
(Retired) Professor and Former Head
Department of History
D.D.U. Gorakhpur University, Gorakhpur
rizvisnr65@gmail.com

Foreword

History is a complex discipline and History writing is a difficult and time-consuming task. It requires mastery over facts, the will and courage to face the facts that do not support the thinking/ideology of the historian, the skill to analyse the facts in an objective and impassioned manner, the knowledge of the sources required for writing the history of a particular age/event and last but not in the least the command over the language/languages of the sources. Every Tom, Dick and Harry cannot therefore claim to be the practitioner of the historian's craft. The current trend of journalists and politicians, masquerading as historian, does not augur well for the discipline of history. The propensity of these so-called historians to distort the facts of history to serve the narrow political end of the party or profession they represent, is equally harmful for the discipline as a whole. For facts of history will always remain intact and the truth representing the facts will always prevail.

Despite all the hazards associated with the profession of history writing, society needs history. Since every society needs a collective memory or self-knowledge to establish its own identity, history caters to a fundamental need of the society. But society also needs a man or a group of men to preserve and communicate this knowledge. History is therefore made only when the historians write it. Renowned historian Ramchandra Guha has rightly suggested that 'By writing in rich detail about other peoples and past times, the historian can expose his fellow citizens to a wider range of human social experience.' The historian however, is required to muster all the aforementioned tools/skills to reconstruct the past. This is particularly true for the historians attempting to write the history of the religion or sect he/she professes. More often than not it becomes practically impossible to rise above ones prejudices and predilections while writing about ones religious beliefs. Objective analysis of facts usually becomes a victim in such circumstances. Needless to say that achieving total objectivity in history writing especially in writings on religious and sectarian issues is beyond the pale of human faculty. The historian is nonetheless expected to bring his account of the events as close to the truth as possible. This has precisely been achieved by Professor S. N. R. Rizvi in the present collection of six essays on myriad facets of history of Shī'īsm in India. As an intellectual as well as a practicing Shi'a Muslim, Professor Rizvi has successfully tread on the difficult path of explaining the intricacies of Indian Shī'īsm without succumbing to the lure of loyalty to his beliefs and inborn perceptions.

Shī'īsm has had a long and chequered history in India. There is evidence that the first encounter of the Shi'a Muslims in the subcontinent took place in Sind as early as the late 7th century AD. Pockets of Shi'a hegemony began to appear in various parts of Sind prompting the migration of Muhammad al-Nafs al-Zakiyah, grandson of Imām Hasan, along with his sons to Sind in 761. Eight years later his son Abdullah Ashtar, known as Abdullah Shah Ghazi, fell victim to the internal squabbles of the contemporary politics and was killed at the orders of the Abbasid Caliph al-Mansur. The Shi'a population in Sind however continued to grow. According to an estimate approximately 14% Muslims of Sind professed Shī'īsm in the 9th century. During his visit to Sind in 915 Al-Masudi, the renowned Egyptian traveller and author of *Muruj al-Zahab*, is reported to have met a number of Shi'as who were the descendants of the sons of Hazrat Ali [d. 661]. Almost fifty years later an Isma'ili state was established in Sind. It was during this period (early 10th century) that the earliest public mourning of

Muharram and the Shi'a call to prayer was introduced in this territory. This state was however not destined to survive for long. In 1005, Sultan Mahmud Ghaznavi [r. 999-1030] invaded and conquered the capital city of Multan.

Information about the presence of Shi'a Muslims in Northern India during the Delhi Sultanate is few and far between. During his sojourn in Delhi, Ibn Battuta is reported to have met members of Shi'a community who had recently migrated from the Middle East. Moreover, the persecution of Shi'as at the hands of Sultan Firuz Tughluq [r.1351-1388], by his own admission, does indicate the presence of Shi'as in and around Delhi. Around the same time the Shi'a community seems to have been thriving in Gujarat. Thanks to the activities of the Isma'ili missionaries, Isma'ili Khoja and Bohra communities came into existence and played a vital role in the spread of Islam in Gujarat. But Shī'īsm in India came into its own after the establishment of the independent kingdoms of Bijapur, Golkunda and Ahmad Nagar in the fifteenth century. In 1502 Bijapur became the first Twelver Shi'a state in India. It was in Bijapur that the Shi'a call to prayer was introduced and names of twelve Shi'a Imāms were included in the *khutba* for the first time. Quli Qutb Shah, the founder of the kingdom of Golkunda, had likewise ordered the *khutba* to be read in the names of Twelve Imāms. The first *Imambarah* in India was also built in the capital city Hyderabad in 1591. *Charminar*, the famous monument of Hyderabad, was built by a Shi'a architect Mīr Muhammad Momin in the same year. Burhan Nizam Shah [r.1508-1553], the ruler of Ahmad Nagar, embraced Shī'īsm in 1537 and the kingdom continued to be a Shi'a state during the reign of his successors. We are told by the seventeenth century chronicler Firishta that the family mausoleum of the Nizam Shahi dynasty was situated in Karbala and that the first four monarchs of the dynasty were buried there. Firishta's testimony is corroborated by an Ottoman document issued on 21 September 1578.

During the Mughal rule, the Shi'a community in India fared relatively better. Barring a few incidents of persecution owing to political intrigues, the Shi'a elites by and large enjoyed peace, prosperity and political power. We know that there were many Shi'a nobles in Babur's entourage when he invaded India in 1526. Bairam Khan, Humayun's most trusted noble and guardian of Akbar during the first four years of his reign, was a twelver Shi'a. According to W. H. Moreland almost 70% of Akbar's nobles were foreigners, many of whom were Shi'a. Jahangir has also testified to the religious, sectarian and communal harmony prevailing in the empire during his father's reign. In *Tuzuk-i Jahangiri*, he has observed that 'the professors of various faiths had room in the broad expanse of his {Akbar's] sway. This was different from the practice in other realms, for in Persia there is room for Shi'as only and in Turkey, there is room for Sunnīs only. There was room for the professors of opposite religions [in the Mughal Empire]. Sunnīs and Shi'as met in one mosque and observed their own forms of worship'. This tradition was continued by Jahangir, Shahjahan and Aurangzeb; they gave important military and administrative assignments to the Shi'as. There is evidence that in the first half of Aurangzeb's reign almost 28% of the high Mughal nobility comprised of the Shi'as.

Indian Shī'īsm however achieved its full potential and blossomed into a force to reckon with in the eighteenth century. The successor states of Bengal and Awadh, that emerged on the ashes of the mighty Mughal Empire, became major centres of Shi'a theology and religious rituals in the eighteenth century. Murshid Quli Khan, the first Nawab of Bengal, was adopted by a Shi'a merchant Hajji Shafi Isfahani and was brought up as a Shi'a. His successors continued to practice Shi'a faith, built huge *Imambaras*, promoted *azādārī* and encouraged Shi'a *ulama* to migrate to Bengal. After the collapse of Muslim rule in Bengal [1757], Awadh emerged as the most important and vibrant centre of Shī'īsm in India.

Professor Rizvi has primarily focused on the history of Shī'īsm in Awadh in the present collection of his essays. He has admirably explained the process of the expansion of Shi'a influence in Awadh as well as the role of S'adat Khan Burhan ul-mulk and his successors in the foundation of Shi'a Islam on a firm footing in this erstwhile Mughal Suba. Efflorescence of Shi'a cultural practices and religious rituals including the institution of Friday prayers for the first time in Awadh followed. Shi'a theologians and intellectuals migrated to Awadh from far and wide, popularised Shi'a religious ceremonies and indulged in polemics against the Sufis and Sufism. Shī'īsm thus emerged as the dominant faith in this region allowing the Shi'a Muslims, in the words of Professor Rizvi, to profess their faith openly for the first time.

Professor Rizvi has done well to explain the subtle differences between the *Usūlī* and *Akhbārī* schools of Shi'a theology and the influence of these schools on the Shi'a community at large. His essay on the career of Sayyid Dildār Ali Ghufran Ma'ab [d.1820] highlights the great theologian's contribution to the public dissemination of Shī'īsm in Awadh. He worked hard to bring his Shi'a compatriots out of the mores of ignorance, familiarized them with the basic principles of *Usūlī* doctrine, cautioned them against the adverse impact of blind faith in Sufis and established a Shi'a seminary to impart religious instruction to the members of his community. In the same vein the essay on Shi'a Madrasas of Awadh is a significant addition to the existing knowledge on the Shi'a education system. In the backdrop of the development of Shi'a learning in Iran and Iraq during the pre-modern era, Professor Rizvi has systemically traced the growth of Shi'a education in the pre- and post 1857 Awadh. The attention of the reader is successfully drawn to the process of the establishment of various institutions of higher learning, the courses offered, the mode of teaching, the syllabus prescribed for various grades of students, the qualification of teachers and information on the contemporary challenges demanding suitable changes in the Shi'a education system. Needless to say that the essay opens new vistas of research and writing on the Shi'a education in India and will go a long way in introducing the required changes in the mode and method of imparting knowledge to the members of Shi'a community at large.

The essay on Muharram in Awadh and Eastern Uttar Pradesh is an equally valuable addition to our knowledge on the commemoration of the martyrdom of Imām Husayn, both in the past as well as in the present. It is known to all and sundry that mourning in the first ten days of the Islamic month of Muharram has always been an integral part of the life of every Shi'a Muslim so much so that it has for all practical purposes become synonymous with the Shi'a Islam itself. But it was only in the eighteenth century, following the establishment of Shi'a state in Awadh, that the public observance of Muharram began. Under the patronage of the rulers of Awadh separate buildings for mourning ceremonies, known as *Imambarah*, were erected and distinct ceremonies for each day of the *ayyām-i-azā* were formalised. Replicas of the mausoleum of Imām Husayn known as *Ta'zia* were constructed and paraded with great fan and fare on the streets, mourning assemblies [*majlises*] were organized and poems narrating the events of Karbala [*marsiya* and *nauha*] were recited with great passion. The essay also provides useful information on the process of observance of Muharram in Gorakhpur and other districts of Eastern Uttar Pradesh where Shi'as and Sunnīs come together to display their love for the *ahl-e bait* and recall the tragedy that befell them in the battle field of Karbala. Muharram continues to be observed today with the same passion and reverence as it was held in the eighteenth century and every member of Shi'a community contribute to its fruition according to his/her status. The remaining two essays on Shaykh Ali Hazīn and Nauroz festival highlight the contribution of Shi'a Muslims to the making of the glorious Indian civilization.

Needless to say that Professor Rizvi has presented an extremely cogent and readable narrative of Indian Shī'īsm in the eighteenth century and its subsequent flowering in the nineteenth century Awadh. He has laboured hard to bring to our notice diverse little known facts about the history of Indian Shī'īsm which will go a long way in enriching our understanding of the Shi'a beliefs and precepts. I am confident that this excellent collection of essays will be welcomed by all students and scholars of Indian history and culture.

330 / 4, Ashok Nagar
Allahabad

N. R. Farooqi

Introduction

Prior to the 1979 Islamic Revolution in Iran, according to Moojan Momen, few people in the west were conscious that a separate sect of Islam called Shī'ī Islam existed. However, even those who were aware of this were not very clear about who the Shī'īs were, where they lived, what they believed or what made them different to the majority Sunnī community. His above statement astonished me because his book entitled, *An Introduction to Shi'i Islam, The History and Doctrines of Twelver Shi'ism* was published from Yale University Press, London, in 1985. He made the same statement in his another book, titled *Shi'i Islam: A Beginner's Guide* published from Oneworld Publications, London, in 2016, i.e. five years back. Then I thought about my own province (Uttar Pradesh, India). The situation was more or less, same except in few districts. The attitude of Sunnī-Muslims to neglect them, was not a matter of surprise to me because Shī'īsm rose as a dissenting group in opposition to the Muslim majority. Their protests were crushed by the Caliphs and for centuries, Sunnīs had been used to discounting the Shi'as, considering them an irrelevance to the politics and economics. Even in many Muslim countries they are treated as a non-Muslim. They are Khariji. In 1973, a Malaysian (a Muslim country of Asia) student of Aligarh Muslim University, Aligarh had told me in a personal talk that in his country, 'Shi'as are treated as non-Muslims.' One decade earlier, same expression was given to me by a scholar, but in a friendly manner. This inspired me to pen down history of some cultural aspects of Shī'īsm because only an *ālim* (scholar) or *mujtahid* can write on theological or philosophical aspects. In this context, it is mentionable here that about two decades ago five out of six articles presented in this volume, were already published in different journals, Proceedings of Indian History Congress and edited books by other scholars. So, I decided to update the earlier articles and also to write a new article, in the light of the recent researches. This book is the outcome of my decision and effort and is now for the readers to evaluate it.

There are six chapters related to scholars, madrasas and festivals of joy and mourning. In the section one, there is only one article which is exceptional. It deals Polemic and Identity formation of Shī'īsm in Awadh. According to Mana Kia (Associate Professor, Columbia University), "Sufism was popular in Iran during the political rule of Sunnī leaders. Ironically, it was the proto-Shia concept accepted by many Sufi orders, such as devotion to a charismatic leader, that aided the mass conversion to Shī'īsm in Iran. But after the establishment of the Safavid state (1501-1722), Sufis were considered outside orthodoxy and often violently repressed by both the Ulama and the Shahs". The situation in Awadh was somewhat similar to Iran. In Awadh, also, Sufis were in dominating position, but after the establishment of Shī'ī nawabi-rule in Awadh and tirade against the Akhbārīs and Sufis by the First Shi'a mujtahid, the identity of Shī'īsm established in the region.With this the position of Sufis changed among the Shi'a Muslims. The chapter discusses the contributions of Awadh rulers, aristocrats and mujtahid for giving the identity of Shī'īsm, the main points of differences between Shi'as and Sufis and the origin and rise of the usūlī-fiqh. The differences between Akhbārī and Usūlī have been specially discussed. Actually, the defining feature of Shi'a jurisprudence is the use of the reason to interpret law (ijtihād) versus the more restrictive practices used by Sunnī Ulama to derive law from holy sources. In this context, the Akhbārī Shi'as position was no less rigid. They include only the oral sayings of holy Imāms after

Qur'ān as the source of law. The Usūlīs, added reason and consensus to the Qur'ān and Hadīs (traditions) as sources of law. They also maintained that in matters not explicitly covered by the Qur'ān or Hadīs (traditions), the lay believer should emulate a mujtahid in religious practice or else their ritual acts of Ibādat (worship) were considered invalid. This point was essential for the understanding of general people. The article deals with all these aspects.

Section two contains two chapter related to two Shi'a scholars, both mujtahids, but not in to the rank of 'ayatollah' (eye of God). One of them was of Irani-origin, who was also a great Persian poet of his age and another was an orthodox ālim from India. First was Shaykh Ali Hazin, who wrote his autobiography in about 1742 AD but survived till 1766 AD. The fact that, he criticized the Mughal Emperor, Indians and Persian poets of contemporary Mughal court and showed his superiority, that is well known. Though, the article covers all these aspects, but the main focus is on his activities, during his stay at Benares, where he promoted the Persian language. Being a Shi'a- mujtahid, he also attempted to fulfill his responsibility and produced religious literature. He taught many Shi'a scholars and promoted the usūlī thought in the region. But his main teaching to Shi'a community was that how a Shi'a should live in the Hindu - dominated region without annoying them and follow his own right path.

Second scholar is the first mujtahid of Awadh, Sayyid Dildār Ali 'Ghufran Ma'ab'. With the help and support of the Awadh rulers, he changed the ignorant Shi'a society of his time into a usūlī-society. His successful confrontation with Akhbārīs and Sufis for usūlī fiqh, is noteworthy. He also wrote several tracts in refutation of views expressed by Shah 'Abdul Aziz Dehlavi in *Tuhafā-i Isnā Āshariyyā*. One of them, the 'Zulfiqar' is noticeable. He rendered great services to the Shi'a society.

To get the rank of a 'mujtahid' is not so easy for a Shi'a scholar. This qualification is bestowed only on receiving a formal, signed permission from a recognized high ranking-cleric (mujtahid). It usually takes 15-20 years of study in a seminary school (madrasa) to earn this permission and the title of Hojjat al-Islam (Proof of Islam). Sayyid Dildār Ali 'Ghufran Ma'ab' had received the Ijāzā (permission) after the study of two years. Therefore, his contemporary opponents raised the question about his Ijāzā and critics made this a point against him. Ahmad Behbahānī, an Irani scholar, who was not satisfied with 'Ghufran Ma'ab' on personal ground, wrote about this issue in guarded language. But it should be noted that even today, no time is fixed for getting the permission. All these aspects have been highlighted in this article.

Section three deals with Shi'a madrasas of Awadh which is recent in origin. This chapter puts light on the Shi'a education system from the beginning and points out the causes for the establishment of separate Shi'a madrasa. As madrasa is needed for the society and not for the rulers, perhaps this was the reason that Shi'a Nawabs of Awadh promoted the scholars and Shi'a ulama but did not take interest in establishing Shi'a madrasas. The first and the last Shi'a madrasa was established by King Amjad Ali Shah (1843 AD), named Madrasa-i Sultaniyya or Shahi madrasa. The revolt of 1857 closed this institution. After few years Shi'a scholars felt the need of establishing madrasa for the Shi'a society. Thus, with their efforts few madrasas were established which are still in existence. The article traces their history, courses, subjects, syllabi and sanads (degree). The changes in madrasa system are also depicted.

The section-four is dedicated to the Shi'a culture. It contains two articles, one on Nauroz—the festival of joy and second on the commemoration of Muharram. The first article traces the origin of the festival of Nauroz, its celebration style during the Sultanate and Mughal period as a court-festival, later during the ta'lluqdari period in Awadh and in the last, by the common people. Previously, Sunnīs celebrated this festival with enthusiast but now they do not take interest in it but Shi'as celebrate it with pomp and show. The article includes the description of the festival presented by Mrs. Meer Hassan Ali', which is bewitching.

The last chapter, entitled "Muharram in Awadh and Eastern Uttar Pradesh" is coming forth for the first time. The commemoration of Muharram has been portrayed as synonymous with the religion itself. The work traces its causes, history of its commemoration in earlier period, as how did the nawabs of Awadh, his aristocracy and ta'lluqdars commemorated the Muharram, as devout Shi'a, their contribution in constructing the Imāmbārahs, zari, tā'zias, 'alams and organizing the majlises. It talks about the participation of Shi'a women in Muharram, and also the later development during the colonial period. But the special feature of this article is that for the first time it gives the details of Muharram commemoration in the district of Gorakhpur of Eastern Uttar Pradesh, where the Shi'as are still in absolute minority, so much so that even today there are not more than forty to fifty families of this community. The details of commemoration of Muharram since the post-independent period is described by the author on the basis of his personal observations. In Gorakhpur, Hindu community recognizes Shi'as as, "Ma'tam waale Musalman", when they see their flagellation in the procession of Muharram and the Sunnī Musalmans call their procession as "Shi'a logon ka Jaloos" which exhibits their presence. In brief, the article gives us a real picture of Muharram commemoration in Awadh during the Nawabi-period on the basis of contemporary eyewitness, Mrs. Meer Hassan Ali, a British lady. It also mentions the later development during the colonial period and personal observation of the author for the post-independent period, especially for the region of Eastern Uttar Pradesh.

For collecting facts and information to write the abovementioned articles, I have consulted Persian, Urdu, English and Hindi sources. For Arabic sources I have used the English translations. The English or Urdu translation of Persian sources is also preferred. The recent writings have been consulted to know the modern views regarding Shī'īsm. Among them, *The Origins and Early Development of Shi'a Islam* by S.H.M. Jafri; *A Socio-Intellectual History of the Isnā' Ashari Shi'is in India*, two volumes by Saiyid Athar Abbas Rizvi; *SHI'A* of Allamah Sayyid Muhammad Husayn Tabātabāī and translated by Sayyid Nasr (Qum, 1989); *SHI'ITE ISLAM* of Yann Richard (translated by Antonia Nevill, Cambridge, 1995); Moojan Momen's *An Introduction To Shi'i Islam: The History and Doctrines of Twelver Shi'ism* (Yale,1985) and *Shi'i Islam A Beginner's Guide* (London, 2016.); *The Shi'a of India* by John Norman Hollister (London, 1953 and second edition,1979); *Shi'a Women: Muslim Faith and Practice*, by Diane D'souza (Zubaan Publication, New Delhi, 2012); *Roots of North Indian Shi'ism in Iran and Iraq* by Juan R.I. Coles (Oxford University Press, Delhi,1989); *Shi'a Islam in Colonial India* by Justin Jones (Cambridge University Press, New Delhi, 2012); *Shi'ism in America* by Liyakat Nathani TAKIM (New York, 2009); *Delhi: Pages From A Forgotten History* by Arthur Dudney (Hay House, India, 2015); *A Desire for Meaning: Khan-I Arzu's Philology and the Place of India in the Eighteenth-Century Persianite World*, by Arthur Dudney (Doctoral Theses, Columbia, 2013) and *Persianate Selves: Memories of Place and Origin Before Nationalism* by Mana Kia (Stanford University Press U.K., 2020) have been constantly consulted for writing this book. Besides, for the sake of simplicity and elegance, long vowels are marked as ā, ē, ī, ō, ū in the book.

On 1st February 2021, while I was going to collect my recently published book from publishing house, I met an accident when a high-speed car hit me from behind. Thankfully, with God's grace, there were no severe injuries although next few days were quite painful. After one month, when I recovered, though not fully, a thought came to my mind that God has given some life to me to do something. Therefore, I decided to contribute some more writings for the enhancement of the knowledge of the students and common men. This book is a small contribution (*Hadia*) in the decided direction. Therefore, I must thank almighty God (Allah) for the completion of my small project.

21st July, 2021

Syed Najmul Raza Rizvi
Gorakhpur (U.P., India)

Section 1: Identity

Shī'īsm and Sufism: Polemic and Identity Formation

As a religion, Islam has had and continues to have a significant impact on the course of world history at various times, because of either inter-religious or intra-religious factors. Since this article deals with *Shī'īsm* and *Sufism* in relation to polemics and identity formation at a particular time in the later medieval period in India, a question of intra-religious nature, no worthwhile discussion is possible without a look at the history from the earliest days of Islam. Polemics between *Shī'īsm* and *Sufism* did not appear suddenly; it is a manifestation of the socio-economic and religious processes in the Islamic world during the past several centuries. As far as this article is concerned, *Shī'īsm* refers to *lthnā-Asharī* (or The Twelver) *Shī'īsm* unless specifically mentioned otherwise.

About Sunnīs, Shi'as and Sufis

Though, according to a tradition of Prophet Muhammad, which is not included in the collection of Bukhārī and Muslim, 'His people (Muslims) will be divided into 73 'firqā' (sects)', but how many sects are there at present in Islam, is not a matter of discussion here. Today, Islam, as conceived by its followers can be broadly defined as Sunnī and Shi'a Islam. The reason is only that the Shi'a alone have continued all these fourteen hundred years to preserve their faith or stand.

There is a broad consensus and similarity of beliefs between these two groups on the basic tenets of Islam. Like Sunnīs, a Shi'a also believes in Tauhid (Oneness of God, or "There is no god but Allah"), the Qur'ān, Prophet Muhammad, the mā'ad (Resurrection or the last Judgement) and in the fundamental obligations or duties of Namāz (five times prayers), Roza (fasting), Haj (pilgrimage), Khums, Khairāt (alms giving) and Jihād (holy war).

However, differences exist, sometimes very sharply. For example, there is the basic difference on the institution of Imamate or say, Khilāfat or on the question of leadership of the Muslim community after Prophet Muhammad In some practices also, we find differences between them. For example, the Shi'as regroup the five obligatory prayers into three points in the day; 'Zuhr' and 'Asr' [the mid-day and afternoon prayers are performed together, as are those of the 'Maghrib' and 'Īshā' (the evening and night)]. A tradition affirms that the Prophet considered this practice permissible.

Their az'ān, is same with some exception.[1] The Shi'as ritual of ablution (Wūjū) is slightly different from the Sunnīs. They perform Namāz on a little prayer mat unsullied by impurities. Customarily, they place a tiny tablet (Sijdā-gaah) of clay brought from a holy place on the spot where their forehead will touch the ground. Shi'as also believe in the 'ziyārat' of tombs of Imāms. They, too, believe in Haj, at least once in their life. Despite, the faith of both communities on basic tenets of Islam and minor differences in performing the duties, Shi'as and Sunnīs are still on dragons drawn on the principle of Imāmate or say Khilāfat. Sunnīs believe that the Prophet was selected and appointed by God, but the Ummah had the right to choose his successor. They also believe that Prophet Muhammad did not nominate anyone to succeed him. So, they elected his nominee, while Hazrat Ali and his party were busy in the funeral of Prophet and they did not participate in the deliberation of Saqifa or election. After the first three Caliphs, Sunnīs accepted Ali as their fourth Caliph. They also put all these four caliphs in the category of 'Khalifā-i-rāshidūn'. Later, they also accepted the Ummayid and Abbasi caliphate and in the last, the Khilāfat of Turkey, though the nature was hereditary. Now the institution of caliph is no more. During, this long period they also accepted the Muslim rulers of different parts of the world, as the representatives of Caliph of their time.

On the other hand, the Shi'as believe that like Prophethood, the institution of Imāmate is also from the God (Min Jānib Allah).[2] To them, Prophethood ended after the death of Prophet Muhammad, but God selected and appointed Imāms to protect the religion and guide its followers till the Day of Judgement. In other words, they do not believe in the election of Prophet's successors. To them, there are twelve Imāms, Ali is the first and The Mahdi, is the twelfth Imām. He (The Mahdi) is in great occultation (*ghaybat-e Kubrā*). All the Imāms are descendants of Fatima, the daughter of Prophet Muhammad and are also known as *Ahl-e bayt*.

The exalted position of '*Ahl-e bayt*' during the lifetime of Prophet Muhammad and the harsh treatment that were meted out to them by his followers, immediately after his death stands in sharp contrast.

Neither was the people's memory so short that they forgot the words of a person like Muhammad, nor their senses were so weak that they could not feel the unjust attitude and atrocities perpetrated by the Ummayids, on *Ahl-e bayt*. Thus, was generated a strong undercurrent in favor of Ali, Fatima, Hasan, Husayn and their descendants among the masses. However, their love for *Ahl-e bayt* could not find an overt manifestation for fear of reprisal from the then ruling class. It was this undercurrent that was utilized by the Abbasids to dethrone the Ummayids in the 2nd century Hijri.

Though the Abbasids came to power by exploiting people's love for the Prophet and his progeny, they proved equally repressive, if not more, towards the followers of *Ahl-e bayt*.[3]

It was around this very time that Sufism first surfaced. The origin of the word *Sufi* is shrouded in mystery. Though it is not known exactly how or from where the word came into circulation, it is said that the word *Sufi* has its origin in the Arabic word 'Soof', which means 'wool'. People who used to wear woolen or sack-like clothes throughout the year were known as Sufi. They were ascetics, not given to worldly lavishness and did not wear fine clothes.

There is another belief that the word *Sufi* came from the term *Ahl-e Safā*, those who lived in the front outer portion of the mosque of Prophet Muhammad (Masjid-e Nabavi) during the time of Prophet. They were the people who were busy in prayers and were fed by other persons of the society.

Some people have opined that the word *Sufi* might have come from the clan Bānū-Sūfah which was a Baddū clan of Arabia, since they were simple people and Sufis also are simple persons, hence the name. For yet another few, the word *Sufi* is derived from the word, 'Saufanatā' which is a kind of vegetable popular among ascetics and to a few other Saf, Watal, Quzā, meaning bunch of long hair over the rear portion of neck is the source of the word *Sufi*.

Apart from the abovementioned sources there are persons who trace the roots of Sufism beyond Islamic days down to the ancient Greek period. They understand that the word *Sufi* might have come from the word "Theosophist", a group of ancient Greek philosophers. Ibn e Juzy puts for word that the word *Sufi* came into existence just before the end of the 2nd century Hijri.[4]

Saad ibn Khaldun has expressed his opinion that there appeared a group of people among Muslims, towards the end of the 2nd century Hijri who spent their lives in a strange way. Their apparent way of life was not in keeping with the directives of Islam, it was but natural that they were to be given a new name and the name was *Sufi* because they wore woolen clothes.[5]

On the basis of the views of a Shi'a ālim, Mohammad Ali Behbahānī (d.1803 AD), Ali Dāvanī, a clerical historian, who died in 2007 AD at Tehran (Iran) writes that "There are several explanations of the term "Sufi" and the Sufis themselves are unable to make sense of them. The first to claim it were heretics, then schismatics influenced by the Brahmans of India. In the Islamic world, those people were enemies of the Family of Prophet, like

Hasan Basrī and others. Keyvān Qazvīnī dwelt for 40 years on the plain of Sufism, even becoming one of the heads of the order; he denounced the Indian origin of Sufism and showed that the terms "Sufi", "Sufism"(Sufiya, tasavvuf) are meaningless. The Sufis are people who wear wool (according to one of the etymologies of the term "Sufi") and disguise themselves in the attributes of ascetics and Christian monks in order to attract the esteem of Muslims and to realize their evil designs... ."[6]

Whatever be the source of the word 'Sufi', in today's world Sufis are related to Islam and quote extensively from the Qur'ān and the Prophet's traditions for the legitimacy of their existence. Today's Sufism is deeply rooted in Sunnīsm though there is a group of Sunnīs (Wahabīs and Salafī groups) that opposes Sufism, the same as the Shi'as. Some of their objections are:

1. The Sufi concepts of a secluded and ascetic way of life are not permitted in Islam.
2. The hermitage or the Khanqah and the present-day Sufi ways were absent during the time of the Prophet.
3. The practice of limited starvation (fāqā-parastī) and observance of silence and so on are alien to Islam.
4. *Ghusl-e Islam*, *Ghusl-e Taubā*, *Ghusl-e Ziyārat*, *Ghusl-e Hājat*, all variants of ritual baths prevalent among Sufis, are not prescribed by Islam.
5. The *Pir-o-Murshid* and Murid relationship and the rituals of initiation into a particular order and zikr are not acceptable to many, particularly the Shi'as.
6. The concept of wahdat ul-wūjūd (Existential Monism) is considered to be blasphemous by many Muslims.[7]

There are certain similarities as well among Shi'as and Sufis, of which a few are enumerated here:

1. The Sufi concept of Qutub or *Insān-e Kāmil* (Perfect Man) resembles the Shi'a concept of *Imām ul-Waqt* (Imām of the Age),

although the Imām is infallible (mā'sūm) and should be a descendent of 'Ali or Fatima, which is not required for a Qutub.

2. Shi'as believe that there exists one and only one Imām for a particular age and followers have to identify and recognize him. Sufis hold the same about a Qutub.
3. Shi'as believe that the Universe would not survive without the existence of such an Imām. Sufis hold the same belief about the Qutub.
4. Shi'as trace their ideological and spiritual ancestry of Hazrat Ali (as Khalifat ul Bilā fasl to Prophet Muhammad) through the descendants of 'Ali and Fatima. Sufis, except a branch of the Naqshbandi order, also derive their spiritualism through Ali though not necessarily through the progeny of Ali and Fatima.
5. *Ahl-e bayt*, the five Pure Souls are revered very highly by Sufi's and Shi'as alike, both revering them as being infallible (mā'sūm).
6. Shi'as observe Muharram to mourn the death of Imām Husayn and his companions; so, do the Sufis.

The 2nd century Hijri is very important to both Sufi's and Shi'as. While the famous ascetic Hasan al-Basrī was spreading Sufi thought, Imām Mohd. Bāqir,(a.s.) (contemporary of Hasan al-Basrī), followed by Imām Jafar al-Sadiq,(a.s.) were producing thousands of students of Islamic Jurisprudence during this time.

Though, Chisti Sufis claim that Khwājā Hasan al-Basrī was a faithful disciple of Hazrat Ali, Shi'as do not agree, claiming instead that Khwājā Hasan al-Basrī never fought on the side of 'Ali, Hasan or Husayn although he was alive when the battles of Jamal, Siffin and Karbala took place.

The Emergence of 'Usūlīsm'

After the martyrdom of Imām Husayn, it was Jafar as-Sādiq(a.s.) who preached and spread the knowledge of Islamic Jurisprudence, traditions, teachings and family accounts of the events. He utilized the opportunity when the Ummayid rulers were busy in controlling opposing forces and, as a result, official repression and surveillance by Ummayid rulers was temporarily reduced.

From 'Ali to Jafar as-Sādiq(a. s.) and up to the eleventh Imām Hasan al-Askarī,(a.s.) there is an unbroken chain of guidance available to Shi'as. The Twelfth Imām went into lesser occultation (*Ghaibat-e Sughrā*) as per the Shi'a belief, in 874 AD and this continued till 941 AD. Thereafter, he was forced to go into the greater occultation, which is continuing till date. During the lesser occultation there were four abwābs (Gates) or Safirs (Ambassadors) or Naibs (Nawab) through whom believers were provided guidance. Thus, a real gap in direct guidance from an infallible Imām arose among Shi'as only after the death of Imām Hasan Al-Askari (a.s). Since four abwābs were successively available for guidance during the period of lesser occultation the question of deputyship or Nayābat arose prominently during the period of greater occultation. Questions about who would lead the Friday congregational prayer or jihād in the absence of the Imām, arose. Around this time, the Shi'a Buyid dynasty (932-1055 AD) came to power in Iran and Iraq. The Twelver Shi'a scholars held a conclave to study oral reports from the Imāms. These reports to Baghdad originated in Kūfā (in Iraq) and Qum (in Iran). However, around this time the practice of employing Greek logical tools, such as syllogism, to theology started among a section of the Shi'as in Baghdad, but the notions of rationality were rejected by most of the Shia scholars. They favored instead the quotations from the Imāms. It is in this period that the rationalist theologians began to be called Usūlīs and the other group Akhbārīs.

This was the beginning of the concept of Ijtihād (reasoning), introduced by the Usūlīs. The Usūlīs divided the Shi'a society into two groups, the *mujtahid* and the *muqallid*, the learned ones and the laymen, respectively. Those without a formal training in Islamic, i.e. Shi'a jurisprudence and bereft of a particular level of learning, were henceforth considered laymen, who ought to consider

Usūlī School	Akhbārī School
A. On the Sources of Doctrine and Law	**A. On the Sources of Doctrine and Law**
1. The Usūlīs accept four sources of authority in matters of doctrine and law: the Qur'ān, the Sunna, consensus (ijma) and the intellect ('aql).	1. The Akhbārīs only accept the first two and some often only the second (since the Qur'ān can only be understood with the help of the Traditions).
2. Accept and use the literal meaning of the Qur'ān and the Traditions claiming that it is possible to know the meaning of these through the use of the intellect ('aql);	2. Consider that; the Qur'ān and Traditions can only be understood where their meaning has been made explicit by the commentary (tafsir and tawil) of the Imāms;
3. Consider the four 'canonical' books of Traditions to contain many unreliable Traditions.	3. Consider the four books to be reliable.
4. Accept as authoritative only Traditions from the Imāms transmitted through reliable Shia's.	4. Allow a much wider search to be made for Traditions bearing on a particular problem, allowing Traditions from Sunnī or other-sources (provided the transmission is 'protected from fabrication') and even from the unknown source if there is good evidence, supporting it.
5. Divide the Tradition into four categories: sahih, hasan, mutawatir and da'if.	5. Recognize only two categories sahih and da'if.
6. Consider that doctrines or	6. Consider that what is derived

legal decisions derived from transmitted (naqlī) sources (i.e. the Qurān and Traditions) cannot contradict what is derived from rational principles.	from naqlī sources always has precedence over what is derived from the use of reason.
B. On the Principles of Jurisprudence	**B. On the Principles of Jurisprudence**
1. The usūlīs accept ijtihād.	1. The Akhbārīs reject ijtihād.
2. Consider that decisions can be given on the basis of 'zann' (valid conjecture) achieved through ijtihād, in cases where certain knowledge ('ilm) from an explicit text in the Qur'ān or Traditions is not available.	2. Consider that decision can only be given where there is certain knowledge through a relevant Tradition from the Imām.
3. Consider that knowledge was only obtainable directly from the Imāms by those who were in their presence (i.e. that the legal decisions of the Imām may have been affected by individual circumstances and do not necessarily have general applicability) and so, during the Occultation, it is necessary to resort to ijtihād, and fatwas (legal decisions) can only be issued through use of this.	3. Consider it obligatory to refer to the Imāms even if through an intermediary (i.e. a transmitted Tradition) and that these have general applicability and that, the fatwas can only be issued on the basis of a relevant Tradition.
4. Consider that through the use	4. Use only explicit texts from

of ijtihād, the Traditions can be examined, one Tradition can be preferred over another contradictory one and practices can be derived from unclear and ambiguous texts.	the Imāms.
5. Act on the basis of freedom and the permissibility of all actions if there is no clear text against it.	5. Consider that in case where there is no clear text, caution must be exercised.
C. On the Position of Faqīh (Jurist)	**C. On the Position of Faqīh (Jurist)**
1. The Usūlīs divide men into two groups: mujtahid and muqallid.	1. The Akhbārīs hold that all men are muqallid to the Imām and it is not permissible to turn to a mujtahid.
2. Consider that the unrestricted (i.e. fully competent) mujtahid is learned in all of the ordinances of the religion since the condition for issuing legal decisions is knowledge of a large number of sciences, the most important of which is usul al-fiqh (principles of jurisprudence).	2. Consider that only the Imām is informed of all of the ordinances of the religion and that the only condition for issuing legal decisions is a knowledge of the terms used by the Imāms and knowing of a Tradition conforming the matter.
3. Forbid following (taqlid) a dead jurist (marja).	3. Allow use of the decisions of a dead jurist.
4. Consider it obligatory to obey a mujtahid as much as it is, obey the Imām.	4. Reject this.
5. Consider that the use of ijtihād	5. Consider that the issuing of a

will result in a (heavenly) reward even if the decision is incorrect.	decree except on the basis of a reliable and explicit Tradition is blameworthy.

mujtahids as general representatives of the Hidden Imām and follow them. The Usūlī School, in this manner, strived for a balance between reason and authority.[8]

The Akhbārīs, on the other hand, depended on the Qur'ān, the oral reports from Prophet Muhammad and from the Imāms and did not employ logic or rationalism to interpretation of religious questions or socio-political problems (maslehat). They favored the suspension of reason in favor of a more totalitarian kind of authority.[9]

Thus, for the Usūlīs, the Friday congregational prayers could be held in the absence of the twelfth Imām on the condition that it would be *wājib-e-takhiyaree* and not *wajib-ul-aiynē*, that is to say that it is obligatory for a person to assemble for Friday congregational prayers but it was not necessary for him to Friday prayers as wajib or must in place of *Namāz-e-zuhr*. Once a person became a part of the Friday congregation, it was optional for him to offer either zuhr or Friday prayer as wajib during the occultation period of the twelfth Imām.

Differences between Akhbārīs and Usūlīs

The differences between the Akhbārīs and the Usūlīs, according to Froncis Robinson, revolved around two issues. First, regarding the sources of law, the Akhbārīs restricted them to the Qur'ān, the Hadiths, and the Imāms, while the Usūlīs asserted that both the consensus (ijmā) of the jurisprudents (mujtahids), as well as the independent reason (ijtihād) of a jurisprudent, could also serve as a source of legal judgement. Second, regarding the capacity to represent the Hidden Imām, Akhbārīs agreed in principle that a relater of Hadīths from the Imāms could act as a judge, but often forbade such action in practice in the absence of an infallible Imām. Usūlīs, on the other hand, asserted that the mujtahids, as a general representative of the Hidden Imām, could substitute for him in giving legal judgements, collecting and distributing alms, ordering defensive holy war, and leading Friday prayers.[10] However, the following chart shows the differences between Akhbārīs and Usūlīs:

[***Source:*** Momen, Moojan, *Shī'ī Islam*, p.109.]

Spread of Shī'īsm in the World: A brief sketch

It may be mentioned that the mid of 10th century AD was a favorable period for the Shi'as as far as their political condition was concerned. The Shi'a Buyids were ruling over Iraq and Iran, while the Hamadānis, who are considered as Nusayiri, though the exact nature of their Shī'īsm is not clear, were ruling over Syria. It may be mentioned that the Twelvers do not approve of Nusayiri thought, but it remains a fact that the Nusayiris exalt 'Ali and his progeny. Simultaneously, the Ismailis were ruling in Egypt and North Africa and Yemen was under the Zaydi Shi'as.

By the middle of the 11th century AD, the various Shi'a dynasties began to lose control of their respective kingdoms. The Buyids were overcome by the Sunnī Seljuks by 1055 AD. The Hamadānis in Syria fell and the Fatamids in Egypt became weak.

In all these countries, Sunnī Islam was making a comeback to power. As a natural outcome the Shi'a intellectual center moved from one place to another. Baghdad, the main center of the Twelver Shi'as so far, had now to be shifted to Qum where the traditionalists (Akhbārīs) were prominent. After the death of Ibn Babuya in Qum, Baghdad again came into prominence as the most prominent Shi'a center. When the Seljuks captured Baghdad, Shaykh al-Taifa was forced to leave. He settled in Najaf, which is till today a prominent center of Shi'a learning.

During the reign of the Buyid, Muizud-Dawla, the public observance of two great commemorative occasions for the Shi'a was established in Baghdad in 962 AD. The first was the martyrdom of Imām Husayn and the second was the anniversary of the incident of Ghadir-e Khum on 18th Zil Hij.[11]

In India, the Arab invasion dates back to 712 AD led by Mohd.

b. Qasim during the Ummayid period. Later intruders like the Ghaznavids, rulers of the slave dynasty the Khaljis, the Tughlaqs, the Lodis and the Mughals were all Sunnī dynasties. The persecution of minority Shi'as during the West and Central Asian Sunnī regimes of the 11th century AD pushed them towards India, but once again the rulers were Sunnīs. Though less acrimonious than it had been in their earlier homelands, the atmosphere of Mughal India was not congenial for the Shi'a faith either. The correspondence between Mīr Yusuf Ali Astarābādi and Qāzī Nurullah Shushtri shows that even in the reign of Akbar, the Shi'as were not in a position to abandon taqiyyā.[12] The apprehensions of Mīr Yusuf Ali were vindicated when Nurullah Shushtri was executed for his writings on the orders of Jahangir.[13] Hence, there was no question of an open declaration of their faith by the Shi'as.

The permitted practice of dissimulation (Taqiyyā) allowed many of the emigree Shi'as to hide their real identity and overtly profess the religion of the court. Thus, the Shi'as in medieval India remained a dispersed and unorganized lot maintaining a very low profile. Though on individual merit, they held, at times, prominently high positions in the Mughal army and administration. For example, out of the nine jewels of Akbar's court, five were Shi'as. Sādāt-e Bārahā, a Shi'a Sayyid family became so powerful after the death of Aurangzeb as to become the virtual rulers and kingmakers of the Mughal dynasty until 1720 AD. They were eventually, and ironically, suppressed by Burhan ul-Mulk, a fellow Shi'a. It was only with the establishment of Shi'a rule in Awadh that the Shi'a could profess their faith openly.

Several Shi'a dynasties came to power in the southern parts of India after disintegration of the Bahmani kingdom, contemporary to the Safavids in Iran. Yūsūf Ādil Shah, of Persian or Turkoman origin and an adopted son of Mahmūd Gawan, the Shi'a chief minister of the Bahmani kingdom, proclaimed his independence in 1489 AD and, following in the Safavids' footsteps, declared Shī'īsm as the official religion of the state of Bijapur.

The second ruler of this dynasty Ismail ibn Yūsūf established links with the Safavids in Iran so much so that his troops wore the red twelve- pointed cap of the Qizilbash, the symbol of a Shi'a in those days.[14]

A converted Brahmin, Hasan, established a Shi'a dynasty in Ahmad Nagar in 1490 AD under the name of Ahmad Nizam Shah. This dynasty lasted for about 143 years before being subjugated by the Mughals in 1633 AD.[15] Golconda also declared its independence from the Bahmani kingdom in 1512 AD under Sultan Qutub Quli Shah.[16]

During this period a number of Shi'a ulama also migrated to India with the purpose of establishing Imāmi (Shi'a) Islam. Tahir of Qazvin and Qāzi Nurullah Shushtri (1542-1610 AD) were among them. Nurullah was made the chief qāzi of Lahore by Akbar and later on was executed by Emperor Jahangir for his Shi'a pronouncements. Nurullah, who lies buried at Agra, is reverently called by the Indian Shi'as as Shahīd-e Saalis.[17]

In 1492, Mīr Shamsuddin Iraqi from Gilan in Iran came to Srinagar. He was a follower of Muhammad Nurbaksh, a Sunnī with strong Shi'a learning, so much so that he had visited all major Shi'a shrines in Iraq and quoted from Shi'a works. However, he considered the first three caliphs of Islam as Sufi saints. The followers of Nurbaksh gradually adopted Shī'īsm. Mīr Shamsuddin Iraqi converted a few notables of Kashmir to Shī'īsm, particularly the chak family that eventually became the rulers of Kashmir in 1561 AD till Akbar displaced them in 1586 AD.[18]

Thus, we find that the Shi'a kingdoms that rose in the south and in the extreme north of India were eventually suppressed by the Sunnī Mughals by the end of the 17th century. However, it is the irony of fate that the strongest Shi'a kingdoms in India arose during the 18th century AD upon the decline and disintegration of the same Mughal empire.

The Rise of Shī'īsm in Awadh

The Mughal emperor Muhammad Shah assigned the governorship of Agra in 1720 AD to Mīr Muhammad Amīn Nishāpurī, who had come to India from Iran in 1708 AD. This was a reward for freeing the throne of Delhi from the political control of the Sā'dāt-e Bārahā.

However, when Nishāpurī, decorated with the title Sa'adat Ali Khan Burhan ul-Mulk, failed to suppress the peasant uprisings in 1722 AD, the emperor demoted him to the governorship of a less remunerative state, namely Awadh.[19] Burhan ul-Mulk selected Faizabad as his capital. He was a staunch Shi'a. Munshi Jawala Prasad 'Akhtar' writes:

> "Since Burhan ul-Mulk himself was a Shi'a, he and his entire family members used to put on black attires and the ladies would take off their all jewellery and break or remove their bangles from their wrists as soon as the moon for the month of Muharram was sighted. Public holidays were declared from the seventh of Muharram in Awadh and the Hindus and Muslims along with Burhan ul-Mulk used to mourn the death of Imām Husayn. Thus, it would not be wrong to say that the first public dissemination of Shī'īsm (in Awadh) is dependent of Burhan-ul-Mulk."[20]

Burhan ul-Mulk died in 1739 AD After much political manoeuverings, Mirza Muhammad Muqeem Abul Mansur Khan Safdar Jang succeeded him to become the Nawab Wazir of the Mughals in Awadh (1739-1753 AD). He was a nephew and son-in-law of Burhan ul-Mulk.

Nawab Begum (Sadr e Jahān Begum), the wife of Safdarjung was a wise lady blessed with a strong personality. She was liberal in the distribution of largesse to her employees and to the poor and destitute. She put together a sum of rupees fifteen lakh, in those days, by curtailing her personal expenditure alone, in order to undertake a pilgrimage of Shi'a shrines in Iraq and Iran but could not proceed due to ill health. Her devotion to the Shi'a faith can be gauged from the fact that she donated all this money for construction of Āsfi Imāmbārah in Lucknow in 1784 AD, entrusting her grandson, Nawab Āsafud-Daulah, with the task. Munshi Jawala Prasad writes:

> In the construction of Āsfi Imāmbārah, Nawab Āsaf ud-Daulah expended Rs.15 lakh received from his grand-mother Sadre Jahān Begum which she had kept for ziyārat along with his own wealth.[21]

Nawab Shujā ud-Daulah took the reins of Awadh in his hand in 1753 AD on the death of Safdarjung. The interest of Nawab Shujāud-Daulah in Shī'īsm is discernible in the following lines by Muhammad Khan Shāhjahānpurī:

> Nawab Shujā ud-Daulah had a special inclination towards azādarī. If as per chance Muharram fell during his military expedition, he used to postpone his schedule of battle during the mourning days. In the military camps, majlis-e azā were organized. The soldiers used to keep with them the bamboo and articles for the construction of tāziā.[22]

Another writer, Syed Ghulam Ali in his book *Imad us-Sa'adat*, writes:

> "Once in 1760 AD due to the ensuing battle of Panipat, Shujāud-Daulah was staying in the suburbs of Delhi when the moon of Muharram was sighted and Nawab enwrapped himself in black-colored clothes. Along with other mourners, open head and barefoot, holding 'alam in hand he passed through the residence of Ahmad Shah".[23]

Though Shī'īsm was becoming popular during the reign of the Nawabs of Awadh, and the public observance of Muharram was also growing, it is interesting that the procession carrying the 'alam which is attributed to the brave Abbas ibn- Ali, a half-brother of Imām Husayn and his commander-in-chief in Karbala, was started by a Dervish Sufi, Kamal Shah in Awadh. According to an account by Munshi Jawala Prasad 'Akhtar':

> "The first 'alam procession attributed to Hazrat Abbas was started at Ayodhya from Babri Masjid built by Mīr Baqi and the credit for this procession goes to a Rajput official Dharam Singh of Mughal Army who, as per the wishes of Sufi Kamāl Shah deliberated the matter with the local notables among Hindus and got their consent for the procession on the day of Āshurā".[24]

It is said that Nawab Shujā ud-Daulah visited Ayodhya along with his mother, Sadr e Jahān Begum, to perform ziyārat of his 'alam. The 'alam procession was discontinued when Kamāl Shah died in 1777 AD.

The practice of azādārī (the mourning-session and processions) was formalized in Awadh, when Sadr e Jahān Begum built an Imāmbārah at Moti Bagh (Faizabad) in 1764 AD.

One of the notables, Sarfaraz ud-Daulah Nawab Hasan Riza Khan, was also a staunch Shi'a, with a strong interest in azādārī. Initially, he used to hold mourning sessions at his residence, but subsequently he had an Imāmbārah built specifically for this purpose. He used to visit it every day after namāz to perform ziyārat of the zarih (cenotaphs). Despite the adverse political conditions, Nawab Shujā ud-Daulah took many steps to popularize Shī'īsm in Awadh, as attested by Munshi Jawala Prasad:

> Nawab Shujā ud-Daulah was a Shi'a by faith, therefore, in spite of adverse conditions, he protected and disseminated Shī'īsm during his reign. Under the guidance of Mīr Muhammad Husayn Nishāpurī more than two dozen Iraqi and Irani ulama were employed for spreading Shī'īsm in different parts of Awadh. They were paid from the royal treasures.[25]

After the death of Shuja ud-Daulah, Āsaf ud-Daulah became Nawab (1775-1797 AD). He was under tremendous pressure from the East India Company for political reasons. Seven years after coming to power, he shifted the capital of Awadh from Faizabad to Lucknow. Consequently, the notables and other important persons also shifted to Lucknow. The center of Shi'a activities was still in Faizabad due to the presence of Sadr e Jahān Begum and Sultan Jahān Begum, who had remained behind. But Lucknow also began to attract notable Shi'as from different parts of Awadh, and also from Delhi where anarchy had become the order of the day. According to Yann Richard, "Lucknow became the 'Home of Shī'īsm' (Dar ash-shi'a) in competition with Faizabad, which was briefly the capital."[26]

Āsaf ud-Daulah was also a devout Shi'a, much interested in fine art and architecture. In 1784 AD, a severe famine broke out in Awadh. Even the well-off were affected, and many came to the verge of starvation. In order to help people, who were flocking to Lucknow from nearby areas, to earn their livelihood, the construction of Āsfi Imāmbārah was started. The poor use to work during the day and those who were higher in the social strata (shurfā) worked at night in order to avoid identification. It was in this manner that a fine Imāmbārah, a manifestation of Āsaf ud-Daulah's religious inclinations and his generosity in creating employment to avoid social unrest due to the famine was erected.[27] After completion of the Āsfi Imāmbārah, he concentrated on the construction of Dargah-e Hazrat Abbas in Lucknow. The personality of Abbas ibn-e 'Ali has a special significance for all the Shi'as. Born of 'Ali and Ummul Banin in 26 Hijri (15 May 647 AD), Abbas lived for 14 years with 'Ali, then10 years with Imām Hasan and the last 10 years of his life with Imām Husayn. He was so handsome that he is known as Qamar-e Bani Hashim (the moon of the Bani Hashims). It is said that even sitting on horseback, his feet would touch the ground. Imām Husayn considered him as commander-in-chief of all persons present at the time of the battle of Karbala. Mirzā Faqir Beg, a Sufi, upon his return from the Haj, established the Dargah of Hazrat Abbas in his house at Lucknow. It is said that he had a dream during his Haj, ordaining him to do so.[28]

Āsaf ud-Daulah extended financial help in the establishment

of this dargah, which was later renovated and expanded by Nawab Sa'adat Ali Khan (1798-1814 AD).[29] The line

"Eeen Gumbad-e Jadeed Bina-e Sādāt Ast".

(This new Gumbuz has been built by Sādāt), composed by Mirzā Muhammad Husayn 'Qateel', gives the date of its construction as 1217 AH./1802-03 AD.[30]

Another epoch-making event of the times of Āsaf ud-Daulah was the commencement of congregational Friday prayers among Shi'as. Till then some Shi'as used to participate in Friday prayers along with Sunnīs. Seeing this, a Sufi Shaykh Ali Akbar Maududi, who was attached to Bahu Begum in Faizabad, advised Āsaf ud-Daulah to arrange for Shi'a Friday prayers.

Around the same time, one Muhammad Mullā Ali Kashmiri wrote a pamphlet describing the importance and praising the holding of Friday congregational prayers and sent it to Āsaf ud-Daulah. The treatise was so compelling in its argument that Āsaf ud-Daulah called his chief minister Nawab Hasan Riza Khan and ordered him to arrange for the Friday prayers. Thereupon, on the same day, the 13th of Rajab 1200 Hijri, (May 1786 AD) the first Shi'a congregational prayer was led by Sayyid Dildār Ali Nasirabadi, Ghufran-Ma'ab in the mosque located at the residence of Hasan Riza Khan.[31] The 13th of Rajab is considered a very auspicious day by Shi'as all over the world as this is the birthday of Hazrat Ali.

J.R.I. Cole writes: "When he first led them, in May 1786 AD (13 Rajab 1200 Hijri), some believers from notable class gathered at the palace, where they offered the noon and the afternoon prayers in congregations. But they followed the same ritual form as if they were praying congregationally on any other day of the week, rather than the special Friday form. Two weeks later the same group offered the Friday congregational prayers (Juma'h) according to the prescribed form. Some sources indicate that before he agreed to preside over this ceremony, Nasirabadi wrote a treatise on the congregational Friday prayer, showing it to be an 'obligation of preference' (*Wūjūb-e takhyirī*) rather than an individual absolute duty (*Wūjūb-e aynī*)."[32]

Construction of Masjid-e Āsfi was completed in 1201Hijri/ 1786-87AD and since then the Friday congregational prayers are held there. It is adjacent to Āsfi Imāmbārah, which came up later. Both the buildings are, however, majestic to look at. The famous poet Pandit Brij Narain 'Chakbast' wrote on Āsfi Imāmbārah:

Jagmagātā hai shuaaon mein yeh aiwān-e bulund
Jis ki sanat ka hai duniyā mein nirālā andāz.
Iske taammer ko aaye nahin mā mār-e firang
Hai ye tahzeeb Awadh ke liye sarmāya-e naaz. [33]

[This great structure shines in the celestial lights,The style of which is unique (among the other structures of the world). European architects were not required for its construction and it is the crown jewel of Awadh's ethos.]

Nawab Āsaf ud-Daulah himself wrote about Masjid-e Āsfi.

Masjid kā gar che sab se badā ihterām hai
Lekin Imāmbārā bhi aalī muqām hai
Woh aastān-e haq, ye makān-e Imām hai
Bande jo hain so raat din unkā ye kām hai
Sajdā agar udhar to idhar bhi salām hai.[34]

[The mosque may be held closest to the hearts,
The imambarah too is seen in high regards,
One serves as shelter to the truth,
The other is house of Imām.
As believer one is dutybound to bow at the former (mosque),
And salute to the latter (Imambarah.)]

The personal devotional and interest of the Nawabs of Awadh towards Shī'īsm greatly helped in its spread in Awadh. One can say that a kind of intellectual fervor must have been already present among the notable Shi'a of Awadh, as is indicated by the fact that the Muharram mourning-session (majlis-e azā) became an intellectual platform. Those who addressed the majlis-e azā began to educate people about the early history of (Shi'a) Islam and essentials of religion, engendering discussion on various aspects of Shi'a Islam. Thus, they prepared a large group of people among Shi'as, who could be described as being learned in Islamic, though even without the formal education necessary to be included in the ranks of the pesh-e namāz or ulama. Since there were no Shi'a Madrasas or seminaries, it was out of the question to bring forth Shi'a ulama at that point of time. The court in Faizabad, however, had a good number of knowledgeable persons, such as physicians or hakeems. As physicians used to have a deep knowledge of Arabic, Persian and Urdu and were trained in Avicennian medicine and logic, they had a virtual monopoly in matters of intellectual interest and played the role of ulama in Awadh.[35]

However, around 1766 AD, intellectuals like Mawlana Sayyid Atā Husayn Zangipuri (Ghazipur), Shiekh Muhammad Hazin Gilani and their-like had a profound impact on society. Atā Husayn was associated with the Mughal court of Delhi,[36] whereas Ali Hazīn Gilani (1692-1766 AD) had a patron, Raja Balwant Singh of Benares. Hazin had come to India in 1734 AD from Isfahan (Iran). He arrived in Benares in about 1742 AD. Being from Isfahan, he was an Usūlī while his contemporaries in Awadh were mostly Akhbārīs at this time. Hazīn was the arbiter between Shujā ud Daulah and Balwant Singh. He chose a few Shi'ites from the suburbs of Benares as his students.[37]

The most important 'ālim of Awadh Court—Sayyid Dildār Ali Nasirabadi 'Ghufran Ma'ab', was from Nasirabad, a village in Rai Bareli. Nawab Hasan Riza Khan had persuaded him to go to Iraq for studies at state expense. Before leaving for Iraq, Dildār Ali was an Akhbārī-Shi'a; however, on his return from Iraq after about two years' sojourn, he had a completely changed mindset. He declared himself an Usūlī, perhaps being influenced by the great Usūlī Ulama in Iraq. One of his teacher was Aqā Muhammed Bāqar Bihbahāni.

On wayback to India, Sayyid Dildār Ali visited Kazmain, Tehran, Mashhad and Khurasan. He started disseminating his knowledge by writing and teaching; his energies were directed at attacking the Akhbārīs and supporting the rationalism of Usūlīs. The family of Dildār Ali later played a very important role in the spread of Shī'īsm in Awadh.[38]

J.R.I. Cole has indicated that the emergence of Ulama of Dildār Ali corps was a necessity of the state and such a corps was raised as a deliberate policy. He writes "The clash of physicians with foreign Ulama pointed to the need for an indigenous trained ulama corps who could help to articulate symbolically the growing autonomy of Nishapuri Avadh and spread Shī'ī sciences. Sayyid Dildār Ali's two-year sojourn in Iraq and Iran was a first step towards the formation of such a corps."[39] He further says, "Until his death in 1775 AD Shujā ud-Daulah still minted coins and had the khutbah read in emperor's name for the sake of protocol, but for all practical purposes he was an independent prince. A further declaration of independence could only come when Friday prayers sermons were read in the name of Nishapuri but that required the emergence of Shī'ī ulama corps loyal to the regional dynasty."[40]

The observations made by Cole do not appear to sustain in the light of following facts:

1. Why no such necessity of indigenous ulama was felt by the Shī'ī kingdoms of South in 17th century AD where they managed their affairs with the help of ulama of foreign roots.
2. Sending Dildār Ali to Iraq with a view to establish Friday congregational prayers and thus declaring autonomy of Awadh in Friday Khutba was out of question as Dildār Ali was an Akhbārī while going to Iraq and Akhbārīs do not believe in Friday congregational prayers. No one knew that Dildār Ali will return as an Usūlī to lead Friday prayers.
3. Even after availability of Dildār Ali Nasirabadi's establishment of Friday prayers in 1786 AD and a weak

Mughal center at Delhi, the Nawabs of Awadh never declared themselves independent of Mughals until 1818 AD, i.e., 31 years after the establishment of Friday prayers.

4. For reading out Khutba in the name of Nawab the availability of the ulama of the brand of the court physician or those of foreign origin could have been utilized for their loyalty to Nawab of Awadh was never under question.
5. The first ruler of Awadh who declared himself as Badshah was Ghaziuddin Haider (1814-1827 AD), that too with the blessings of East India Company and not the Mughal king at Delhi. Abdul Haleem 'Sharar', a native of Lucknow and a student at Farangi Mahall, essayist, novelist and historian, writes about Ghaziuddin Haider "The English court bestowed upon him the title of Badshah. The earlier rulers of Awadh were considered as Vizier and were not remembered with any other title than Nawab."[41]

The fact that Dildār Ali had completed his basic education in his village (at home), went to Allahabad and Firangi Mahal to get educated in theology, depicts his strong personal interest in religious education. Coupled with this was a sea change in the public observance of Muharram in Awadh. Muharram processions were more in number, there was public holiday from 7th of Muharram till Āshurā. Personal passion of all the Nawabs for Muharram mourning, right from Burhan ul-Mulk to Āsaf ud-Daulah must have created a very encouraging atmosphere to the ones like Sayyid Dildār Ali. The shurfās (notables) like Hasan Riza Khan who were deeply religious and interested in matters relating to theology inspite of not being formally literate, must have seen their unfulfilled desire of religious education being realized in the education of Sayyid Dildār Ali and thus a support was extended to Dildār Ali for higher education in Iraq by the notables and Nawab of Awadh. It is said that before sending him to Iraq, Hasan Riza Khan had read all the works/writings of Dildār Ali and started liking him.

It may further be pointed out that the assessment made by Cole that, "Burhan ul-Mulk did make an assault on Sunnī ulama and Sufi holders of revenue free land grants"[42] has no justification as there was no general order to assault madrasas or Khānqāhs based on religion taking back of revenue free land from their institutions were the necessity of the state keeping in view the crunch in economic conditions. Had it been under a general repressive policy against Sunnīs and Sufis, Firangi Mahal and the madrasa in Salon would not have survived. Not only the Firangi Mahal survived during the time of Nawabs of Awadh but also their authority never eroded completely so much so that Dildār Ali's suitability for leading prayers on return from Iraq was ratified by the Firangi Mahalis.[43]

The question of taking back land from the Shī'ī madrasa did not arise as there was no such madrasa till then. But the more important fact that the Burhan ul-Mulk did not establish any Shī'ī madrasa is indicative that he was not repressive on Sunnī and Sufi institutions.

Attack on Sufism

It is already mentioned that the key figures in Islam have been the personalities of *Ahl-e bayt*. There has always been an undercurrent in favor of these pious souls. Whenever the followers of *Ahl-e bayt* were put under pressure they found out one way or the other to protect and profess their love for *Ahl-e bayt*. Since Sufis were also great admirers of 'Ali and his family members, the Shī'īs were attracted to Sufism as a natural course and vice versa. Commenting on the period—ranging between 1000-1500 AD, Moojan Momen wrote "The rapprochement between Shī'īsm and Sunnīsm was to have an even greater impact on Sunnī Islam. Firstly, among Sunnīs there developed a tendency to what is called tashayyu Hasan (good or moderate leaning towards Shī'īsm). This meant extolling the virtues of 'Ali and condemning Muaviyya and Yazīd but without going to what was considered the extreme of Twelver Shī'īsm and rejecting the first three Caliphs and exaggerating the position of

'Ali and the Imāms. But, even more importantly, the Sufi orders, which were in the process of being formed into organized schools with chains of successive leaders during this period also took a pronounced pro-Shī'ī turn in their mode of thoughts and expressions. It was an era when the majority of the great Sufi Shaykhs claimed to be descendants of 'Ali, such figures included al-Rafiai (d. 578 Hijri /1182 AD), al-Badāwi (d. 675 Hijri /1276 AD) and al-Dasuqi (d. 676 Hijri /1279 AD). Simultaneously the Sufi concept of the position of the Shaykh came to be increasingly parallel to Shī'ī Imāmate while 'Ali came to occupy almost an important position in Sufism as he did in Shī'īsm. These changes resulted in several Sufi orders gradually evolving from Sunnīsm to Shī'īsm.

In Khurasan, the Kubrawiyya order, which started as an orthodox Sunnī order in the early 13th century AD adopted an increasingly Shī'ī orientation. As-Simnānī (d. 1336 AD) a Shaykh of the major line in the order, although still regarding himself a Sunnī, regarded 'Ali as superior to the first three caliphs and the qutb (axis) of his time. Another prominent Shaykh of the Kubrawiyya, Ali Hamdānī (d. 1385 AD) although described as a Sunnī, greatly venerated "Ali and the House of the Prophet. He played an important part in taking this Sufi- Shī'ī admixture to India. Later several lines in this order became openly Shī'ī."[44]

In India, under the Sultans and Mughals' rule, Shī'ī were discriminated and there were lots of restrictions on their social and religious practices. But many famous Sufis of the age praised the Imām Husayn and condemned the umayyid caliph, Yazīd son of Muaviyya. For example, Khwājā Muinuddin Chisti praised Imām Husayn in following words:

Shāh ast Husayn, Badshāh ast Husayn,
Deen ast Husayn, Deenpanāh ast Husayn.
Sar dād, na dād, dar daste Yazīd,
Haqqā ke binā -e Lā-Ilāh ast Husayn.

[Husayn is shah, Husayn is Badshāh (Emperor). Husayn is Deen (faith) Husayn is Deenpanāh (defender of faith). He sacrificed his head, but did not give his hand (allegiance) into the hands of Yazīd. By God the foundation of Lā Ilāh (There is no God but Allah) is Husayn.][45] These lines are still quoted by many Shi'a Zakirs in their Khitābat (addreses). Khwājā Banda Nawāz Gesudarāz, Sayyid Muhammad Jahangir Simnānī (d.1436-37AD) and many other Sufi saints openly expressed their grief for the martyrs of Karbala. It is also said that many Shi'as followed taqiyya, and became Sufi in this period. Qāzi Noorullah Shustrī in his book *Majālis-ul-Momineen*, provides many such names.[46] Heydar Āmuli, a Shi'a theologian of north Iran (d.1385AD) tried to integrate Sufism with Shī'īsm. He said, "Among all the branches of Islam and the various Mohammadan groups, there is none which has vilified the Sufis as much as the Shi'ites have done, in return, no group has railed against the Shi'ites as much as the Sufis. And that despite the fact that both groups have one and the same origin; that they drink from the same fount; that the end to which they refer is one and the same."[47] Hence, many Shi'as were practicing taqiyya (dissimulation) and found solace with Sufis.

However, to the Usūlī Shi'as, many of the tenets of Sufism were not acceptable. To them, the two basic dogmas—incarnation and monism (*hulul-va-ettehad*) of Sufism, were against the Islam. During the Safavid period, their differences and enmity increased. Shi'a ulama openly attacked on Sufism. Ali Dāvani, writes:

> "We draw the conclusion that the branches of Sufism, are all false, erroneous, and deviant, and differ totally from the religion of Islam, above all from the road to salvation of Twelver Shī'īsm.....they regard the doctors of the Shi'ite faith as purely superficial people, considering their own mystic leaders as the only ones to represent the substance of Islam. They insult the ulama in their writings. They attribute an apocryphal hadīth to the Prophet, taken up by the Sunnīs, in which Muslims are divided into two groups, those who follow the Law and those

> who follow the mystic path (shari'at, tarīqat).Their spiritual leaders, Hasan Basrī, Ma'ruf Karkhī, Shaqīq Balkhī, Bāyazid Bastāmi, Mansūr Hallāj.....were all Sunnīs and enemies of the Imāms, uneducated, unbalanced people, who had no contact with our Imāms while none the less regarding them as guardians of supernatural secrets.....As for their claims to ecstasies and visions, these are the result of hashish or cannabis, drugs forbidden by religion, which some admit to using regularly. They impose excessive privations on themselves and practice an asceticism that upsets their temperaments... . It is very astonishing that despite all the warnings which have come down to us through tradition and the teaching of the most important ulama—those through whom religion has been maintained during the course of the centuries—there are still people who are victims of these charlatans and seek to reach God through their mediation, abandoning any spirit of criticism".[48]

Adhering to Usūlī school of thought, Sayyid Dildār Ali trained under Iraqi and Irani mujtahids, did not like the practices and belief of Sufism. It is difficult for anybody to say for sure that the polemics of Usūlīs towards Sufism was purely for power's sake to dislodge them from the position of power or it was derived from religious fervor and force filled with which Dildār Ali had returned from Usūlī Iraq. Since Dildār Ali was the first Indian to return to India as a recognized mujtahid (1785 AD), there was no one competent enough prior to him to oppose Sufism on doctrinal grounds. Also, never before the environment was so conducive for a Shī'ī ālim in India to oppose Sufism.

Dildār Ali attacked in his writing the very philosophy of metaphysical Sufism such as the concept of wahdat ul-wūjūd (existential monism or unity of all creations), the doctrine of kashf (inspiration), wajd (mystical ecstasy) and practices like singing, dancing and beating drums. He cited oral reports from Prophet and

Imāms in condemnation of Sufism.[49] Sayyid Dildār Ali branded the Sufis as innovators (*ahl al-bid'ah*).

Sufis retaliated by writing against Dildār Ali. They said that the mystical knowledge referred in Imāmi oral reports were nothing but the Sufi-path. They cited that many Shī'ī ulama did not like to criticize Sufism. They defended the listening of music and bestowal of cloak of initiation. They charged Dildār Ali for associating himself with notables and to accept grants from them. These charges were not accepted and were explained by Dildār Ali.[50] Also, one should keep in his mind, the attitude and behavior of the Chisti leader Shah 'Ali Akbar Mawdudi (d.1795 AD), the keenest competitor of Dildār Ali. He refused to accept the leadership of Shi'a mujtahid, for Fridays-prayers.[51] However, under the leadership of Mawlana Sayyid Dildār Ali, Usūlīs tirade against Sufism had deep impact on Shi'as. They stopped visiting Sufi-centers (Khanqah). Therefore, the Sufi-influence on general people decreased. In nineteenth century also the Shi'a scholars (maulvis) did not stop the polemic against the Sufis and Sufism. But one can find that many practices of sufis were infused in Shi'a society in a changed form. For example, visiting of Shi'as to Shi'a mazārs and shrines was becoming popular.The ulama corps produced tracts railing against the mystical tradition (tasawwuf).[52]

Nawab Āsaf ud-Daulāh was succeeded by Yāmeen ud-Daulah Nawab Sa'adat Ali Khan (1798-1814 AD) by setting aside the accession of Wazir Ali Khan which lasted only for a few months. This was done with the help and understanding of East India Company. The scope of this article does not permit to go into the details of these events. However, Abdul Haleem 'Sharar' in his *Guzishta Lucknow* has praised him as being intelligent and open minded.[53] It is stated in the *Tarikh-e Sultan-e Awadh*[54] that Nawab Sa'adat Ali Khan was a devout Shi'a like his step-brother Nawab Āsaf ud-Daulah. During his period azādārī was not only maintained but it flourished also. He established a practice of regular visit to Dargah-e Hazrat Abbas on every Thursday. He also established the Karbala of Talkatora at Lucknow in preference to the place 'Suppa' for the burial of tāziās.[55]

The reign of Awadh came to Ghāzi ud-din Haider in 1814 AD who assumed the title of Badshāh in 1818 AD and issued currency in his name. The Imāmbārah of Shah-e Najaf at Lucknow was built by him which is a replica of the tomb of Hazrat 'Ali at Najaf (Iraq).[56]

Summing up the rise of Shī'īsm during the period of Ghāzi ud-din Haider, Abdul Haleem 'Sharar' writes:

> Royalty and especially queens, showed great enthusiasm for religion. From the days of the Safavi dynasty the religion of Persia had been that of the Asna Ashari Shia sect of Islam, but most of the Muslims in India were Sunnīs. As Nawab Burhan ul Mulk had recently come from Persia, his sect and that of his family was Shia. In spite of this, for a time in Lucknow the government followed the old practices which had prevailed in India since the start of Muslim rule. But from Ghāzi-ud-din Haider's time, owing to the religious fervour of the King and his household, the Shia faith became an important element in the Lucknow government. The ruler disregarded the religious heads of the Firangi Mahal, and the family of Shia priests (Mujtahid family), who had gained ascendancy, established a close contact with the court.[57]

By the time Nawab Ghāzi ud-din Haider died on 20th October 1827 AD, Shī'īsm had fully established in Awadh and the religious leadership had come to the family of ijtehadis that is to the Khandan-e Dildār Ali Ghufran Ma'ab.

Badshah Begum, the wife of Ghāzi ud-din Haider had a great influence even during the times of Naseeruddīn Haider. She extended the days of mourning (*ayyām-e azā*) till 8th Rabi ul-Awwal. In her enthusiasm she prohibited the ceremonies of happiness during *ayyām-e azā* by issuing a farman. However, the resident intervened and Naseeruddīn Haider made it optional.[58] However, the roots of azādārī were so deep by this time that most of the people by their own choice avoided celebration during *ayyām-e azā*.

Mrs. Meer Hassan Ali, an English woman writes:

> Hindus' faith in Tāziah is also common. These people bow before Tāziah and attend majlis. Muslims happily ask them to sit together. While entering Imāmbarah, everyone takes off his shoes; except Englishmen, no one is to be reminded of this.[59]

Mrs. Ali also describes the involvement of women in Muharram rituals in detail. Her narrative is well informed.[60] Another Englishman William Knighton's account is also very interesting. From the reign of Ghazi ud-din Haider, Shah Najaf or the royal Imāmbārah became the centre for the royal commemoration of Muharram. According to Knighton's estimate the reigning Nawab spent "upwards of three hundred thousand pounds" on Muharram celebrations.[61]

During the times of Naseeruddīn Haider, the practices of azādārī had blossomed fully. Maulavi Najmul Ghani has given details of azādārī in his work, *Tarikh -e Awadh*. He writes that "the birth and death of all the Imāms were observed by organizing mahfils or majlis. Fragrant flowers were offered so much so that there was a shortage of flowers in the market. The Badshah himself used to carry tāziās on his head from his house to Imāmbarah on first of Muharram. This was done walking a few miles bare foot on uneven roads."[62]

Urdu literature in general and religious literature in particular was also developing fast. Marsiyah, the mourning poetry pertaining to the events of Karbala assumed the four line "Musaddas" form during this period. The noted ones among the marsiyah composers of the times were Ahsan, Ejāz, Afsurdah, Razā, Sauda, Meherban, Mirzā Dabir and Meer Anees (1803-1874 AD).

Some unparalleled marsiyahnawis lived during these times. On the death of Shah Naseeruddin (1837 AD) his uncle Nawab Muhammad Ali Khan became the king under the title of "Muhammad Ali Shāh " after a battle between the forces of Badshah

Begum and East India Company. Muhammad Ali Shāh had unwillingly agreed to sign an agreement put forward by the Company.[63]

Shī'īsm continued its journey under this Badshah also. He got the Imāmbārah of Husaynabad built in his reign and established a trust for azādārī by depositing Rs. 1,20,00,000 with East India Company in 1839 AD. The interest, amounting to Rs. 48,000 per annum, was bequeathed for the maintenance of the Imāmbārah.[64] Muhammad Ali Shah was succeeded by Amjad Ali Shah in 1842 AD. His father wanted to bring him up as per Islamic teachings. So he was brought up in the company of Ulama. This had a greater influence on his life-style. His piousness did not allow him to accept and assimilate the Aabkari (Excise) tax of Rs. 16 lakhs per annum collected on wine, ganja, bhang and opium, in the royal treasure. So, he had given this department to the eldest son of Dildār Ali Ghufran-Ma'ab, Sultan ul-ulema Syed Mohammad Rizwān Ma'ab. Sultan ul-ulama was authorized to collect these taxes and either distribute it among poor and needy or utilize it for himself as he deemed fit.[65] Shī'īsm flourished during his reign and azādārī continued with enthusiasm.

In 1847 AD, Amjad Ali Shah expired and his son Jaan-e Ālam Wajid Ali Shah became the king of Awadh on 13th February, 1847 AD. By this time the East India Company had made deep inroads in the affairs of Awadh. Thus, the Badshah had little freedom. Owing to political situation the East India Company took up the affairs of Awadh in 1856 AD and Wajid Ali Shah was put under house arrest at Calcutta. After the Mutiny of 1857 AD, Awadh was fully taken over by East India Company. Wajid Ali Shah died in 1887 AD

Wajid Ali Shah was known for his secular temperament. He did not differentiate people on the basis of religion. His chief minister Qaisar ud-Daulah Bahadur was a Sunnī and management of most of the Imāmbārahs was in the hands of Sunnīs.

Manzar Husain Rizvi writes: "Wajid Ali Shah in addition to being a pious and religious man used to write and recite marsiyah.

He was highly devoted to Ahl-e bayt. He built and Imāmbārah, Quasar ul-Azā at Qaiser Bagh....The famous Nauha *Ae kul ke madadgar, madad karne ko aao* was written by Wajid Ali Shah which is still recited world over." [66]

The establishment of a Shī'ī state in Awadh created the need for the Shī'ī ulama to cater to the religious and social needs of the society. Thus, the cadre of Dildār Ali's came into existence. It seems that the 'ulama trained in the tradition of Dildār Ali were required more by the Shi'a society of Awadh than by the Shī'ī state of Awadh. If Awadh's need for Shi'a 'ulama was greater, the establishment of Shi'a madarīs with arrangement for higher studies could have been quiet early in Awadh, something which never happened. On the other hand, we notice that it is the family of the Mujtahids which became prominent, rather than the class of the Mujtahids.

With the availability of the Shi'a 'ulama and a congenial atmosphere for Shī'īsm and a clear-cut identity formation, the separation of the congregational prayers and the establishment of the Namāz-e Jumā were natural culminations. Also, with the development of organized Sufi order, their rituals and the mixing of 'irfān and tassawuf,' the Usūlī Shi'a became highly non-compromising towards Sufism. Mawlana Sayyid Dildār Ali being an Usūlī, severely condemned Sufism and played an important role in bringing the masses out of the Sufis' control. The over-whelming love and respect of the masses and notables towards the *Ahl-e bayt* were the twin factors for the establishment of a Shī'īte state in Awadh.

The polemics between Sufis and Shi'as was also part of the process of Shi'a identity formation and can be seen as an exercise in religious academics by the enthusiastic on both the sides. This is to be emphasized that the state was not a direct party to such polemics. However, the personal devotion of the Nawabs and the expenditure from the state exchequer on the spread of Shī'īsm in a very natural way is conspicuous in the establishment and identity formation of Shi'as in Awadh.

Notes and References

1. Richard, Yann, *Shi'ite Islam*, (Translation by Antonia Nevill), p. 8, Blackwell Publisher, Cambridge, Massachusetts, 02142, U.S.A.,1995; Shia recites [(hayyā 'alā kheyrol-'amal) twice after (hayyā 'alal-falāh) and (ash-had anna'Alian vali'ol-Lāh....) twice after profession of faith (ash had an, na Muhammad ar Rasul-Allah)], (Hereafter referred as, Richard, Yann).
2. Saiyid Dildār Ali Ghufran Ma'ab, *Husām-i-Islam*, pp. 56-67; c.f. Rizvi, Saiyid Athar Abbas *Shāh 'Abd al-'Aziz*, Puritanism, Sectarian Polemics and Jihad, p. 395, Canberra, Australia, 1982; Jafri, S. Husayn M., *The Origins and Early Development of Shi'a Islam*, pp. 289-291, Qum (Iran), second edition, 1989.
3. Rizvi, Saiyid Athar Abbas, *A Socio-Intellectual History of the Isnā' Ashari Shi'is in India*, vol.-I, pp. 54-65, Delhi, 1986. (Hereafter referred as, S.A.A.Rizvi, Vol.-I or Vol-II.); John Norman Hollister, *The Shi'a of India*, pp. 72-73, 77, 79, 82, 87-92, London,1953. (Hereafter mentioned as, Hollister)
4. Syed Taqui Wahidi Saleh Ali Shah,*'Az Kue Sufiyan Tā Huzur-e Ārifān'* (Urdu, translation by Nisar Ahmad Jainpuri), chapter on Talqees-e Iblees, pp. 171-73, Rajab 1419 Hijri (1998), Qum (Iran).
5. Ibid., pp. 53-54.
6. Ali Dāvani, 'Aqā Mohammad-Bāqer', p. 289. Cf: Richard, Yann, op. cit., pp. 59-60.
7. Syed Taqui Wāhidi Sāleh Ali Shāh , op. cit., pp. 37-38.
8. Momen, Moojan, *Shi'i Islam*, pp. 91-92. Oneworld, Paperback, London, 2016; Cole, J. R. I., *Roots of North Indian Shi'ism in Iran and Iraq*, Religion and State in Awadh, 1722-1859, pp. 17-18, OUP, Delhi, 1989. (Hereafter mentioned as, Cole.)
9. Ibid., pp.104-106; Cole, op. cit., pp.18-19.
10. Robinson, Francis, *The Ulama of Farangi Mahall and Islamic Culture in South Asia*, p.26, Footenote no. 28, Permanent Black, Delhi, 2001.
11. S.A.A. Rizvi, vol.-I, pp. 549, 553, vol.-II, p. 288.
12. Ibid., vol-I, pp. 358-60.
13. Ibid., pp. 376-84.
14. Ibid., pp. 262-81.; Hollister, op. cit., pp. 111-117.

15. S.A.A. Rizvi, pp. 281-92.; Hollister, op. cit., pp.117-120; Cole, op. cit., p. 23.
16. S.A.A.Rizvi, Ibid., pp. 292-341; Hollister, op. cit., pp.121-123; Cole, op. cit., pp. 22-23.
17. Ibid., pp. 341-87.
18. Ibid., pp. 366-86.; Hollister, op. cit., pp. 143-50; Rizvi, Saiyid Athar Abbas, *A History of Sufism in India*, Vol.-I, pp. 298-99, New Delhi, 2003.
19. Cole, op. cit., pp. 40-41.
20. Munshi Jawala Prasad, 'Akhtar' Farrukhabadi, *Anwār ul- Sa'ādat*, vol-I, pp. 27-28, (Published in 1296 Hijri/1878 AD), c.f, Kazmi, Allama Farogh, *Shahaan-e-Awadh Aur Shi'at* (Hindi – translation by Ali Imam Zaidi "Gauhar Lucknavi") p.65, Abbas Book Agency, Dargāh Hazrat Abbas, Lucknow, December, 1999.
21. *Anwār ul Sa'adat*, vol.-I, p.156.
22. *Malfuzāt-e Razzāqi*, p. 104; Husayn, Dr. Safdar, *Luckhnow ki Tahzibi Mirās* (Urdu), p. 67, Lahore, 1976.
23. Imād us-Sa'adat, vol.-I, p. 83; Kazmi, Allama Farogh, op. cit., pp. 62-63.; Umar, Muhammad, *Islam in Northern India During the Eighteenth Century*, p. 194, Delhi, 1993.
24. *Anwār ul-Sa'adat*, vol-I, p. 156., c. f, Kazmi, Allama Farogh, op. cit., p. 63.
25. Ibid., pp. 151-52, c. f. Kazmi, Allama Farogh, op. cit., p. 66.
26. Richard, Yānn, op. cit., p. 144.
27. S.A.A. Rizvi, vol-II, p. 76; Hollister, op. cit., p. 157; Cole, op. cit., pp.95- 96; Abdul Halim,'Sharar', *Guzishtā Lucknow* (Translated and edited by E.S. Harcourt and Fakhir Hussain, as, Lucknow: *The Last Phase of an Oriental Culture*, p.47, OUP, Paper Back, India, 1994; (Hindi translation as, "Purana Lucknow", by Noor Nabi Abbasi) p. 24, *N.B.T.* New Delhi,1971; Mohd. Ishāq Siddiqi, "Lucknow ke Imāmbāre", in *Naya Daur*, (Awadh-Number), pp.105-08, U.P. Govt. Publication.
28. Cole, op. cit., pp. 98-99.
29. Ibid., S. A. A. Rizvi, vol-II, p. 79.
30. Kazim, Mirzā Mohammad, *Risālā Sawānih Umrī*, pp. 47-48, cf: Kazmi, Allama Farogh, op. cit., p. 101.

31. Cole, op. cit., pp. 128-29.
32. Ibid., pp. 129-30.
33. Brij Narain 'Chakbast', *'Subah-e Watan'*, pp. 98-99, Second Edition, Allahabad; Kāzmi, Allama Farogh, op. cit., p. 103; *Hamāri Tauheed,* (Editor: Naqvi, Sibte Muhammad), *Āsaf-ud-Daulah Aur Azādāri,* Arba'in Numer, p. 97, 15 September, 1997, Imambarah, Ghufrān Ma'ab Lucknow, (Hereafter mentioned as, Āsaf ud Daulah Aur Azādāri).
34. *Kulliyat -e Āsaf-ud Daulah*, cf: Allama Farogh Kazmi, op. cit., p. 87.
35. Cole, op. cit., pp. 55-56.
36. Ibid., p. 50.
37. Ibid., For details, see, S.A. A. Rizvi, vol.-II., pp. 107-117.
38. Cole, op. cit., pp. 61-66.; S. A. A. Rizvi, vol.-II. pp. 128-29.
39. Cole, op. cit. p. 66.
40. Ibid. p. 50.
41. Abdul Haleem 'Sharar', *Guzishta Lucknow* (Hindi Trans.) op. cit., pp. 57-58; *Lucknow, The Last Phase of an Oriental Culture,* (trans. and ed. by E.S. Harcourt and Fakhir Hussain), op.cit., p. 54; Kazmi, Allama Farogh, op. cit. p. 130.
42. Cole, op. cit., p. 57-58; Ghulam Ali Āzād, Ma'āthir ul- Kirām, vol.-I, pp. 221-22, Kanpur, 1913.
43. Cole, op. cit., p. 102.
44. Momen, Moojan, *An Introduction to Shi'i Islam, The History and Doctrines of Twelver Shī'īsm,* p. 96, Yale University Press, London, 1985. Also see, the Momen's, *Shi'i, Islam* (2016), pp. 93-96.
45. cf : S. A. A. Rizvi, vol.-II, p. 294.
46. Section-III of *Majālis-ul-Mominīn*, Waizin Publication, Lucknow; S.A.A. Rizvi, Vol.-I, pp. 352-56.
47. Jāme' ol -asrār (Collection of Mysteries), cf. Richard, Yann, op. cit., p. 56 and footnote no. 8.
48. Ali, Dāvani, 'Aqa Mohammad-Bāqer', pp. 290-94. c.f. Richard, Yann, p. 60.
49. Cole, op. cit., pp. 152-57; S. A. A. Rizvi, vol.-II, pp. 133-39.
50. Ibid.
51. Cole, op. cit., pp. 150-51.
52. For details, see, Jones, Justin, *Shi'a Islam in Colonial India*, pp. 109-10.

Cambridge University Press, New Delhi, 2012.

53. *Guzishta Lucknow* (Hindi trans.), p. 33; Kazmi, Allama Farogh, op. cit., pp. 115-16.
54. Kazmi, Allama Farogh, op. cit., pp. 116-17.
55. S. A. A. Rizvi, vol. II, p. 79.
56. Ibid., pp. 80-81; *Lucknow, The Last Phase of an Oriental Culture*, op. cit., p. 55 and footnote no. 171 on p. 248.
57. *Guzishta Lucknow*, (Hindi Trans.), p. 36; *Lucknow, The Last Phase of an Oriental Culture*, op. cit., pp. 54-55; Kazmi, Allama Farogh, op. cit., p. 131.
58. Ahmad, Muhammad Taqī, *Tarīkh Badshah Begum* (English translation of Waqaa-e Dil pizir, 1253 AH/1837 AD by Abdul Ahad), p.14, Allahabad, The Indian Press Ltd., 1938; S. A. A. Rizvi, vol.-II., pp. 81-82; Cole, op. cit., pp. 189-92; Also see, Fisher, Michael, H., *A Clash of Cultures: Awadh, The British, And The Mughals*, p. 174, New Delhi, 1987.
59. Ali., Mrs. Meer Hassan, *Observations on the Mussulmans of India*, pp. 27-28, Deep Publications, Delhi, 1975.
60. Ibid., pp. 23-27.
61. Knighton, William, *The Private Life of an Eastern King*, p. 186, Oxford, 1921.
62. Najmul Ghani, *Tarikh-e Awadh*, vol. 4, pp. 396-97; Kazmi, Allama Farogh, op. cit., p. 142; Also see Fisher, H. Michael, op. cit., p.174.
63. *Guzishta Lucknow*, (Hindi trans.) pp. 41-43; *Lucknow: The Last Phase of an Oriental Culture*, pp. 58-59; S. A. A. Rizvi, vol.-II., pp. 82-83.
64. S. A. A. Rizvi, vol-II, p. 83; *Lucknow: The Last Phase of an Oriental Culture*, op. cit., p. 247, footnote no. 164.
65. Ibid., p. 84; Rizvi, Manzar Hussain, *Tarikh e Sultan-e Awadh*, p. 361; Naqvi, Sibte Muhammad, Amjad Ali Shah (Urdu), pp. 117-18, Lucknow, 1976.
66. Rizvi, Manzar Hussain, op. cit., p. 361; Allama Farogh Kazmi, op. cit., p. 185.

Section 2: Scholars

Shaykh Ali Hazīn: An Irani Shia-Scholar

Shaykh Ali Hazīn was the most notable Shia-scholar and poet of the eighteenth century. He is one of the immigrants of Iran who came to India during the reign of Muhammad Shah in 1734 AD to avoid the persecution from Nādir Shah.[1] He is known as a great Shia ālim, prolific writer and a poet of a unique style in the tradition of Indian Persian poetry, known as *Sabk-i Hindi*.[2] He is also considered as one of the most prominent scholars of the Safavid era, whose knowledge extended over the theological learning of his time as well as Natural Science.

Shaykh Ali Hazīn's name was Mohammad Ali.[3] 'Hazīn' was his pen-name or "takhallus."[4] He is also known as Hazīn Lahji, Lāhijani, Zāhidi, Jilani and Banārasi etc.[5] Ali Hazīn was from an elite family of Iran. His lineage goes back to the celebrated Sufi Pir, Shaykh Ibrahim known as Zāhid Jilani (Gilāni) who was the preceptor and spiritual guide of Shaykh Safi-ud-Din Ardbili, the ancestor of the Safavid Kings of Iran.[6] Shaykh Hazīn has mentioned his *nasabnama* (geneology) in his autobiography. He writes, "I, a suppliant to the giver of all good gifts, Mahammed, called Ali, am the son of Abū Talib, son of Abd Allāh, son of Jamaluddin Ali, son of Atā Allāh, son of Ismail, son of Is-hac, son of Nūrūddin, son of Mohammad, son of Shihābuddin Ali, son of Yāqub, son of Abd al Wahid, son of Shamsuddin Mohammad, son of Ahmad, son of

Mohammad, son of Jamaluddin Ali, son of Tajuddin Ibrahim known as Shaykh Zāhid Gilāni". [7] Zāhid Gilāni's home and burial place was in the town of Astra, but Shaykh Shihābuddin Ali, one of the ancestors of Shaykh Ali Hazīn, moved to Lahijan, the administrative centre of the province of Gilan, and settled there.[8] Shaykh Jamal-ud-din 'Wahdat', a member of this family and the great grand-father of the Shaykh Ali Hazīn, was one of the distinguished scholars of his time. Ahmad Khan, the king of Gilan, out of regard for his ability, honored him in many ways and took several degrees of science at his instruction.[9]

Shaykh Jamal-ud-din had only one son, named, Shaykh Abd Allāh, who had acquired the various sciences from his father became endowed with the qualities of piety and of abstinence from the worldly pleasures.[10] Shaykh Abd Allāh left three sons—Shaykh Atā Ullah, Shaykh Abū Talib and Shaykh Ibrāhim.[11] Among them, Shaykh Atā Ullah was a scholar of jurisprudence and sacred history. He was also known for his devotion and his frequency in divine worship. He died without off spring.[12] Shaykh Ibrāhim, the youngest of the brothers, was a clever man in business and an acute genius. He was also expert in writing. He wrote exceedingly well in seven different forms of penship.[13]

Shaykh Abū Talib (the father of Hazīn) received most of his early education from Mulla Hasan, the Shaykh ul Islam of Gilan. At the age of twenty he migrated to Isfahan in order to keep the company with learned men in Iran. In Isfahan he continued his studies under Agha Husayn Khonsāri and Rafiai Yazdi and became proficient in Mathematics.[14] The Shaykh devoted so deeply to reading and disputation that till the end of his life he continued steadily in the same course. He had more than 5000 volumes in his library. He corrected all of them and wrote commentaries on most of them, illustrating the greatest part of them with marginal notes.[15] He was an expert calligrapher and transcribed a large number of books both to earn a living and to sharpen his intellect.[16] Hazīn, himself, writes about him that. "He copied with his own hand about 80 volumes, such voluminous books as Tafsīr-i-Baidāwī, Qūmūs-ul-Lughat, Sharah-i Lumā, the whole of Tahdhīb-i-Hadīth....His writing was exceedingly beautiful and clear".[17]

After his father's death, Shaykh Abū Talib dropped the idea of returning to Lahijan and, having bought a house at Isfahan, settled there. After sometime he went to perform the Hajj. He also visited the holy places of Iraq. After completing the pious journey, he came back to Isfahan. There he married the daughter of Haji Ināyatullah of the same place.[18] His offsprings were limited to four sons.[19] Ali Hazīn was eldest among them. Thus, he (Hazīn) belonged to the learned scholars, Sufis and poets' family.

Shaykh Ali Hazīn was born on Monday, 27 Rabi ul ākhir 1103 A.H. (18 January 1692 AD) at the royal residence in Isfahan.[20] At the age of four, Hazīn was placed for instruction under Mulla Shah Mohammad Shirāzi. In about two years' time he was capable of reading and writing. He took so much interest in his studies that no occupation was dear to him than reading and writing and he perused a number of Persian books in prose and verse.[21] When he was eight years old, his father directed him to perfect his 'Qirat' under Mawlana Malik Husayn Qari. He studied two years under the guidance of Mawlana and completed the course of study. He became expert in recitation.[22] In this period he found in himself the tendency to compose poems, but since his master and his father had prohibited him from writing poems, he tried to hide it. Hazīn tells us in one of his verses that he was forbidden by the Preceptor of intellect, not to versify; lest it may bring him infamy.[23] However, Shaykh Khalil AllāhTāliqāni, his master of mysticism, encouraged him and added fuels to the fire. He also gave him the pen-name of 'Hazīn' and thus publicized him as poet.[24] Later Hazīn's father also gave him the permission to poetise and presented him his own pen-case, when one day he witnessed Hazīn's skill of composing an ode consisting of subtle extempore verses in the presence of a number of learned men, which earned him the praises of all those who were present in discussions at his father's house.[25] On this occasion his father also said that, "Now, I give you leave to cultivate the Muses, but not to such excess, as to waste your time".[26] When Hazīn was ten years old, his father, himself, took up as his teacher and taught him many books on different subjects.[27] Hazīn read *Sharh al- Tajrid* and *Zubdat -al-Usūl* from his father when he accompanied him to Lahijan in 1113 AH (1701 AD) and stayed there for one year till his return to Isfahan. At his father's direction, he studied the treatise called, Khulāsat-ul-Hisāb under the guidance of his uncle.[28] During this period he also came in contact with Mirzā Hasan, son of Mawlana Abdur Razzāq, Hāji Mohammad Sharif, Mīr Mohammad Ibrāhim of Qazvin, Mirzā Qawāmuddin Mohammad of Saif (near Qazvin) and Shaykh Ibrāhim (Hazīn's uncle).[29] Again at Isfahan, He came into contact with Mirzā Kamaluddin of Fasa, Hāji Mohammad Tāhir of Isfahan, Shaykh Ināyatullāh of Gilan, Amir Syed Hasan of Taliqan, Āghā Jamāluddin Mohammad Khonsāri, Akhund Maula Mohammad 'Sirāb', Mirzā Masih (a physician) and Mirzā Mohammad Tāhir. All these learned scholars taught him.[30] His father also taught him advanced works of logic, rhetoric, grammar, philosophy, fiqh and Hadīs.[31]

As Shaykh's father himself was a very learned and pious man and was held in high esteem for his abilities among his contemporaries, he always conducted his son to the company of learned and pious people. Consequently, Hazīn came into contact with a large number of eminent scholars while still young. Among them were Mawlana Mohammad Bāqar Majlisi of Isfahan (whom he had seen three to four times, only), Mirzā Alauddin Mohammad, known by the surname of Gulistān, Shaykh Ja'far Qāzī, the Shaykh -ul Islam, Shaykh Ali, the younger brother of Shaykh ul Islam, Mawlana Hāji Abū Turāb, Akhund Masihai 'Shāhidi, Hāji Abū Talib, Āghā Razī-uddin Mohammad, Mirzā Bāqar Qāzī zadeh, Mawlana Shamsuddin Mohammad, Āghā Mehdi, Mawlana Hāji Mohammad of Gilan, Mawlana Mohammad Bāqar of Khurasān.[32] Hazīn studied a number of books of eminent scholars on various aspects of religion as well as other fields of study like Mathematics,

Medicine, Algebra, Astronomy, Law, Logic etc. His teachers were learned scholars of contemporary times as Ahmad Behbahānī , an Irani-Shia ecclesiastic, who visited Benares in the first decade of the nineteenth century writes, "He (Hazīn) received instructions from eminent scholars, like his father and others such as Shaykh Khalilullah Tāliqānī; Mawlana Mohammad Sādiq Ardistānī; Aqā Hādī, son of Mullā Mohammad Sāleh Mazandarāni—the commentator of the Usūl-e-Kāfī, the late Mirzā Kamaluddin Mohammad Fasāvi, the son-in-law of the MawlanaTaqī Majlisi; Amir Syed Hāji Mohammad Tāhir Isfahānī, the distinguished Traditionalist; Shaykh Enayat Gilani, the celebrated philosopher, Syed Hasan Tāliqāni, the most erudite and learned scholar of his time; Mirzā Mohammad Tāhir, the renowned investigator, son of Mirzā Abdul Hasan Qaini—a wonder of the age in the science of Mathematics; Shah Mohammad Shirāzi, a preceptor of the learned scholars and encyclopaedia of rational and traditional learnings; Akhond Masiha-i-Fāsāvi, a disciple of the most learned teacher Aqā Husayn Khawansari, Mawlana Lutfullah Shirazi, a pupil of the most eminent Traditionalist Mawlana Mohsin Kashani and other great scholars of the time".[33] He further writes that "He (Shaykh Hazīn) in a short span of time had acquired such celebrity and perfection that he came to be regarded as an ecclesiastic of a high order of his time."[34] He had attained a high degree of proficiency in theological decision, and had the honor of obtaining the sanction of the distinguished Ulama for that purpose.[35]

One of the artistic attainments of Hazīn, during this period, was that he was well-versed in different type of writing (calligraphy). He might have learnt the different styles of penmanship from his uncle, Shaykh Ibrahim whose writings served as models. Shaykh Ibrahim could write in seven forms of penmanship. Hazīn is particularly known for his Shikasta. His extant writings are in that style.[36]

Towards the end of his studies, Shaykh Hazīn's interest grew in the learning of other religions. He visited many Christian priests and Jewish rabbis. One of them was Khalifā Avānūs. He was an expert in Arabic, logic, astronomy and mathematics. Hazīn was greatly impressed with him. He studied Bible and some commentaries on it.[37] But he did not receive the similar encouragement from the Jewish rabbies. They were reluctant to teach him the Judiac works. But however, with the help of Shu'ab, one of their ministers, Hazīn read the book of Moses (Torah) and had a translation of it made for his own use.[38] He also came in contact with scholars of other religions. A Zorāstrian Dastūr (priest) taught him the book of that religion.The ancient Iranian astronomy was taught to him by Rustam, a Māgus, or another Zorastrian.[39]

During his study period, Hazīn visited many places. He spent most of his time, near about 12 years, in travels and visited Shirāz, Faras, Iraq, Arab, and Ajam, Khurasan, Tabaristan, Hejaj, Yaman and Oman. He stayed in Karbala and Najaf for about three years and consulted the libraries.[40] He tried to perform Hajj twice but due to one or another reason his attempt failed. At last, in 1145 AH/ June 1732 AD he successfully accomplished the pilgrimage.[41]

In his youth, Hazīn was attracted by the beauty and allurement of an accomplished lady which drove his heart to distraction. As a result of pangs of love, Hazīn was under severe physical and mental affliction for a space of two months. But at the end of that period, he recovered and returned to his occupation of teaching and learning. Later, his parents and others had also persuaded him to marry but he did not give his consent because of his excessive love for learning and teaching. Hazīn remained a bachelor throughout his life. [42]

Since Hazīn spent much of his life learning Islamic and intellectual disciplines with eminent scholars of his time, he also wrote many works in Islamic disciplines with a clear and mature prose. Ahmad Behbahānī writes, "He (Hazīn) has left behind a number of books and treatises containing the rarities of thought as a monument of his profound learning and scholarship."[43] The Nujūmū's-Samā, quotes a tract by Hazīn which gives a list of 189 books of which he was author. [44] Ahmad Behbahānī also gives few names of his writings such as:

1. *Risālā-dar-Wūjūb-i-masah-i-rij'lain*
2. *Risālā-dar-Qazā wa qadr,*
3. *Risālā-dar-Hūdūs-i-a'alam,*
4. *Risālā-i-Taufiqe,*
5. *Sharah-i-Hikmat-i-Ashrāque,*
6. *Risālā-dar Ibtal-i-Tanāsukh,*
7. *Hāshiyā-i-Illāhiyā-i-Shafā,*
8. *Risālā dar Madārij-e-Hūrūf,*
9. *Sharh-i-Hayakil'un-Nūr,*
10. *Sharh-i-Risālā-i-Kalāmāt'ut-Tassawuf of Shaykh Ashrāque,*
11. *Fārs nāme,*
12. *A Risālā containing the solution of the most ticklish and knotty problems, he came across during the course of his acquisition of knowledge.*[45]

Sayyid Athar Abbas Rizvi also mentions his writings. According to him, "Thirteen of his treatises are mentioned in the manuscript catalogues in various parts of the world." They are:

1. *Al-Lam'ah min Mir'at Allāh fi sharh āyāt Shahidu'llāh* (an Arabic Commentary on Chapter III, 16 of the Qur'ān composed in 1139 AH/1726-27 AD).
2. *Shajrāt al-Tūr fi sharh āyāt al-Nūr.* (An Arabic commentary on Chapter XXIV, 35 of the Qur'ān (composed in 1140 AH/ 1727AD at Mashhad).
3. *Mawā'idu'l-ashār* (deals with Shi'i theology).
4. *Muzākarat fi'l muhāzarāt* (deals with the Shi'i theology).
5. *Tahqīq-ma'ād* (discuss the resurrection).
6. *Mas'ala-i hudūs-u-qidam* (comprise a philosophical discussion on the Divine essence and created matter).
7. *Risālā fi tahqiq ma'ni'l-wāhid* (contains a note on Divine unity composed in 1134 AH/1721-22 AD).
8. *Untitled Arabic treatise on Divine unity,* written in 1133 AH/ 1722 AD).
9. *Fī Tahqīq rafa' shubhāti'l- mushābbīh* (tract on the unity of God).

10. *Fi tahqiq ismu'la'zam* (a philosophical discussion on the Divine names in Arabic).
11. *Risālā dar tahqīq-i nafs wa tajarrud* (a discussion on the physical nature of man and his relation to the material world.)
12. *Risālā dar tahqīq-i awzān -i shari'i wa 'urfi.* (a treatise on the weight of dirham and dinar in Khurasan).
13. *Fāras-nāma* (Its simplified version was written by Hazīn in India also). The book discusses horses, generally their diet, diseases and treatment.[46]

The titles of these treatises show that they were abridgements, glosses, commentaries, and translations of standard works on Qur'ānic studies, Hadīs, fiqh, kalam, Sufism, religious polemics, comparative religion, philosophy, mathematics, prosody and poetics. Unfortunately, most of them were lost during his travels.[47]

Hazīn continued to write in India also. He wrote his autobiography, *Tazkirāt al Ahwāl*, at the end of 1154 AH/1742 AD in Delhi.[48] The *Tazkirāt al -mu'āsirin*, consisting of an account of about one hundred contemporary Iranian scholars and poets, was completed towards the end of 1165 AH/1752 AD. It was written in nine days. The Tazakirah is divided into two *Firqāh* (section), the first is about the Ulama, which contains twenty contemporary-Ulama, (scholars) and the second is about 80 poets.[49] He also wrote a treatise, entitled the *Dastūru'l-'Uqālā* on administrative ethics and measures to improve government efficiency. It was written in Rabi' II, AH1153/ July 1740 AD The *Hidāyatnama Padshāhān*, is a detailed version of this work. It is said that this work impressed the Mughal Emperor (Muhammad Shah) so much that he had offered the post of Vizier of Mughal empire to him[50] but he refused the offer. He also compiled, *Masābihal-zalam fi arā' al-Kalām*. It concentrates on the origin and significance of kalam (scholastic theology). It was completed in Ramazān 1157 AH./September 1744 AD.[51] In 1178 AH/1764 AD he wrote Sharh-i Qasida-i Lāmiyya, a Persian commentary on his own qasida in praise of Imām 'Ali.[52] Saiyid

Athar Abbas Rizvi also mentions a collection of his letters, preserved in Mawlana Azad Library, Aligarh Muslim University, Aligarh and a short history of Nadir Shah's invasion of India.[53]

About his prose style, Abu Ayman Md. Razwanul Haque Khan, a modern scholar writes: "Hazīn in his prose works has employed both ornate and lucid style".[54] But in the eyes of Iranians, "Hazīn's prose style is remarkably simple and direct".[55] His words are free from any artificial arrangements and his sentences have very few metaphors. At his best he wrote as he talked, but sometimes his sentences are too long and contain too many clauses which spoil their unity. However, his style is neither labored or heavy nor pompous or artificial.

Shaykh Ali Hazīn is famous as a poetical genius. He had shown great promise as a poet from his childhood despite his father's order to stop composing poetry. The reason was simple that the cultural interest of Safavid rulers, which was confined to the consolidation of Shī'īsm and non-religious poetry was discouraged by the people. But he could not abandon it. He compiled four Divāns. His first Divān called, *Saqīnāmā*, includes 1000 verses.[56] His second Divān known as, *Tazkirāt ul 'Āshiqīn* was written after return from Shiraz and his sojourn in Isfahan. This includes 10,000 verses.[57] He composed his third Divān in Shiraz with 4000 verse.[58] The fourth Divān together with a masnavi was called *Kharabat*, includes 1200 verses. It was composed in Mash-had.[59] His fifth Divān was composed during his residence in India. This is mentioned in the preface of *Tazkirāt al mu'āsīrīn*.[60] But the statement of Shaykh Ali Hazīn as given in his *Tazkirāt al Ahwāl*, shows that he had compiled four Divāns only. The first two Divāns were compiled while he was still in his youth. The third Divān was collected in about 1715 AD and fourth, between 1726 and 1729 AD. In 1742 AD he compiled a recension of the fourth Divān in India. The first three were lost. Ahmad Behbahānī, praises his poetry and writes: "Besides the numerous treatises, he has left behind four monumental divāns comprising thirty thousand excellent verses, each of which is itself an ocean replete with precious jewels and gems, and is garden of florid flowers. The excellence, force and vigour of diction, extreme eloquence, flow of words, depth of thoughts and facility of which can be comprehended only by the learned, unbiased and impartial scholars."[61]

Hazīn's collection of poems is known as "Kulliyāt-i-Hazīn." It was published by Nawal Kishore Press, Lucknow in AH 1293/AD 1876 and from Kanpur in 1893 AD. The Kulliyāt includes the fourth Divān—his qasidā, ghazals, rubā'is, qatā'at and masnavis under Safir-i-Dil, Chaman-o-Anjuman, Kharabat, Dibāchā-i-Matmahul al Anzār, Farhangnāmā and Tazkirah-ut-Āshiqīn- together with a preface, written in 1172 AH/1759 AD.[62]

The number of Qasidā in the Kulliyāt is about forty. No Qasidā is written in praise of any noble or king. They are devoted to the praise of the Prophet Muhammad, Hazrat 'Ali and other Imāms. Hazīn was a learned poet, that reflects very well in his qasidā.[63]

There are six masnavis in Kulliyāt. The first masnavi, entitled Safir-i-Dil begins with the verses of 'Hamd and N'at'. In this masnavi, he has not only praised 'Āl-i-Rasool' (Members of the house of the Prophet) but also extolled the virtues of the companions of the Prophet.[64] Other verses of this masnavi describe the miraculous events. After the verses dealing with 'Hamd' and 'N'at', Hazīn pays his tribute to the human faculty of speech. According to him, "a poet is the king of the world and is gifted with many virtues."[65] But Hazīn attacks the so-called poets of his time who are pretenders. He says: "They have converted this world into a frightful place." But he consoles himself with the idea that this world is an admixture of good and bad elements. It is the world where the Prophet of Islam is confronted with Abū Jehal, Imām Husayn is beheaded by a soldier of Yazid's army and so on and so forth.[66] Hazīn then goes on to pay tribute to love and declares himself to be slave of the love. According to his thinking, a man's ultimate worth is determined by love. If the spark of love is in his heart, the man, although a drop, can assume the dimensions of an ocean. Love can dispel darkness. Love is responsible for sunshine, and the pious heart remains alive because of love. He then narrates an anecdote in this connection. Hazīn narrates the story of Zulekha.[67]

A commendable part of this masnavi, according to Kirmani, are those verses, which Hazīn has written in praise of his father. This shows that Hazīn's temperament was basically pious and spiritual instead of being inclined towards carnal desires. Hazīn writes : "Had I praised the kings and rulers I could have accumulated great wealth but I have rejected it scornfully. I feel that praising my father and ancestors, I am only discharging the duty of my faith".[68] This statement proves that Hazīn gave greater importance to his faith than to the material wealth.

The verses of Munajat of this masnavi reflects Hazīn's piety, modesty, humility and religious mindedness. The diction is soft and simple, the feelings sincere and the words melodious.[69] Hazīn gives his comments on the importance of Zikr-i-Ilāhī. His conviction is that one should keep one's tongue always busy in praise of Almighty God.[70.] The masnavi consists fifteen anecdotes also. The anecdotes narrated by Hazīn are didactic for the readers.[71] Remaining five masnavis are also of high standard.[72]

The last part of Kulliyāt comprises fragments on different themes related to the poet's life. Some of them are of didactic nature, while others have been written in condemnation of India and its people. The first two are dedicated to the praise of the Prophet and Hazrat Ali.[73] The poetry written under "Fragments" is important and helpful in understanding Hazīn's nature and circumstances in which he passed the later part of his life in India. A fragment written as an apology is very important and informative regarding his literary controversy.[74]

Hazīn was a great ghazal writer. His best performance can be seen in the field of ghazal. Despite unhealthy and artificial trends of his time, Hazīn was able to keep the emotional spark alive in his ghazals. He seems to be specially influenced by Hāfiz, Rūmī and Sa'dī. He faithfully imitates them in his ghazals. In his ghazals, one can see his melodious style, lyrical expressions and ecstatic outbursts, which are reminiscent of the great masters of ghazal whose influence he had imbibed. Hazīn's ideas are sublime and his language is chaste. A marked feature of his ghazal is its Pathos, a clear indication of his painful life. He is considered to be a model for pathetic poetry. When we take into consideration Hazīn's life, his learning and his high-mindedness, we feel that he attempted to make his poetry a medium of self-expression and not just mean of recreation and enjoyment. The feeling of loneliness as well as home-sickness is of basic importance in Hazīn's ghazal. Time is supposed to be a great healer but in Hazīn's case, it was just reverse.[75] Although a scholar and widely read man, he never bothered to express his scholarship and philosophical thinking in poetry. Hazīn felt pride in belonging to Isfahan, and wrote his verses in the Persian language commonly understood in Isfahan. We can see the simplicity of expression and flowing language with beautiful ideas in his poetry which has a direct appeal and goes into the hearts of his readers.

The best critic of Hazīn's poetry was Wahshat. According to him "Hazīn's special field was ghazal and ruba'ī, in both of which he attained perfection. His style of poetry is best suited for ghazal and is fit to be imitated. It combines depth of thought, clearness of speech and construction, elegance of words, relish, pang, amorous purpose of conversation and Sufism; which has greatly added to its value".[76]

Hazīn was busy in learning and peaceful pursuits in Isfahan. He was leading a life of honor, dignity and authority. His family had decent income from his property of Lahijan. He was care-free from the pecuniary survival problems. But the vicissitudes of time took turn. In 1127 AH/1714-15 AD his father passed away.[77] Two years later, his mother also died. In 1134 AH/ AD 1721, his maternal grand-mother and his two brothers also passed away in the prime of their youth.[78] After the death of his uncle (Shaykh Ibrahim), the property income from Lahijan also came to an end because of the mismanagement.[79] A political turmoil in Iran began at this time.

The rebellion by Mīr Ways, the Afghan leader of Qandhar, destroyed the Safavi empire. Shah Sultan Husayn was unable to crush the Afghan rebellion. After Mīr Ways' death in 1715 AD his son Mahmud seized Kirman in 1722 AD and marched on to Isfahan. He defeated the Safavid army at Gulnabad, an Isfahan suburb, in March. The capital was besieged. Hazīn's library, containing 5000 volumes was plundered and many of his valuable writings were lost forever. The Shaykh had to say good-bye to his birthplace. He escaped from the capital, disguised as a villager.[80] Shaykh was forced to wander for ten years in different places such as Kurramabad, Hamdan, Nahavend, Dezful, Shuster, Loristan, Kirmānshāh, Baghdad, Karbala, Nazaf, Kāzmain, Mash-had, Kurdistan, Azarbaizan, Gilan and Tehran.[81] In these travels, Hazīn had to suffer a lot of mental and physical afflictions and tortures because of the vagaries of weather, difficulties of the unfamiliar ways and the chaotic condition prevailing in Iran due to the invasion of Afghans, Turks and the Russians. During this period, he came in contact with Shah Tahmasp more than once and gave him advice on the preservation of dynasty.[82] But the Safavid dynasty ended due to the rise of Nadir Shah.[83] Under the new regime of Nadir Shah, Shaykh Hazīn was charged with high treason and for the safety of his life, he left his motherland in 1734 AD and sailed to Thatta, a port of Sindh in India.[84] He had wished to remain unknown in India but the Iranian merchants and noblemen learned of his presence and reputation. The climate in Thatta and the neighboring towns affected his failing health adversely. He stayed reluctantly in the region as he was unable to return to Iran. From there he travelled through Sindh and the Punjab cities of Bhakar, Multan, Lahore and Sarhind, from where he made his way to Delhi.[85] According to Ahmad Behbahānī, "In Iran, the abode of righteous, Hazīn lived a life of honor, dignity and authority and held a very respectable position in the courts of Shah Sultan Husayn (1694-1722 AD) and Shah Tahmasp II (1722-1730 AD) and was highly honored and esteemed by them and regarded as the light of their eyeball. During the days of the Afghan supremacy over the land and the decay of the justice-dispensing dynasty (of the Safavid) and coming of Nadir Shah Afshar to power, he behaved with great sense of self-respect and in recompence to the gratitude he owed to the (Safavid) dynasty, and knowing fully well of the debts of the Safavid to the account of the Babarid kings but unaware of the ways and manners of the Indian people, he came (on behalf of the Safavid king) to India to seek the help of Mohammad Shah (1719-1748 AD)".[86] He entered Delhi in about 1146 AH/1734 AD in the hope of high hospitality and warm welcome but received only disappointment. There he saw in the words of Ahmad Behbahānī, "the utter helplessness of the emperor and of his virtual captivity in the hands of the nobles (of the court)".[87] So he felt very much frustration and disappointment. Hazīn also found the men of this country familiar with corruption and depravity.[88] Moreover, he did not find this country fit for a long abode. He writes that "No man, who has a residence and place of abode such as the provinces of Persia afford, which in their nature and essence are the best adjusted and most noble, and to all outward appearance are the most beautiful and perfect habitation in the known world, will ever be able of his own choice to reside in Hindostān. Every person's nature is so formed that without necessity he will never consent to a long abode in this country; and this feeling is common to the King, the peasant, and the soldier."[89] However, in Delhi he stayed more than twelve months, but he wanted to go back to his own country. Therefore, he returned to Lahore again, determined to move to Khurasan via Kabul and Qandhar.[90] In Lahore, he heard the news about the march of Nadir Shah's army to crush the Afghans in Qandhar. It was an obstacle in his further journey. There was no way to go to Khurasan. So, he stayed there and waited for the clearance of the road line of Khurasan. But the siege of Qandhar and disturbances took much time. This lasted near twelve months.[91] Then Nadir Shah pitched his camp near Kabul and stayed there about seven months.[92] In the end of 1737 AD Nadir Shah took decision to march against Lahore. On this Hazīn felt himself unsafe. When Nadir Shah's troops massing in Peshawar, Hazīn fled with a troop were of hired bodyguards via Sirhind to Delhi and took up a corner in that tumultuous town.[93] After the Karnal victory, Nadir Shah entered Delhi on 20 March, 1739 AD. During Nadir Shah's occupation of Delhi, Hazīn remained concealed in the house of his friend, Ali Quli Wālih Dāghistāni.[94] During his stay at Delhi, he witnessed the fall of city with general massacre of its inhabitants. After Nadir Shah's departure, Hazīn again came to Lahore, but there he quarreled with its governor, Zakariya Khan. His friend, Wālih Dāghistāni intervened and saved him. [95] He returned safely to Delhi. The Mughal emperor Muhammad Shah and some noblemen patronized him liberally. Umdat ul Mulk Amir Khan Anjām, a minister of the king, secured a *madad-i-ma'sh* for him from the Emperor.[96] This improved the financial condition of Hazīn but he tactlessly ridiculed the Emperor, his nobles and Indian people.[97] Wālih Dāghistāni warned him but to no avail and finally he was forced by self-interest to sever his relations with him.[98] Hazīn also came into conflict with the celebrated Persian poets at Mughal court. He made a derogatory remark about Nasir's poetry and Bedil's 'prose'. He says:

> "Nazm-i Nāsir Ali [Sirhindi] va nasr-i Bidil bi faham nami-āyad agar murāji'at bi Irāndast dahad barā-yi rishkhand-i-bazm-i ahbāb rahāvard-i bihtar az ni nist."

[The verse of Nāsir 'Ali [Sirhindi] and the prose of Bidil are incomprehensible; if the opportunity to return to Iran were to present itself, no souvenir would be better than [their works] to lampoon at a gathering of friends].[99]

The reason behind this disliking was that they used the subjects which were metaphorical and the meanings that were far-fetched. He also had similar observations about Muhammad Afzal Sabit Illahabadi, a leading Persian poet of the time and a protégé of Umdat-ul-Mulk, Hazīn's own patron. Wālih Dāghistāni mentions about the controversy between Muhammad Azim Sabit and Hazīn, in these words, "Mīr Muhammad Sabat, who is the true son and successor to Mīr Muhammad Afzal Sabit has brought up five hundred she'rs (verses) from the Divān of the Shaykh (Ali Hazīn) where the 'mazmuns' are precisely those of others (Poets). The reason for this matter was this "One of his relations had occasion to send to the Shaykh a verse from the Divān of Muhammad Afzal Sabit. He (Shaykh Ali Hazīn) wrote back to say that the 'mazmun' of this she'r is quite lowly, the 'mazmun' itself is from such and such poet and Sabit has stolen it from him. Mīr Muhammad Azim saw that note and his sense of honor was greatly aroused. Within a few days he trashed five hundred of the Shaykh's verses: —."[100] Hazīn also wrote some satires against the people of Kashmir.[101] In the same way, he criticized Mīr Shamsuddin Faqir and Sirajuddīn Ali Khan, Ārzū. Hazīn was generally dismissive about the Indo-Persian poetry, just because in his assessment it did not come up to the contemporary Iranian linguistic standard. Therefore, Indian scholars took it as an insult for the Indo-Persian poets. They rose up to pay Hazīn in his own coin. Ārzū, who was Bedil's student, collected numerous wrongly constructed verses of Hazīn and criticized them at length in his work, entitled, *Tanbih-al Ghāfilīn*, [Admonition to the Heedless], composed in about 1156 AH/ 1743 AD.[102] He pointed out the mistakes, in four hundred verses in the fourth Divān of Hazīn which were either defective or of disjointed composition, or opposed to the usage of the ancients and the modern. In the Preface of *Tanbih-al Ghāfilīn*, Ārzū states that, "the verses, which I have recorded, are those whom I could not understand on account of my defective intelligence and with a view that the same be corrected by Hazīn".[103] The publication of *Tanbih - al Ghāfilīn* went a long way to damage the literary reputation of Shaykh Ali Hazīn. Ārzū also wrote another tract, entitled, *"Ihqāq ul Haqq."* [Administering Justice or Establishing The Truth], in which he objected those verses of Hazīn, which were not included in *Tanbih-*

al Ghāfilīn. It was a smaller volume in comparison to *Tanbih-al Ghūfilīn*.[104]

It seems that rivalry between Ārzū and Hazın was at personal level. Ārzū offers no assessment of Hazīn's poetry in *Majmā'al-nafā'* is, but he concentrates on summarizing Hazīn's flight from Nadir Shah. He practically rants that Hazīn is an ungrateful guest in India after being welcomed (and provided from the imperial treasury) and that his purpose in writing a particular treatise was to denigrate everyone there,' from the beggar to the king.' Ārzū notes that while Hazīn was free with his criticism of India before, with the passing of time, he has accepted that there are consequences to insulting his hosts. Ārzū is wonderfully sarcastic on this point: "Thank God that now all the crimes of India have turned into elegances".[105] Ārzū continues by bringing up questions of whether Hazīn actually wrote three divāns before the currently available one which he claims as his fourth divān. He defended Mīr Muhammad Afzal Sabit and his son Muhammad Azim Sabit both. He also mentions the incident of Kashmiri poet Girāmi, when he came to Hazīn with twenty friends and left the Shaykh confused.[106] Wālih Dāghistāni, an Irani friend of Hazīn, also in his book, '*Tazkira riyāzu'sh Shu'ara*' criticized Hazīn's poem but he appreciated his mastery in different types of poetic forms.[107] Now Hazīn found himself caught in a trap because Khan-i-Ārzū had quoted specific examples to prove his point of view. Hazīn had no way out but to write an apology, which is the part of fragment and included in Kulliyāt. He clarified his position in apology. While admitting the repetition of theme, he points out that after all he is a great poet and above such shortcomings as have been levelled against him. He expects the people to take into consideration his outstanding contribution to poetry and brush aside such minor errors as it is part of human nature. Then he gave a lengthy discourse in poetry on his poetic excellence and declares that had my critics experienced my painful creative process and were aware of its subtle nature they would never have objected to my shortcomings.[108]

There is a question that why did Hazīn make satires on Mughal Emperor and his courtiers? It is impossible to justify Hazīn's action. The King had been very kind to Hazīn. He granted him cash and estates through Umdat-ul-Mulk, Nawab Amir Khan poetically surnamed Anjām, which Hazīn accepted; offered him the prime ministership, which he refused called him to his presence which he did not comply with; and himself set out to meet him, which Hazīn avoided. Amongst the courtiers, Hazīn was patronized by Anjām and had friendship with Ummid Khan, a nobleman. Hazīn had also many other friends at the court. In the light of above facts, no one can justify his act.[109] That is why, Ārzū accuses him of having been an ungrateful and insulting guest in India.[110] Shamsur Rahman Faruqi, a modern critic, calls his attitude as 'pure malice'.[111] But Wālih Dāghistāni says that "Hazīn's innate generosity and personal sense of justice led him to write 'cheap satires' on everybody, the King and his nobles included, in spite of the highest degree of affection and consideration showered upon him by the King and the nobles".[112] Mana Kia, in her work says that: "Hazīn's apparent dislike of India needs to be seen through the lens of his personal experience, and should be understood not as indicting Indian culture so much as lamenting his inability to return to his devasted native land".[113] She also writes "The chapter in which he purports to describe India (Life of Shaykh Mohammed Ali Hazīn 1830: 275-83) is devoted to Iranian rulers' relations with India and says practically about the place itself."[114]

As for as Hazīn's relations with Indian poets is concern, we find, only two poets wrote against Hazīn. One is Khan Ārzū who composed *Tanbih-al Ghāfilīn* and *Ihqāq ul Haqq*. Various reasons are ascribed to the enmity that existed between Ārzū and Hazīn and resulted in composition of *Tanbih-al Ghāfilīn*. One of the main reasons was jealousy. The poets of India became jealous of Hazīn's popularity and wrote against him. Ārzū was their leader. According to Mana Kia, "Hazīn diluted Ārzū's prestige and that this was the reason behind his hostility".[115] In Delhi, Hazīn was treated as a celebrity and got more respect because of being a Shia-mujtahid, his connections with Safavid court, his poetic lineage and his command over Persian language.[116] He stood for a literary purism that valorized the works of the *pre-tāzāh-goi* poets and presented himself as a guardian of the earlier poetic style. However, Ārzū's own case against Hazīn rested on real stylistic disagreements. Preferring the style of the Ancients, Hazīn denigrated recent developments in poetry, and positioned himself as able to adjudicate the difference in quality, while Ārzū supported contemporary poetic innovation as an extension of rather than a desperate from the tradition, and basically accused Hazīn of inconsistency and capriciousness in his aesthetic judgements".[117] The effects of this disagreement rippled out in Delhi literary community.

Many scholars refer to the personal enemity between Ārzū and Hazīn also. It is as, follows: "Mīr Muhammad Afzal Sābit (died. 1151 AH/1738 AD) and Sirāj-ud-din 'Ali Khan Ārzū went to see Hazīn, who however did not pay them much attention. They felt it and left him. In a symposium they objected to the verse of Hazīn. When Hazīn came to know of it he remarked: "The Indians have nothing to do with Persian" and added: "Silence is the answer to fools." Another version of the above narrative is as follows: "When Hazīn came to Delhi in 1147 AH/1734 AD), Ārzū went to see him. Hazīn paid him due deference. But imputing arrogance to Hazīn, Ārzū took offence to himself and returned to his home". Āftāb Rai and B.R. Saxena are amongst those who believe in the above story.[118]

Though, there were many friends and supporters[119] of Hazīn in Delhi but his critics and opponents made his life unpleasant. The emperor and the court were also alienated from him. Hazīn found ruined staring him in the face, so around 1145AH/1742AD he left for Akbarabad (Agra). After staying there for a few days, he decided to go to Bengal because many Amirs had written letters to him requesting to come and settle there.[120] Hazīn might had some plan to return to Iran. With that object he went to Benares. At the time that Hazīn entered Benares, the place was under the sway of Rajah

Balwant Singh. The Raja desired to dispatch a noble man of his court to inquire of Hazīn whether he had come down to Benares merely as a traveler or had a mind to settle there. The courtier submitted that he had got not the guts to do it. The Raja there upon determined to go himself. He went to Hazīn and questioned him about the state of affairs. Hazīn replied: "I am a traveler no doubt, but if you allow me to do so, I would construct a hut here and live therein". The Raja consented it.[121] Hazīn was given a land grant and cash gifts.[122] It was a large landed property but apparently, a thorny, uneven and unlevelled land. Shaykh brought it into a cultivable state and allotted a part of it for his tomb.[123]

Raja Ram Narain, the Governor of Azimabad (Patna) invited him to visit Patna and also became his disciple.[124] Hazīn went there and stayed for a few days. There are many indications of Hazīn's returning to Azimabad more than once.[125] In Azimabad, he also got some idea about the bad climate and political atmosphere of Bengal. So, he gave up the thought of Bengal and refused the invitation of Mahabatjang, Sirajud-Daula and other eminent nobles of Murshidabad to settle down there.[126] But he also did not settle in Azimabad, because the atmosphere and topography of the place did not suit him. According, to Munshi Ghulam Husayn Khan Āfāq "During his stay at Azimabad, Hazīn went out, one day, to see the city, he saw the river Ganges flowing to the north of the city, and canal called Jilla to its south. This reminded Hazīn of the deluge in Multan. He thought to himself; 'Should both, the river and canal, flood at any time, the city of Azimabad, which is situated between the two, will invariably be overflooded. It is not, therefore, wise to stay at such place". Hence, he left Azimabad for Benares.[127] Finally, he selected Benares for his abode. There may be a political reason also behind this decision that the Benares was under the control of Awadh, a powerful Shia-State.

Hazīn still hoped to return to Iran but was continually frustrated. Ultimately, he reconciled himself to live in Benares. There he built his tomb, two mosques, a house and a garden during his life.[128] Raja Balwant Singh of Benares occasionally used to visit him to pay respect. The Shaykh also used to meet the Raja very sincerely and for the perpetuation of the life and rulership; as evident from the recommendation that Hazīn made to Shujā-ud-Daulah. Raja Balwant Singh tried to conquer the fort of Chunargarh and Shujā-ud-Daulah took notice of it. A brief account of Hazīn's recommendation of Raja Balwant Singh to Shujā-ud-Daulah is as follows: At the time when Nawab Safdar Jang deprived Mīr Rustam Ali of all the chahār Sarkar and handed them over to Raja Mansa Singh and Shaykh Abdullah, he also separated the fort of Chunargarh and handed it over to Mirzā Ahmad Beg who was an Irani. Mirzā Ahmad Beg died in 1166 AH/1752 AD and left a young son named Āgha Jani. In consideration of the services rendered by Ahmad Beg, the Nawab allowed Āgha Jani to succeed his father and to remain in command of the fort, and appointed Āgha Mīr (a servant of his father) to act as his agent.

In 1169 AH/1756 AD on the death of Safdar Jang, Raja Balwant Singh got an opportunity and conspired with Āgha Mīr. But somehow or other Shujā-ud-Daulah came to know of it. Marching with an army with the intention of deposing the Raja, he camped at Jaunpur. Out of fear of the Nawab, Raja Balwant Singh left his residence at Gangapur and went along with his family to the hilly tract of Latifpur. The Nawab pitched his tents at Benares.

Nawab Shujā-ud-Daulah was highly displeased with the misdemeanor of Balwant Singh and had determined to deprive him of the whole state. At Shujā-ud-Daulah's order a boat bridge was put across the Ganges and artillery and infantry were set in pursuit of the Raja. When Nawab Shujā-ud-Daulah went to see Shaykh Ali Hazīn at Fatimān, the Shaykh gave him a bit of affectionate advice saying: "Raja Balwant Singh pays his instalment of gold in time and keeps his subjects prosperous and happy. He should not be ruined. Moreover the hilly paths are difficult to traverse and the army will not find it easy to pass through them. What is good of taking undue trouble over a smaller affair and destroying the creation of God?"[129] But being extremely angry at the time the Nawab did not listen to his advice. Ghulam Husayn Khan also writes in *Balwantnama*, that, "When in 1756 AD Shujā-ud-Daulah came to Benares to put down the rebellious Raja Balwant Singh, the Nawab conferred with Hazīn. The poet-mujtahid urged him to come to terms with the Raja and political events led Shujā-ud-Daulah to follow his advice."[130]

Raja Balwant Singh loved hunting and was extremely fond of chasing lions. He was dissuaded from doing so by Shaykh Hazīn also.[131]

It is said that Raja Balwant Singh often sent his son Chait Singh to the Shaykh. Shaykh Ali Hazīn made Chait Singh to sit with him on a silver palanquin which he had made for himself and no one was allowed to sit on that palanquin. He also used to give him some silver coins as a gift. It was believed that by the time, that Shaykh died in 1766 AD, he had given forty thousand rupees to Chait Singh.[132] However, Cole in 1998 had given reverse statement that the payments were made to Hazīn by Chait Singh (Jit Singh).[133]

During his visits to Benaras, Nawab-Wazir Shujā-ud-Daulah also used to pay respect to Shaykh Ali Hazīn. He kept shaykh informend of his political decisions and used to seek his opinion on the matter. Before the decisive battle of Buxar, in 1764 AD, Shujā-ud-Daulah and Shah Alam II, the king visited Hazīn. The Shaykh enquired from them about the cause of their arrival to Benares. The Nawab replied, "We are determined to expel English from the province of Bengal and the Peninsula of India". Shaykh Hazīn gave them an unwelcome advice that they should not attempt to fight the English, but if they chose to do so, they should depend on their cavalry. Faqir Khairuddin Muhammad Illāhabadi writes in his *Tuhfa-i- Tazā* alias *Balwant-nama* that: "It is said that one day, during the stay of the emperor and Nawab at Benares, they visited Shaykh Ali Hazīn, one of the holiest men on that time. The Shaykh enquired the cause of their coming to Benares, the Nawab replied that they were proceeding to drive the English from Bengal and the borders of Hindustan. The Shaykh smiled and said, he doubted the chance, the Hindustani army (the greater part of which knew not even how to handle sword or shield and had never seen a battle) would have against the English, who knew the whole art of war and whose troops were experienced soldiers, thoroughly acquainted with the use of their chosen weapon, the musket and that the Hindustanis would be merely slaughtered, therefore it was much better to forego all intention of war and as far as possible preserve peace, that the English also might do the same, but that if the Emperor considered war absolutely unavoidable, he should depend on his trained cavalary".[134] According to the author, on that occasion, Shaykh Hazīn only half bowed to Nawab, saying that a full bow (Sijdā) is reserved for kings and the escorting is reserved for the Mujtahids and the Ulama.[135] His proud behavior astonished the Nawab. [136]

In Benares not only Raja Balwant Singh but local community also welcomed his presence. Many eminent personalities, including, poets, scholars and students of Islamic theology, Persian language and poetry, came to welcome him. Some of them became his pupils also. Raja Ram Narain, the Governor of Azimabad was his pupil. The takhallus, 'Mauzkin' was conferred on him by Hazīn.[137] Kumar Chait Singh often used to go to Hazīn and picked up a good deal of Persian. Bāsit, Hakīm Beg Khān Lāhorī, Mīr Muhammad Husayn of Ayodhya, Mulla Abdullah, poetically surnamed, Sabiq Benaresi, Shaykh Gulshan Ali, Nawab Amin-ud-Daula, surnamed, 'Khalil', Bindra Ban Das, surnamed, 'Khushgu', Sayyid Ghulam Husayn the author of *'siyar ul muta'khkhirin'* are the few names of poets and authors who visited Hazīn in Benares.[138] Most of them became his pupil. But the list is not exhausted. Munshi Ghulam Husayn Khan' Āfāq, Ram Nagar (Benares) in his *Tazkira* mentions the meeting of famous poet 'Sauda' with Hazīn.[139] There is another story which tells us the meeting of a mad poet of Jaunpur who came to see Hazīn in Benares and out of a claim for equality of status, he took his seat on the very bed which was reserved for Hazīn. The Shaykh disapproved it and said: "There is no place for strangers." The poet replied to Shaykh, "who gave the permission to the Moth (a kind of grass)?" The Shaykh was highly pleased on hearing this. On another occasion, the Shaykh saw him on the road, when some boys were pelting stones at him and his head was bleeding. Shaykh inquired about his state of affair's. In his response, he said: "My head has become tulip-bed through the stones of the boys; Madness has destroyed the days of spring." Hazīn facilitated his medical aid.[139] Thus, he devoted the most of his efforts to writing and teaching Persian poetry.

Shaykh Ali Hazīn belonged to the Usūlī school, believing that a religious scholar (mujtahid) has the right to make independent judgements in law based on his own reasoning (ijtihād). He was himself a mujtahid. But in those days the Shias of Awadh were Akhbārī. So, he did not forget his religious duty. He wrote a number of books and treatises on religious subjects and commentaries on the works of mystical thinkers. In his last days, he also taught some students. He inspired many scholars of the region. One of them was Mawlana Saiyyid Muhammad Askari bin Saiyyid Zia-ud-din Jaunpuri and another was Muhammad Iwāz of Jaunpur.[140]

Though Hazīn kept himself aloof from the people, he could not escape the piercing accusations of his sordid fellowmen. Some of them accused him of expounding the doctrine of pantheism (*wahdat-ul-wajood*). He was even accused as a for-saker of canonical prayers. There was also an accusation that the Shaykh did not believe in resurrection.[141] These were false allegations against him. He felt hurt and expressed his feelings in one of his Qasidā, which transpires that he was much more pestered and tormented by his sordid fellow-men.[142]

Hazīn built a rauza of Bibi Fatima (the daughter of Prophet Muhammad) and a mosque on the left side of rauza. Both were for his personal use. Towards the end of his life, he constructed his also tomb.[143] The verses inscribed on his tablet reflect his deep poetical sensibility. At the foot of the table the following verses are:

Raushan shud az visāl e tu shab e taare maa,
Subah e qayaamat ast chiraag e mazaar e maa.[144]
(Our dark nights have brightened up through your union, The morn of resurrection is the torch of our tomb.)

On the eastern side of the tomb is the following verse:

Jabaan-daane muhabbat bude aam digar nami daanam,
Hami-daanam ke az Dosht paigaame Shunidah inja.[145]
(I have been a pupil of Love and know nothing else; only this much I know that, the ear heard a massage from the friend here.)

And on the western side the following verse:

Hazin az Paa e Rah Paima bos e Sharhgastgi Didam,
Sar e Shooridah Bar Baali ne Asa –ish rashide inja.[146]
(Through the path- traversing feet, O Hazīn, I have done a lot of wandering, the agitated head reached here on the pillow of rest.)

During his life time Hazīn used to visit his own tomb on Thursday and after prayer, also distributed some alms. The richness of Hindu saintly tradition in Benares posed no threat to Hazīn being recognized as a saint. His works do assent the importance of Shī'īsm but are not designed to encourage antagonism between Sunnīs and Shias or between Hindus and Muslims.

In Benares, Hazīn did not visit the house of anyone—rich or poor and passed his time in seclusion. The Shaykh did not receive anything from anybody; rather he gave frequently to the poor as his means permitted. His life was irreproachable and he did not cherish any desire except that of union with God. Therefore, the inhabitants of Benares, both Hindus and Muslims, were extremely reverent towards him. They came over long distances to see him. Hazīn lived at Benaras for a long time in such a manner that people suspected him of receiving Divine help and of knowing alchemy, and having the Jinn under his control.[147] He used to spend spent thousands of rupees every month. The people of Banares also belived that Hazīn was a thaumaturge having certain occultism, revelation and the gift of miracles. His reclusive life was the main reason behind this feeling.

Hazīn also paid a tribute to Benares. He composed verses in the praise of the holy city of Benares and its people. One verse reads:

Az Banāras nā rawam mā'bad-i-amm ast inja,
Har Brahman bachchā-i-Laksman wa Ram ast inja.[149]

(i.e., I am determined not to leave Benares, which is the center of worship of all. Every Brahman here is child of Ram and Lakshman.)

In another verse, he says:

Pari Rukhān-e-Benāras be sad karishme o rang
Pae parastish- e mahed ya chun kunand ahang,
Be Gang-gusl kunand wa be- sang pā-maland,
Zahe sharāfat- e sang wa zahe latāfat-e Gang.[150]

(i.e., the fairy-faced ones of Benares, with charisma and colour, when they tend to the temple with the intent to worship, they bathe in the Ganges and rub their feet with stone. How noble the stone and how delicate the water of the Ganges!)[151]

On 10th Jamād- al Awwal 1180 AH/14th October 1766 AD, Hazīn died at the age of 78 years and was buried in the tomb which he had built during his life.[152] The Shaykh's grave in the Benares is known as, Fatmayn (Fatimān). It is covered by graves of different shapes and sizes and constructed of different materials. Amongst other things it also contains the rauza of Bibi Fatima, the daughter of Prophet and the wife of Hazrat 'Ali. The whole place derives its name from Bibi Fatima. Fatimayn also contains the imprint of the right hand of Hazrat 'Ali.[153] Ever since the death of Hazīn, there have been un- interrupted and incessant encroachments from all sides on the land constituting Fatmayn.[154] The earliest instance on record is the sale of seven bighas of land by Mahabbat Ali, the custodian or Mutwalli of Fatmayn, to Qutlaq Sultan Begum, the widow of Prince Jawan Bakht for the grave of her deceased husband at the sum of Rs. 20 per mensem. This relates to the northern portion of Fatmayn which consisted of a garden and which now forms the part of the graveyard of Prince Jawān Bakht. The eastern portion has been occupied by the graves of the Sunnīs and the bracelet-sellers. The southern portion has been encroached upon by the weavers and the bracelet-sellers of Benares. At present, the compound is much reduced in the size.

The tomb was visited by vast multitudes on the nights of Monday and Thursday.[155] But with the passage of time, it has lost a good deal of its original significance. The number of visitors has decreased. But on Thursday, the Shias offer their evening prayer in the compound-mosque and afterwards hold majlis and marshiya-khwani. In Muharram, they hold majlis. Majlis is also held on the 20th of Ramzān and during the days of Chehllum, which falls in the month of Safar. Sometimes religious meetings too, are organized in the compound. On 10th of the Muharram, a big crowed use to gather not only in the compound but also on the roads and the lanes of the area and the tāziās of the most of the city are buried here.[156]

Thus, Shaykh Ali Hazīn enriched the Persian literature and Shia theology through his teaching and writings. Though he sought independence in his private pursuits, he made Benares an important center of Persian language and Shia learning in eighteenth century. His thoughts and role in society, both, were important for the north India Shia tradition. Due to his scholarship, liberal attitude, unbiased thought and simple living, he was equally admired by the Muslims, Hindu and English population of the place.[157]

Notes and References

1. Belfour, F. C., *The Life of Shaykh Mohammed Ali Hazīn*, [written by Himself]; Translated from Two Persian Manuscripts and Illustrated with Notes... . Preface, p. v, Printed for the Oriental Translation Fund, London, 1830. (Hereafter mentioned as Belfour, F.C.)

2. "The term *sabk-e hindi* was coined perhaps by the Iranian poet, critic and politician Malik u'sh-Shu'ara' Muhammad Taqi Bahār (1886-1951) in the first quarter of the twentieth century. It signposted a poetry in the Persian language, especially ghazal written mostly from the sixteenth century onward by Indian and Iranian poets, the latter term to include poets of Iranian origins who spent long periods of their creative life in India." see, Faruqi, Shamsur Rahman, *A Stranger In The City: The Poetics of Sabk-i Hindi*, pp. 2-3, in Annual of Urdu Studies 19: 1-93; According to Dudney, Arthur Dale, Sabk-i hindi, is stylistic category, referring to a specific historical period and not an analysis of linguistic and stylistic variations particularly to Indo-Persian throughout history. see, *A Desire for Meaning: Khan-i Ārzū's Philology and the Place of India in the Eighteenth-Century Persianate World*, p.160, (Columbia University, 2013); According to S.R. Faruqi, Hazīn was a distinguished poet of Indian style., op. cit., p.17.
3. Belfour, F.C., op. cit., p. 1; According to *Siyaru'l -muta'akhkhīrīn*, His name was Shaykh Jamalu'd-din Abu' l- Ma'ali Muhammad 'Ali Hazīn. See, Ghulam Husayn Tabātabāī, *Siyarul mutā'akhkhīrīn*, (Persian), Lucknow, 1897, p. 615, c.f., Rizvi, Saiyid Athar Abbas, *A Socio-Intellectual History of the Isnā 'Ashari Shī'īs in India*, vol. II, p.107. Australia, 1986.
4. Ibid., p. 21; Ahmad Behbahānī, *Mirāt-ul-Ahwāl-i- Jahān Numā* (English translation by Prof. A.F. Haider), Patna, 1996, p. 138. (Hereafter, mentioned as Ahmad Behbahānī); Hazīn is a Arabic word for, Sad, Sorrowful, Melancholic.
5. *Nigāristan-i-Fārs*, p. 226; c.f., Kirmani, Noor Afshan, *Ali Hazīn: A Critical Evaluation of his Poetic Writings* (Ph.D. Thesis, Department of Persian, A.M.U, Aligarh, 1986), p. 53 (Hereafter, mentioned as Kirmani.)
6. Ahmad Behbahānī, op.cit., pp.138-39; Munshi Ghulam Husayn Khan, 'Āfāq' Banarasi, *Risālā-Tazkirāh-i-Hazīn*, pp. 4-5 Lucknow, 1917, (Hereafter mentioned as Risālā -i- Hazīn.)
7. Belfour, F.C., op. cit., p.1; also see the nasabnāmā (genealogy), given in *Risālā-i- Hazīn*, p. 4 and its footnote.
8. Belfour, F.C., op. cit., pp. 1-2; *Risālā -i- Hazīn*, p. 5.

9. Belfour, F.C., op. cit., p. 2.
10. Ibid., p. 5.
11. Ibid.
12. Ibid., pp. 5-6.
13. Ibid., p. 6.
14. Ibid., p. 9.
15. Ibid., pp. 9-10.
16. Ibid., p.10; Rizvi, Saiyid Athar Abbas, op. cit., p. 108. (Hereafter mentioned as S. A. A. Rizvi, vol-II.)
17. Belfour, F.C., op. cit., p. 10.
18. Ibid., pp. 10-11.
19. Ibid., p. 11.
20. Ibid., p. 17; According to Ahmad Behbahānī, and the author of *Risālā-i- Hazīn*,' He was born in Isfahan on Monday, the 27th of Rabi-Awwal, 1103 AH/ (December, 8, AD 1691). See, Ahmad Behbahānī, op. cit., p. 139; *Risālā -i- Hazīn*, p. 6. But Hazīn's own statement is more reliable.
21. Belfour, F.C., op. cit., pp. 17-18.
22. Ibid., p. 19.
23. Kirmani, op. cit., p. 62.
24. Belfour, F.C., op. cit., pp. 20-21; *Risālā -i -Hazīn*, p. 7.
25. Ibid., pp. 27-30; *Risālā -i- Hazīn*, pp. 7-8.
26. Ibid., p. 30; *Risālā -i- Hazīn*, p. 8.
27. Belfour, F.C., op. cit., p. 19, Hazīn mentions the names of those books which he read with his father, see, Ibid., pp. 19-20. & foot-note.
28. Ibid., p. 52.
29. Ibid., pp. 50-51.
30. Ibid., pp. 56-61.
31. S.A.A. Rizvi, vol. II, p. 108.
32. Belfour, F.C., op. cit., pp. 32-39.
33. Ahmad Behbahānī, op. cit., p. 139.
34. Ibid.
35. Ibid, p. 140.
36. Kirmani, op. cit., p. 63.
37. Belfour, F.C., op. cit., pp. 62-63.

38. Ibid., p. 63.
39. Ibid., pp. 92, 102-103.
40. Ahmad Behbahānī, op. cit., p. 139; Belfour, F.C., op. cit., p. 168.
41. Belfour, F.C., op. cit., pp. 215, 218-219; *Risālā -i- Hazīn*, p.16.
42. Belfour, F.C., op. cit., pp. 65-70, 104; *Risālā- i- Hazīn*, p. 10.; Kirmani, op. cit., p. 79; M. Raymond, a French Creole who assumed the Muslim name of Hāji Mustafa and translated the *Si'yar-ul-mutā'khkhīrīn* into English under the pseudonym of Nota Manus, 'according to his own statement', visited Hazīn twice in 1764 and 1765 AD in Banāras. He tells us about Hazīn as late as1765 AD, "He (i.e. Hazīn) told me that he had never loosened the cordon of his drawers neither upon lawful nor unlawful occasion and of course that he had never meddled with a woman." See, *Si'yar-ul-mutā'akhkhīrīn*, vol. II, (English translation by Nota Manus), p. 176, footnote, 84.
43. Ahmad Behbahānī, op. cit., p. 140.
44. *Nujūmū's-Samā'*, pp. 287-293, c f, S. A. A. Rizvi, vol. II, op. cit., p.114.
45. Ahmad Behbahānī, op. cit., pp. 140-141.
46. S. A. A. Rizvi, vol. II, op. cit., pp. 114-115.
47. Ibid., p. 114.
48. Belfour, F. C., Preface, p. ix; Khan, Abu Ayman Md. Razwanul Haque, *Contribution of Shaykh Ali Hazīn to Indo-Persian Prose* (With Reference to *Taz kirāt ul Mu'asereen* and *Tāzkirātul Ahwāl)*, Ph.D. Thesis, Persian Department, A.M.U. Aligarh, 2011, (Abstract), p. 3., For details, see, chapter-4, pp. 134-226.
49. Khan, Abu Ayman Md. Razwanul Haque, op. cit., pp. 2-3.
50. S. A. A. Rizvi, vol-II, op. cit., pp. 112,115.
51. Ibid., p. 115.
52. Ibid.
53. Ibid., Khan, Abu Ayman Md. Razwanul Haque mentions twenty prose works of Shaykh Ali Hazīn. See, op. cit., p. 2.
54. Khan, Abu Ayman Md. Razwanul Haque, op. cit., (Abstract) p. 9.
55. Encyclopedia Iranica, cf Bahar, Mohammad Taqī, Sabk-Senasi, Tehran, 1320-21 S/1942-43, III, p. 304.
56. Belfour, F.C., op. cit., p. 71; en.wikishia.net
57. Belfour, F.C., op. cit., p. 106.; en.wikishia.net

58. Belfour, F.C., op. cit., p. 111; en.wikishia.net
59. Belfour, F.C., op. cit., pp. 176-77; en.wikishia.net
60. en.wikishia.net
61. Ahmad Behbahānī, op. cit., p. 141.
62. Kulliyāt means 'complete'. This is an Arabic term. Kulliyāt represents a poet's complete works.
    A Divān is a collection of poems, either gathered by the poet or by one of his disciples, generally containing short poems but sometimes with longer poems appended. There can be different kinds of poems in divān, such as qasidā, ghazals, rubais, masnavis and tarji-bands: The qasidā and ghazal both consist of couplets in which all the second lines rhyme throughout the poem.
    The qasidā is a very old verse form which originated in pre-Islamic Arabic and is often a lengthy praise poem.
    The ghazal is shorter poem than a qasidā. The opening verse of a ghazal or qasidā is called a matla'.
    A masnavi is a long poem made up of rhyming couplets in which the rhyme changes with every couplet.
    Rubais are quatrrains. See, Dudney, Arthur, *Delhi: Pages From A Forgotten History*, New Delhi-2015, Preface.
63. Kirmani, op. cit., pp. 82-83, but Kirmani does not find him among the great qasidā-writers of Persian. She writes, "It is, however, difficult to place Hazīn among the great 'qasidā-'writers of Persian. Rather, we are afraid he may not be included among the second-best line of qasidā- writers," see, p. 87. However, she admits that, "there is some element of sincere feeling and of course, craftsmanship too, which attracts the attention of readers." See, ibid, p. 87.
64. Kirmani, op. cit., p. 88.
65. Ibid., p. 89.
66. Ibid., pp. 89-90.
67. Ibid., p.90.
68. Ibid., pp. 91-92
69. Ibid., pp. 92-93
70. Ibid., p. 93.
71. For critical details, see, Kirmani, op. cit., pp. 94-102.

72. Ibid., pp. 102-133.
73. Ibid., p. 133.
74. Ibid., pp. 133-134.
75. Ibid., pp. 141-151.
76. Makhzan, July 1909, pp. 12-13; 'Wahshat' was an Irani. He came to India and entered into the service of Sa'adat Khan Burhan-ul-Mulk. His original name was Mirzā Imām Quli Isfahani. See, *Khizānā-i 'Amīrā*, pp. 246-47, c.f. Umar Muhammad, op. cit., p. 243, footnote no. 266.
77. Belfour, F.C., op. cit., p. 110.
78. *Risālā -i- Hazīn*, p. 11; Belfour, F.C., op. cit., p.123.
79. Belfour, F.C., op. cit., pp. 112-13.
80. Ibid., pp. 115-116, 121-124.
81. Ibid., p. 125, 129, 153-156, 162-163, 167-169, 174, 194-95.
82. Ibid., p. 191-192, 205-20; *Risālā-i-Hazīn*, pp. 15-16 and footnote no. 1 of p. 16; S. A. A. Rizvi, vol-II, op. cit., p. 110.
83. Ibid., pp. 220-222, 269-270.
84. Ibid., pp. 229-236, 251-252; *Risālā -i- Hazīn*, op. cit., p. 17; Kia, Mana, *Persianate Selves, Memoirs of Place and Origin Before Nationalism*, Dramatis Personae- Shaykh Muhammad 'Ali' Hazīn' Lahiji (1103-80 AH, 1692-1766 AD) Stanford, California, 2020. Actually, Hazīn was so horrified by the continuing oppression under the regency of the future Nadir Shah that he left Iran for good. See, Encyclopedia Iranica.
85. Ibid., pp. 252-263; *Risālā-i- Hazīn*, op. cit., pp. 18-19.
86. Ahmad Behbahānī, op. cit., p. 141.
87. Ibid., p. 141.
88. Belfour, F.C., op. cit., pp. 277, 307.
89. Ibid., p. 279.
90. Ibid., p. 263
91. Ibid., p. 286.
92. Ibid., p. 289.
93. Ibid., pp. 291-294.
94. Ibid., pp. 295-298; *Siyaru'l-mutā'akhkhīrīn*, pp.118-142; *Tuhfatu'l' Ālam*, pp. 217-219, 518-526., c f, S.A. A. Rizvi, vol. II. op. cit., p. 112.; *Risālā-i- Hazīn*, op. cit., p. 25.
95. Belfour, F.C., op. cit., pp. 298-301; S. A. A. Rizvi, vol. II. p.112.

96. Umdat-ul-Mulk Amir Khan, poetically surnamed 'Anjām' was the first man to entertain Hazīn on his own behalf and on behalf of the King. On Hāzīn's arrival at Delhi, Anjām secured for him a flef of fertile lands from the Mughal Emperor Muhammad Shah; where Hazīn passed his life happily. According to Muhammad Rida, the fief granted to Hazīn consisted of a few villages. See, *Naghma-i-Andalib*, British Museum MS. Or. 1811, f 66a; Ahmad Ali tells us that the estate was worth Rs. 40,000 and situated near Akbarabad (Agra). See, *Makhzan-i-Ghard'h*, Rampur MS. 57, f 263-a.; Ārzū says that it valued, 2,000,000 dams. (Rs. 50000) see, *Majma-un-Nafāis* f. 170. According to Husayn Dust, 'Umdat ul-Mulk, on his return from Illahabad in 1166 AH/1743 AD, gained the confidence of Hazīn and offered him a subvention of a few lakhs' which Hazīn accepted. Umdat ul-Mulk then handed over the grant to a certain man, with the instructions to pay over the proceeds to Hazīn at each harvest time, See, *Tazkirāt-i-Husayni*, p. 106. c.f. Full text of *Muhammad Ali Hazīn*, pp. 65-66, Shaykh ali hazin in archive.org> internet.dli-201580932.
97. For the verses against the king and his courtiers, see, *Divān-i-Hazīn*, Lytton Library, MS.1/32, f. 91b., For satires on India and its people, see, *Kulliyāt-i-Hazīn*, Lucknow, Edition, pp. 168-69, 190-193, 219, 265, 313, 569, 754, 755, 774 and 925.
98. S.A.A. Rizvi, vol. II, op, cit., p. 112; Wālih Dāghistānī had disclaimed his friendship with Hazīn by the time he had finished his *Tazkirāh riyāz al-shu'arā* [The Garden of Poets, 1161 AH/1748AD], see, Dudney, Arthur Dale, op. cit., p. 60.; Wālih Dāghistānī, in his entry on Hazīn, in *Riyāz u'sh Shu'ara*, he even reprimands him for his uncompromisingly harsh attitude, saying that Iranians ought to be grateful to have found a home in India during the time of hardship. Hazīn's caustic comments are deemed by him to be unworthy of the stature of the Shaykh. ["hajv-hā-yirakik ki lāyiq-Ishā'n-shaykh na būda."], c f, Jane Mikkelson, *'Of Parrots and Crows: Bidil and Hazīn in Their Own Words'*, p. 526. [PDF. academia. edu.]
99. Azād Muhammad Husayn, *Nigāristān-i-Fārs*, p. 212, c.f. Jane Mikkelson, *Of Parrots and Crows: Bidil and Hazīn in Their Own Words*, p. 525 and footnote no.65 [PDF.academia.edu].

100. Wālih Dāghistānī, riyāzu'sh Shu'ara. p. 213, c.f. Faruqi, Shamsur Rahman, *A Stranger in the City: The Poetics of Sabk-i Hindi*, p. 27.
101. Lytton Library MS. 1/32, f. 98a, ff. 101a.-101b., c.f. Full text of "*Muhammad Ali Hazīn*" OU 220047, p. 35., Shaykh Ali Hazīn in archive. Org>internet.dli-201580932.; see also, Dudney, Arthur Dale, op. cit., p. 64.
102. Its full and gloriously Arabicised title is *Risālāh-yi-tanbihal-ghāfilīn fī i'trāzāt 'al'a ashar al-hazīn*. [Lit. The Essay of Admonition to the Heedless, in objections to the verses of Hazīn.]
103. Full text of *Muhammad Ali Hazīn*, op. cit., p.37.
104. Full text of *Muhammad Ali Hazīn* op. cit., p. 41; S. A. A. Rizvi, vol-II, op. cit., p. 112; No one of the Hazīn's supporters has taken notice of *Ihqāq-ul-Haqq*. Those who mention the *Tanbih-ul- Ghāfilīn* take it to be the only book of criticism written by Ārzū against Hazīn.
105. Dudney, Arthur Dale, [2013], op. cit., pp. 63-64.
106. Ibid., p. 64; For details of Girami's incident. See, Full text of *Muhammad Ali Hazīn*, p. 108.
107. Ibid., p. 64. Footnote 71.
108. Kirmani, op. cit., pp. 134-135.
109. Full text of *Muhammad Ali Hazīn*, op. cit., pp. 54, 65-66; In support of Hazīn, it is said that, "The actual reasons seem to be, that, Hazīn did not have a nice time in India on account of his bad health and constant variation of weather conditions in India to which he was subjected by his constant tours which in turn were necessitated by local conditions, including jealousies of some of his associates." ibid., p. 36.
110. Dudney, Arthur Dale, op. cit., p. 63.
111. Faruqi, Shamsur Rahman, op. cit., p.13.
112. riyāzu'sh shu'arā, p. 202, c.f. Faruqi, Shamsur Rahman, op. cit., p. 13.
113. Dudney, Arthur Dale, op. cit., p. 154, footnote, 10. (Kia, 2009)
114. Ibid., p. 154, footnote 11.
115. cf: Dudney Arthur Dale, op. cit., p. 62.
116. Ibid., p. 62.
117. Ibid., pp. 62-63.
118. Full text of *Muhammad Ali Hazīn*, op. cit., p. 42; Aftab Rai wrote in the

late 19th century: "Although he (Ārzū) knocked at Hazīn's door, he was completely beyond the pale. Terrible envy is a calamity that makes a man blind." [*tazkirāh-i-riyāz al-arifīn*, 1977], cf Dudney, Arthur Dale, op. cit., p. 62; According to Babu Ram Saxena: Ārzū composed the *Tanbih al-Ghāfilīn* being offended at a show of discourtesy by Hazīn and actuated by jealousy see, Babu Ram Saxena, *A Literary History of Urdu Literature*. p. 47. c. f. Full text of *Muhammad Ali Hazīn*, p. 43.; Babu Ram Saxena writes, "Shaykh Mahommad Ali Hazīn came from Persia to Delhi and everybody wanted to know this distinguished scholar and poet, Ārzū, however did not partake of the general enthusiasm but being offended at a show of discourtesy by Hazīn and actuated by jealousy he picked faults in his divān and embodied his adverse criticism in a treatise entitled, *Tanbih al Ghāfilīn* (Advice to Careless People), see, *A Literary History of Urdu Literature*, p. 47, 1940. (digital library, India, Jai Gyan)

119. Wārastāh was a partisan of Hazīn. Hakim, despite his apparent friendship with Ārzū and respect for him writes in his tazkirāh that, "*Tanbih al-Ghāfilīn*, is mostly unfair, mainly that Ārzū has committed "Sitam-Sharīkī," or "partaking in oppression." See, *Tazkirah-i mardum-i didāh* (Biographical Dictionary of People, composed in 1761-62.)
120. S. A. A. Rizvi, vol. II, op. cit., p. 113.
121. Full text of *Muhammad Ali Hazīn*, p. 105-106.
122. *Risālā-i- Hazīn*, op. cit., p. 26; Cole, J.R.I., *'Roots of North Indian Shī'īsm in Iran and Iraq'*, p. 51, Oxford University Press, Delhi, 1989.
123. Full text of *Muhammad Ali Hazīn*, p. 140.
124. Ibid., pp. 67, 93; *Risālā-i- Hazīn*, op. cit., p. 25.; S. A. A. Rizvi, vol. II, p. 113.
125. Full text of *Muhammad Ali Hazīn*, pp. 94-95.
126. Ibid., 94.
127. *Risālā-i- Hazīn*, op. cit., pp. 25-26; Full text of *Muhammad Ali Hazīn*, op. cit., p. 102.
128. Full text of *Muhammad Ali Hazīn*, p. 95.
129. Full text of *Muhammad Ali Hazīn*, pp. 103-105; Mazhar Hasan, *Tarikh -i- Benaras*, Vol-I, (1916 AD), pp. 191-193.
130. Ghulam Husayn Khan, *Balwant Namah*, pp. 125-126; Cole, J. R. I., op. cit., p. 51-52.; Rizvi, Syed Najmul Raza, *Attharahvi Sadi Ke Zamindar*

[The Zamindars of Eighteenth Century] in Hindi, pp. 22-23, Peoples Publishing House, New Delhi,1988.

131. Full text of *Muhammad Ali Hazīn*, p. 106.
132. *Risālā -i- Hazīn*, op. cit., p. 26.;
133. According to Cole "when Jit Singh replaced his father, Balwant Singh, as ruler, he gave Hazin 40,000 asharfis." See , Cole, J.R.I., op.cit., p. 51; It is well known fact that Chait Singh became Rajah of Benares in 1770 AD, while Hazin had already died in 1766 AD. More over, Jit Singh is wrong name.
134. Khairu'ddin Muhammad Illāhabadi, *"Tuhfā-i-Tāzāh"*, Persian MS. (Bankipur, Patna), fol. 40 a- b. [English Translation by F. Curven, 1875], p. 52; Cole, J.R.I. op. cit., p. 52.
135. Cole, J.R.I., op. cit., p. 52; It may be remarked that independent though he was of the potentates but he was highly respectful towards Ulama. For example, he had a very great respect for Haji Badi'-ud-din of Patna. For details, see, Full text of *Muhammad Ali Hazīn*, p. 132.
136. Ibid.
137. Full text of *"Muhammad Āli Hazīn"*, p. 74.
138. Ibid., pp.69-70, 74-76, 106-110, 114; *Risālā-i- Hazīn*, op. cit., pp. 29,32-33; Khan, Seid Ghulam Hossein, *The Seir Mutaqherin* (English Trans.), Vol. II, p. 323, Reprint, 1990, Low Price Publication, Delhi.
139. *Risālā-i-Hazīn*, op. cit., pp. 27-28; For Sauda, See, Malik, Zahiruddin, *The Reign of Muhammad Shah*, p. 398 & F.N. 06., Bombay, 1977.
140. Full text of *Muhammad Āli Hazīn*, p. 112; Mawlvi Nooruddin Zaidi, *Tazalli-i-Noor*, vol. II, pp. 100-101, (Rampur MS.). According to Iqbal Ahmad, the author of *Sharqi Kaleen Jaunpur Rajya ka Itihas*, "Mulla Iwāz, whose surname was Hikmat, used to be seen sometimes in Jaunpur and sometimes in Benares. Once he entered the meeting hall of Hazīn, bareheaded, without shoes and his clothes were torn. He sat on the masnad without giving any thought. Shaykh Hazīn read this verse:

    "Dareen bazm rah nist begānā, rā."
    [There is no permission to any unknown person to enter the Hall.]
    On this, Mulla Iwāz answered:

"kai parwaanagi daad Parwana rā.?
[Who orders to Patanga (insect) to enter?].
There is another incident related with Mulla Iwāz. One evening, when he reached Benares, the boys took him as a mad man and pelted stone on him. His head was broken. At the same time, Hazīn was passing from the same route. He stopped his palanquin and enquired the matter. Mulla Iwāz answered:

"Saram az sang-e tiflān laal zār ast. Junu Ghul kardā aiyaam-e Bahār ast."
[My head blossomed like flower due to stoning of the children. The season is Spring and love is on its height.]

The author's source is also *Tazalli -i- Noor.* see, *Sharqi Kaleen Jaunpur Rajya ka Itihas*, pp. 524-525.

141. Seid Ghulam Hossein Khan has given the details of Syed Mohd. Askari, see, *The Seir Mutaqherin* (Eng. trans.) Vol. IV, pp. 90-94; S.A.A. Rizvi mentions only Iwāz's name as Hazīn's pupil. See, S.A.A. Rizvi, vol. II, p. 116; Cole J.R.I. writes that, "Still, elite Hindus there cultivated Persian, and the surrounding districts boasted a relatively large Shī'ī population, which provided him with some religious students in his last years." Cole also mentions the name of Tafazzul Husayn Khan Kashmiri (d.1800 AD), who attended the lectures of Shaykh Muhammad Ali Hazīn in Benares. See, *Roots of North Indian Shī'īsm in Iran and Iraq*, OUP, Delhi,1989, pp. 51-53.
142. Ahmad Behbahānī, op. cit., pp. 142-143; Full text of *Muhammad Ali Hazīn*, p. 121-122.
143. Ibid., p. 43.
144. Full text of *Muhammad Ali Hazīn*, p. 135.
145. Ibid., p. 145; *Risālā -i- Hazīn*, op. cit., p. 33.
146. Ibid., p. 146; *Risālā-i-Hazīn*, p.33.
147. Ibid.
148. According to 'Āfāq', Shaykh's servant, named Ramjaani, was Jinn. See, *Risālā-i-Hazīn*, p. 28.; Full text of *Muhammad Ali Hazīn*, p.116; In Islamic doctrines, the jinn are that group of creatures which was made of fire rather that earth and into which God also breathed. His Spirit. Hence like man they possess a spirit and consciousness and

have Divine commands-revealed to then. For details on the Jinn, see, Appendix-iv. A Note on Jinn by Sayyid Hossein Nasr in Allamah Sayyid Muhammad Husyan Tabātabaī, *SHI'A*, translated by Sayyid Husayn Nasr, Qum, Iran, Feb, 1989.

149. *Risālā-i- Hazīn*, p. 32; S.A.A. Rizvi, vol-ii, op cit., p.113.
150. *Risālā-i-Hazīn*, p. 32.
151. English translation by Late Shamsur Rahman Faruqi.
152. *Risālā-i-Hazīn*, p. 33; S. A. A. Rizvi, vol-II, op. cit., p. 113; According to Sir William Ousley, E.G. Browne, Belfour, F.C., Hāzīn died in about 1193 AH/1779 AD; Siyar-ul mutākhkhīrīn tells us that, "Hazīn was 82 years old at the time of his death."; According to Ahmad Behbahānī, "Hazīn died in the year, AH 1181 / AD 1767.", see, *Mirat-ul-Ahwāl-i-Jahān Numā* (English trans.) p. 141; But these dates are incorrect. Only 1180 AH/1766 AD is correct. For details, see, Full text of "*Muhammad Ali Hazīn*", p. 138.
153. Full text of *Muhammad Ali Hazīn*, p. 140.
154. Ibid., pp. 141-145; The mutwallis of Fatmayn have been selling portions of the place on various pretexts. Amongst other things, places are sold to the heirs of the orthodox Shias for construction of graves for their dead. In some cases, sites are bought up by living persons for construction of their graves when they will be no more. The best buyers under both the categories are the Shia prostitutes who overbid one another in getting a place nearest the Rauzā, in an earnest belief that the sins of all those that are buried near the Rauzā will be forgiven for the sake of Bibi Fatima and that thus they will be able to go to Paradise no matter how great or abominable their sins have been. There are two marble graves of the prostitutes named, Husayn Bakhsh Bi. (d.1283 AH/1886 AD) and Bi Yaman (d. 1872 AD) see, ibid., p. 143; The process of purchasing land for qabr (grave) by the Shias is still going on.
155. Ahmad Behbahānī, op. cit., pp. 141-142; Moti Chandra, *Kashi Ka Itihas*, (3rd Edition), Varanasi, 2003 AD (*Fatmayn Ka Mela*), p. 308; S. A. A. Rizvi, vol-II, op. cit., p.114.
156. *Risālā-i-Hazīn*, pp. 33-34; Full text of *Muhammad Ali Hazīn*, p. 147.
157. Belfour, F.C., op. cit., Preface, p. v; The dead body of the Indian wife of Mr. Alfert, the Commissioner of Benaras is also buried here. In

her memory, Majlis was held and for the expenses, a property was attached in waqf. The Commissioner also constructed the gate of Fātimān. See, *Risālā-i-Hazīn*, p. 34.

Sayyid Dildār Ali 'Ghufrān Ma'ab': The First Shi'a Mujtahid of Awadh

During the Nawabi period, many Shī'ī ulama made substantial contribution to Shī'īsm in Awadh. Among them, Mullā Muhammad Ali Kashmiri, entitled, 'Mullā Pādshāh', his three sons—Mullā Ahmad Ali, Mullā Qasim Ali and Mullā Jawād Ali, and Mullā Muhammad Muqim Kashmiri may be mentioned. These Ulama were Kashmiris who came to Awadh and settled here under the patronage of Nawabs of Awadh. But Sayyid Dildār Ali 'Ghufran Ma'ab' who was from Awadh region and was the first Shia Mujtahid stands high amongst all.

Before discussing the contributions of Mawlana Sayyid Dildār Ali 'Ghufran Ma'ab' it is necessary to describe in brief the basic differences between Shia and Sunnī Muslims. It is well known that Muslims are divided into two major sects: the Sunnī[1] and the Shia.[2] Sunnīs believe that Prophets are selected and appointed by God but the community had the right to choose the Khalifa (Caliph). They also believe that the Prophet Muhammad had not nominated anyone to succeed him and that after his death, the leading members of the community elected Abu Bakr (632-634AD) as his successor who was the most intimate friend and ardent supporter of Prophet. He was succeeded by Umar (634-644 AD), Usman (644-656 AD) and Ali (656-661 AD). The period of their rule is called the 'Khilāfat-i- Rashidun' (the rightly guided caliphate). After them came the

Umayyads (661-750AD) who were replaced by Abbasids (750-1258 AD).[3]

The Shias, on the other hand believe that like prophethood, the institution of Imāmate is also from the God (Mansus min Allāh). They believe that the Imāmate is a pillar of religion without which Islam would vanish. Shia faith speaks that Ali was the immediate successor of Prophet in real terms though the caliphate was usurped by Abu Bakr, Umar and Usman before it could come to Ali. According to them, Prophet Muhammad had, by divine command, proclaimed 'Ali as his successor. This event took place at Ghadir Khumm, while he was returning from his last Pilgrimage (Haj) in 632 AD.[4] On other occasions too, Prophet had already indicated Ali as his successor.[5] Shi'as further maintain that differences within the Muslim community regarding succession to the Prophet began even before he died, referring specifically to the Prophet's companions' refusal, at his deathbed, to give him pen and article so that he could dictate his wishes to them.[6] Shias believe that the companions conspired to dispossess Ali of his rights as the rightful and divinely appointed successor of the Prophet. So, they reject the authority of the first three caliphs.

With the coming of Ali to power in 656 AD, Shī'īsm emerged as an effective religio-political movement. The massacre of Imām Husayn, the son of Ali and his family members along with some closed followers at Karbala by the Umayyad caliph Yazīd (d. 684 AD) in 680 AD was an important milestone in Shī'ī history; it affirmed notions of injustices endured by the progeny of the Prophet and exacerbated a passion of martyrdom.[7] Thus, Shī'īsm rose as a dissenting group in opposition to the Muslim majority (Sunnīs) from the very beginning. This dissent manifested itself in different forms during the course of Shī'ī history. Later conflicts between Ali and Mu'awiya ibn Abu Sufiyan (d. 679 AD), Husayn and Yazīd, and the various Shi'a revolts against both the Umayyad and Abbasid dynasties were further manifestations of the differences.[8]

Shī'ī theology and jurisprudence took definitive shape in the times of the fifth and sixth Imāms, Muhammad al-Bāqir a.s. (d. 733) and Ja'far as- Sādiq a.s. (d. 765). Imām Ja'far as- Sādiq taught the doctrine of dissimulation (taqiyya) rather than political activism because he realized the futility of armed struggle against the political authority (Caliph).[9]

The Shias are divided into many sects. Among them, the Kaisanis, Zaidis, Ismailis and Isnā' Asharis may be mentioned. Kaisanis exist only in name. The Zaidis are mostely in Yeman and majority of Ismailis are in India few in Iran and in Africa. The Isnā' Ashari Shias are found in Iran, Iraq, Pakistan and Hindustan. According to Isnā' Ashari Shias, there are twelve Imāms. Hazrat Ali, the cousin and son-in-law of the Prophet, being the first and the Mahdi, the twelfth Imām, who, since 940 AD is in great occultation (*Ghaybat-i-Kubrā*) being at present the last Imām.[10]

The Isnā Ash'ari Shias are also divided into Akhbārī and Usūlī.[11] The Akhbārī are those who depend on Qur'ān and oral reports from Prophet and Imāms and do not employ logic. The Usūlī Shias are those who are rationalist.[12] They divide the Shia society into two groups—Mujtahid and Muqallid (A learned ones and laymen) respectively. Those, who are trained to the highest level in Shia-Jurisprudence are knows as mujtahid.[13]

Sayyid Dildār Ali 'Ghufran Ma'ab' was the first mujtahid and most outstanding Shia scholar of Awadh. Before him, as Kamaluddin Haider remarks, "The Muslims in Lucknow were Shia only for namesake. Due to their ignorance, they acted against the teachings of their faith. Those who were familiar with it owing to their education, they did not openly offer their prayers in congregation and deliver sermons."[14] In his '*Haft Tamasha*', 'Mirzā Qatil' also gives a detailed account of the ignorance of Shias. He writes: "The Shia Muslims put on the baddhi (thread) of Shah Madar, with a black mark, every year on the necks of the children for their safety and long life and he-goat was sacrificed for the niyāz (offering) of Shaykh Saddu as well. That is, it was due to the ignorance of their own religious beliefs. Because, if the religious sciences had been popular in these cities such customs had not become popular.[15] Sayyid Ali Naqi Naqvi, a great Shi'a alim (scholar) of mid-twentieth century, also confirms the above mentioned statements. Describing the ignorance of Shi'as he writes, "In those days, the Shia community of Hindustan was passing through the age of ignorance. Being a minority and without a religious Ālim they had adopted the customs of other communities. The cow of Ahmad Kabir, he-goat of Shaykh Saddo, Mirān Ji ke Gulgule (baked floor balls mixed with sugar) and the Mannat (Vow) of Bhawaniji etc. were prevalent in the Shia community".[16] Even Nawabs of Awadh did not follow the religious rules. Another modern scholar Sibte Muhammad Naqvi writes in his article that, "even Nawab Āsaf ud Daulah was himself a cannabis addict."[17] But after completion of his study in Iraq and Iran and coming back from Mash-had (Iran) with Ijāzā (certificate or letter of permission) for ijtihād (a legal ruling where no certain proof exists) Sayyid Dildār Ali 'Ghufran Ma'ab' changed the whole scenario of Shi'a society. He familiarized the Shi'as with the basic doctrines of Usūlī sect, prayers and religious rituals. With the support of Awadh-State he established separate Juma-Jamāt (congregational Prayer of Friday) of Shias and established a separate Shi'a Madrasa to impart the religious education in the community. Through his teachings and writings Sayyid Dildār Ali fought vehemently against those forces who were propagating against the Shia faith. He also tried to remove the social evils of Shia society and firmly established a separate identity for Shias.

Mawlana Sayyid Dildār Ali's ancestors were descendent of the tenth Imām Ali Naqi (a.s.). According to a legend, his forefathers came to Lucknow with the army of Salār Masud Ghāzi (a nephew and one of the Commander of Mahmūd Ghaznavi's army) and conquered a fort called Adyanagar and renamed it Jai'Aysh (Land of Luxury). Gradually it was corrupted to Ja'is.[18] It is also being said that Sayyid Zakariyya, one of the Mawlana's ancestor captured a fort and named it 'Nasirābad' after his ancestor Nasir'ud-Din's name.[19] It seems that Mawlana Dildār Ali's family, like many other

Sayyid families left Nishapur, or some other town in Khurasan, and settled in the east of Lucknow in Ja'is. This family also obtained madad-i ma'ash grant and lived in affluence.[20]

According to J. R. I. Cole, "The Sayyids of Ja'is and Nasirābad in Rai Bareli district hold themselves to be in the line of Sayyid Najmu'd-Din Sabzavāri, who, they say, accompanied Salār Mas'ud Ghāzi on his eleventh-century expedition into North India. The Sayyid qasbah at Ja'is split seven generations after Sabzavāri's arrival when Sayyid Zakariyya moved three miles away founding a new settlement inside a fort at what became Nasirābad The Sayyids of Ja'is and Nasirābad held land grants from the central government".[21] Cole also says that, during the reign of Bahadur Shāh (1707-12), a few Sayyids in Nasirābad embraced Imāmi Shī'īsm. Later Shī'ī Nawābi rule in Awadh accelerated the adoption of Shī'ī beliefs. Nasirābad produced an important Shī'ī cleric, Sayyid Dildār Ali (1753-1820).[22] Cole also provides us the genealogy of Sayyid Dildār Ali of Nasirābad, which follows as:[23]

1. Sayyid Najm'ud-Din Sabzavāri
2. S. Sharaf'ud-Din
3. S. 'Alamu'd-Din
4. S. 'Alīmu'd-Din
5. Sayyid Nasiru'd-Din
6. S. Taju'd-Din
7. S. Khidr
8. S. Zakariyya
9. S. Sulaymān
10. S. Muhammad
11. S. Ishāq
12. S. Mustafa
13. S. Talib
14. S. Ibrāhim
15. S. Abdu'l- Hādi
16. S. Muhammad Mu'in
17. Sayyid Dildār 'Ali (1753-1820)

Sayyid Dildār Ali was the son of Sayyid Muhammad Mu'in bin Sayyid Abdul Hādi. He was born in 1166 Hijri (1752-53 AD) at the large Sayyid dominated village of Nasirābad (Ja'is) in the modern district of Rai Bareli in Uttar Pradesh.[24] He received his early education in Nasirābad. There he learned Arabic and studied some basic texts. Then he left for other towns in order to pursue the rational sciences with individual scholars. Most of them were small town, dominated by Muslims. He received his higher education from Sayyid Ghulam Husayn Dakani Illahabadi and Maulvi Haider Ali Sandilawi. At Allāhabad he joined the classes of the Imāmi philosopher, Ghulam Husayn Dakani with whom he studied most of the basic textbooks for the rational sciences. His another teacher, Mawlvi Haider Ali Sandilawi was a Sunnī but his father Mullā Hamdullah was a Shia. He had written commentaries on the Sharh Sullam and Shams Bāzigha by Mullā Mahmūd Jawnpuri and the Zubdat u'l-Usūl by Shaykh Bahā'ud-Din Āmili. He was a great scholar and famous teacher of his time. His disciple, Mawlvi Babu'llah of Rai Bareli also taught Mawlana Dildar Ali.[25] According to Professor Saiyid Athar Abbas Rizvi, "most of his teachers were Maturidiyya to Hanafis."[26] Mawlana Dildār Ali travelled a lot and came in to contact with both Sunnī and Shia Ulama (scholars). At Shahjahanpur, he met Mullā Abdu'l- Ali Bahru'l-Ulum (d.1801 AD) who was the son of famous scholar Mullā Nizāmu'd-Din of Firāngi Mahal (d. 1748 AD). Sayyid Dildār Ali furthered his exploration of the rational sciences at the hands of Mullā Abdu'l-Ali Bahru'l-'Ulum. Bahru'l-'Ulum considered one of the statement of Maulvi Hamdu'llah, ungrammatical. Sayyyid Dildār Ali defended the statement of Maulvi Hamd'u-llah and at one point engaged in a heated debate with his distinguished tutor. Mullā Hasan, another teacher of the institution, also debated Sayyid Dildār Ali on matters of metaphysics.[27] Sayyid Dildār Ali left Shahjahanpur for Nasirābad as he started feeling unsafe there. After sometime he travelled to nearby Faizabad, where a number of Shī'ī Ulama were gathering under the patronage of Nawab Shujā-ud-Dullah and his notables.

There he fell ill and was chided by the Nawab for studying too hard.[28] From there he went Lucknow where he taught and also completed his studies.[29] The student days of Sayyid Dildār Ali were hard. At one point he reportedly made a deal with a Hindu shopkeeper to serve as a night watchman for his shop if he could be permitted to sleep on its doorstep.[30]

Finally, Sayyid Dildār Ali's diligence was rewarded. Within a short span of time his reputation and ability as well as some of his early writings was brought to the notice of Nawab Hasan Riza Khan, the chief minister of Awadh, who was an illiterate but a staunch Shia. When Mawlana's writings were read to him, he got impressed and awarded him a stipend of rupees thirty per month and included him among his companions.[31]

Sayyid Dildār Ali, like other Shī'ī scholars, became an Akhbārī and a rationalist. He greatly admired the *Fawāid-i Madaniyya*, a book of Akhbārī faith written by Mullā Muhammad Amin Astrabadi. It was written nearly two centuries ago. In 1193 AH/1779 AD Sayyid Dildār Ali, financed by Hasan Rizā Khan, left for Iraq and Iran for further studies.[32] He also took the *Fawāid-i Madaniyya* with him. During his long boat journey and also en-route to Najaf, he became friend with an Arab scholar. Both discussed about the jurisprudence. His Arab friend upheld the Usūlī basis of fiqh but Sayyid Dildār Ali defended the Akhbārī point of view.[33] At Najaf, he met Sayyid Muhsin Baghdādei, a renowned Usūlī scholar and submitted him that the *Fawā'id-i Madaniyya* had converted the Indian Shī'ī Ulama to Akhbārī point of view and even he himself was confused. Sayyid Muhsin told him that the ignorance of the Usūlī theories was responsible for the popularity of the Akhbārī traditions. The Sayyid then gave him the *Fawāid al-Makkiyya* written by Nūru'd-Din' Ali bin Husayn (d.1068 AH/1657-58 AD) for study and said that this book would clear his doubts regarding the Usūlī fiqh. Sayyid Dildār Ali studied some chapters of it but he found the refutation unconvincing. Then he met Shaykh Ja'far Najafi, who also could not resolve his doubts. Next day Sayyid Muhsin again explained the Usūlī theory of ijma' and the circumstances under which it was permissible. Though, Sayyid Dildār Ali was still not convinced but he did not press his points to him in the interest of his further studies because he knew that the Iraqi Ulama were touchy on this point.[34]

From Najaf, Mawlana Dildār Ali moved to Karbala. But there he did not raise the controversial question again. He studied under Aqā Muhammad Bāqir Bihbahānī and Sayyid' Ali Tabātabāī. The libraries in Karbala contained a large number of Usūlīs and Akhbārī works and this prompted the Mawlana to study the problem thoroughly. His intensive reading convinced him that the author of *Fawā'id-i Madaniyya* had condemned the Usūlī mujtahids unjustly.[35] At Karbala, he also studied under Sayyid Mahdi Shahrastāni. Later on, Sayyid Dildār Ali visited Mashhad (Iran). There he took lessons from Sayyid Mahdi bin Sayyid Hidayatullah Isfahāni. From Mashhad he returned to Lucknow (India) with Ijāzā (certificate or letter of permission) of ijtihād (Right to give a legal ruling where no certain proof exists, or decision based on qiyās or fatwā) from Sayyid Mahdi Tabātabāī and Mirzā Mahdi Isfahāni.[36] Now, he was mujtahid of Usūlī fiqh.

After his arrival in Lucknow, Sayyid Dildār Ali started his mission of bringing all the Shi'as under Usūlī fiqh. But he found Akhbārīs as a barrier in his mission who were in majority in Awadh. Most of the notables in Nawab's court in Lucknow and also in Faizabad were Akhbārī.[37] Even two years earlier he himself was a staunch Akhbārī. Akhbārīs did not believe in ijtihād.[38] In their view, all men were muqallid to the Imām and it was not permissible to turn to a mujtahid.[39] They were also against the holding of Friday congregational prayers in the absence of Living Imām.[40] So, he set out to refute the thought of Akhbārī school. He wrote a book on the subject entitled, *Asās al-Usūl*, in Arabic and attacked on the Akhbārī position. Mawlana also defended the *Ilm al-Usūl*. In this book, Mawlana has not only refuted Mullā Muhammad Amin Astrabadi's *Fawa'id-i- Madaniyya* but also has spelled out in detail the process of *zan* (opinion) and *qiyās* (analogy) in the Shi'a ijtihād. The book also removes the misunderstanding regarding ijmā (consensus).[41] Mawlana also says that, "although a mujtahid might commit an error, he would still be rewarded by God".[42] In brief, the book discusses the main issues in jurisprudential method between the two major schools giving both rational and traditional proofs for the stances.[43] Meanwhile Mullā Muhammad Ali Kashmiri, known as 'Mullā Pādshāh', who was settled in Faizabad in about 1785 AD wrote a treatise on the virtue of congregational Friday-prayers for Shi'as. He dedicated the book to Nawab Āsaf-ud-Daulah[44] and urged him to establish Friday, congregational Prayers. He also wrote that, Mawlana Dildār Ali was a most competent and pious 'ālim. The outstanding 'ulama of Karbala and Mashhad had authorized him to perform ijtihād. Therefore, he should be invited to lead the congregational prayers. When Hasan Riza, the Chief Minister went to Faizabad on a visit, Mullā Kashmiri presented him a copy of the treatise. He also urged the minister to make his obligatory five times a day prayers behind Mawlana Sayyid Dildār Ali.[45] The treatise was so compelling in its argument that NawabĀsaf-ud-Daulah called his chief minister, Hasan Riza Khan and ordered him to arrange for the Friday prayer. But when the chief minister sounded out Sayyid Dildār Ali about the idea he rejected it. Mawlana feared that such a public display would arouse the hostility of the majority Sunnīs and he asked the chief minister to dismiss the proposal. Not only this, to avoid the further pressure, Mawlana retired with his family and attendants to Nasirābad.[46] But later on, he agreed to lead the congregational prayer. On 13th Rajab 1200 Hijri' (May 1786 AD), Sayyid Dildār Ali led the first congregational Friday prayer. It was organized by the chief minister in the mosque of his own palace and only some believers of notable class participated.[47] This was the anniversary of Imām Hazrat Ali's birthday. But, according to J.R.I. Cole, they followed the same ritual form as if they were praying congregationally on any other day of the week, rather than the special Friday form.[48] According to him, this might have been an attempt to compromise though it lasted only for a short time.[49] After two weeks the same group prayed the Friday congregational prayers (Jum'ah) according to the prescribed form.[50] Some sources say that Mawlana wrote a treatise on the congregational Friday prayer, showing it to be an obligation of preference (*Vujub-e-takhiyiri*) rather than an individual absolute duty (*Vujub-e-aynī*), that is to say that it is obligatory for a person to assemble for Friday congregational prayers but it was not necessary for him to offer Friday prayers as *Wajib* or must in place of Namāz-e-zuhr (noon prayer). Once a person became a part of the Friday congregation it was optional for him to offer either zuhr or Friday prayer as Wajib during the occultation period of twelfth Imām. He firmly disputed the most conservative and earliest post-occultation view that the Friday congregational prayers are forbidden in the absence of Imām.[51] The beginning of Friday prayers in Lucknow was a great victory for Usūlī ulama. This was an epoch-making event in the history of Shi'a sect at Lucknow, which placed it among the few Indian towns where Shi'a's congregational prayers were held.

Mawlana Sayyid Dildār Ali led the prayers and gave the sermons on historical, ethical and religious topics. His fifty sermons were compiled into a book, entitled *Fawāid-i Āsafiyya wa Mawa'iz-ī Husayniyya*. The preface says that the rule of tyrants had prevented the Shī'ī dignitaries from implementing the obligatory Friday congregational prayers. This led the Sunnīs to believe that the Shī'ī faith forbade these prayers although it was the sunna (tradition) of the Prophet and Imāms. Consequently, they ridiculed them. Unfortunately, for them the illiterate and ignorant Shī'īs also believed that until the twelfth Imām re-appeared congregational prayers were prohibited.[52]

The early sermons deal with the ahādis relating to the Friday congregational prayers. In his sermon on 27th Rajab, Mawlana said that according to Imām Bāqir (a.s.), if seven persons happened to assemble somewhere and there was no danger to life in congregational prayers, it was incumbent them to perform it.

According to Imām Ja'far as- Sādiq, if five people met in a village and one of them could recite the khutba, they should hold congregational prayers. The Mawlana also said that according to Mawlana Muhammad Bāqir Majlisi and Mawlana Muhammad Taqī Majlisi, Friday congregational prayers were *wājib-i'aynī* (unavoidably obligatory).[53]

In his third sermon, Mawlana said that the Shī'īs and Sayyids should not be unduly proud of their faith and lineage. They should not ignore prayers and must avoid sins. He also added that, Imām Muhammad Bāqir (a.s.) had declared that, "those who did not participate congregational prayers were not his Shi'as and friends. The true Shī'īs were humble and courteous to their brethren, prayed regularly, observed fasts, were good to their parents, helped the poor, the beggars and those who were unable to pay their debts".[54] The sermons and teachings of Mawlana Sayyid Dildār Ali raised the ethical and moral standard of the Shi'a aristocracy of Awadh.

The practice of holding Shi'a Friday prayers and building of Shi'a mosques also spread to the other cities of Awadh. In the same year, the Friday prayers began in Faizabad In 1812 AD Sayyid Dildār Ali constructed a Friday prayers mosque in his home town of Nasirābad Maulvi Sayyid Muhammad 'Ibādat began leading Friday congregational prayers in Amroha at an old Imāmbārah. In 1808 AD, Hāji Ashraf Ali of Patna built a Friday prayers mosque in Amroha.[55] Thus, Usūlī fiqh took place among the Shia population of Awadh.

But the Akhbārī Ulama did not left Mawlana unchallenged. His most colorful enemy from the ranks of the Akhbārī ulama was Mirzā Muhammad Nishāpuri Akbarabadi (1764-1817) of Agra. Akbarabadi originally wrote his attack on Sayyid Dildār Ali's work in 1792 in Iran. He denounced the Usūlī principles but he was killed in February 1817 AD by a mob in Baghdad.[56] Similarly, in 1818 AD another Akhbārī scholar—Husayn Ali Khan had issued a wide-ranging criticism of Usūlīsm in which he admitted that the Usūlī fiqh has been widely accepted. He rejected Usūlis' claims that the Ulama represented the hidden Twelfth Imām, accusing mujtahids of love of high position and a desire to rule over others, even though only the Imāms were worthy of obedience and emulation.[57]

Mawlana Sayyid Dildār Ali produced a number of works discussing the basic principles of the Shi'a faith and fiqh related to the history of Imāms, tragedies suffered by the Prophets and Imāms and also for the promotion of the mourning ceremonies. His writings enriched the Shī'ī literature to counter the critics of the Shī'ī faith. His book on Kalām, *Mirā'u'l-uqūl fī 'ilmu'l-Usūl*, popularly known as *Imādu'l-Islam*, written in Arabic language counters the anti-Shī'ī arguments in *Nihāyahu'l-uqūl* by Fakhru'd-Din Rāzi (467 AH/1075 AD-538 AH/1144 AD). It is divided into five maqāsid (volumes). The first volume deals with Tawhid (Divine unity) which contains 400 pages, the second discusses 'Adl' (Divine justice) in 200 pages, the third deals with prophecy (Nabū'at) in 300 pages, the fourth with Imām and the fifth with al-mā'ad (eschatology). The first volume was printed in 1319 Hijri (1901 AD) and the next two in 1320 Hijri (1902 AD), but fourth and fifth volume are still unpublished. The fourth volume contains about 600 pages while fifth is of 500 pages. In its preface, Mawlana says that he is fully conscious of the Ulama's duty to defend the faith and disseminate the knowledge. He quotes Imām Ja'far as- Sādiq's statement to the effect that the Shī'ī 'ulama' were the custodians of the frontiers of Shī'īsm, which were threatened by the incursions of the devil and slanderers. Those who prepared themselves to defend it were bound to receive unlimited Divine rewards. Those who busied themselves in the acquisition of knowledge were reminded that the Qur'ān urges the Prophet to pray for the enhancement of knowledge. Further Imām Hazrat Ali says, "My Shi'as, who are endowed with knowledge of the shari'a, who help the ignorant Shī'īs to enter into the realm of the light of knowledge and leave the darkness of ignorance, are guaranteed salvation on Judgement Day."[58]

The writings on fiqh by Mawlana Sayyid Dildār Ali are also

significant and a definite contribution to the subject. Mirzā Qatil, who was writing his book, '*Haft Tamasha*' in 1812 AD writes, "there had been scholars of fiqh in India, but there had not been the Shi'a scholars. Now with the grace of God, they are also to be found. It was the result of efforts of some of those Indian scholars who went to the countries of Wilayat and studied there religious sciences under the guidance of the 'ulama of those places. After they came back, they popularized in this country all those sciences. Even some of those scholars, who appeared to be inferior in their erudition, were hundred times better than those who flourished during the reign of Shujā'-ud Daula, and made tall claims of their scholarship."[59] Till that time Mawlana Sayyid Dildār Ali's fame, as a Shi'a scholar had spread in north India. He wrote two books on fiqh. One of them entitled, *Muntahiu'l-afkār* contains a detailed exposition on the principles of fiqh. It is written in Arabic. Another important work on fiqh is a commentary on the *Hadiqatu'l-muttaqin*, written in Persian. It is divided into three volumes, dealing with purification, fasting and zakāt respectively.[60] His *Risālā–i Jum'*a is well argued treatise on Friday prayers. It is written in Persian.[61] The *Jawāb-i masāil-i fiqhiyya* written in Persian deals the rules of fiqh.[62] The Mawlana wrote the *Risālā-i Arzayn* on the problem of land ownership particularly the rights of Hindus over land and property under an Islamic government.[63] The *Zahabiyya* is a short treatise on the use of gold and silver utensils.[64]

Mawlana wrote an account of the martyrs of Karbala in Arabic. Its title is *Atāra tal-ahzān' alā'qatil al-'atshān.* [65] The another work, *Musakkin al-qulūb* deals with the tragedies, suffered by the Prophets and Imāms.[66]

There are two important works on logic written by Mawlana Sayyid Dildār Ali. One of them is *Hāshiya Sharh Musallam al-'ulūm* in Arabic. It is a commentary on Mullā Hamdu'llāh's *Musallam al-'ulum*. Another work, *Hāshiya Sharh Hikmatu'l-ayn*, is also a commentary. It is on Mullā Sadra's philosophical and mathematical theories in the *Hidāyatu'l- hikmā*. In this book, the author refutes

Mawlana Abdul Ali's objections against Mullā Sadra. He also takes issue with the Shī'ī rationalists such as Mawlan Tafazzul Husayn.[67]

Before the arrival of Mawlana Sayyid Dildār Ali from Mashhad to Lucknow, the notables in Awadh did not originally hold the Ulama and Mujtahids in high esteem, rather honoring Sufi pirs. Sufis believed in the doctrine of wahdat al-wujūd and claimed to enjoy divine grace (karāmāt) to perform miracles and also to be privy to inspiration (kashf) from God. Indian Muslims practiced Sufism widely. Even many high notables and several powerful court physicians in Faizabad attended them and believed Sufism to be a path to spiritual well-being. Sufi pirs often benefited from the largesse of Awadh's rulers. Some pirs had also shown Shī'ī sympathies. In Awadh, Sufi adoption of Shī'īsm may often have aimed at gaining court patronage. The name of Chisti leader Shāh 'Ali Akbar Mawdudi (d.1795 AD) may be mentioned who contested with Sayyid Dildār Ali for the superior position.[68]

Having been of Usūlī school of thought, Mawlana Sayyid Dildār Ali did not like the practices and beliefs of Sufis. Therefore, in 1786 AD, about four months after the congregational prayers began, Sayyid Dildār Ali launched a stinging attack on the Sufis in his afternoon sermon. He condemned those who claimed to meet every day with God, or even to be God Himself and who said they knew the condition of the seven heavens, though, they even did not know the Islamic laws. Mawlana accused them of innovating heretical rituals and laws. In later sermons, Mawlana criticized Sufi ascetic ideas and what he saw as pantheism. Besides sermons, Mawlana Sayyid Dildār Ali also wrote *Shihāb-sāqib*, refuting the Sufi doctrines and condemning the leading Sufis. The principal target of his attack was the Wahdat al-Wujūd (Unity of Being) of ibn'Arabi. He cited verses and ahādis which contradict the Sufi views of Wahdat al Wujūd. The book also shows that the best description of God and His Attributes is available only in the sayings of Imāms of the Prophet's family.[69]

A chapter of the work deals with the definition of Kashf (Sufi revelations) and asserts that knowledge obtained through this process was not necessary correct. Kashf did not discriminate between truth and falsehood and so could not be made the basis for a final decision. If it could, the past masters of Kashf would have been infallible.[70] In a section of the chapter, Mawlana points out the faults of eminent Sufis starting with ibn Arabi. He quotes the correspondence between ibn Arabi's supporter, Abdu'r Razzāq Kashi, and ibn Arabi's opponent, Alā'ud-Dawla Simnāni and refutes the statements made by his followers, including those of Haydar Āmili. According to Mawlana, the Imāmiyya works did not justify Āmili's statement that Hasan Basrī was one of Imām Hazrat Ali's most eminent disciple.[71]

In the section three of the same chapter, Mawlana accuses Safyān Sawri of hostility to *Ahl-i bayt* and blames him for disseminating many baseless ahādis. He also condemns the famous utterances of Abū Yazid Bistāmi as heretical. Referring to Abū Yazid's services to sixth Imām Ja'far as- Sādiq (a.s.), Mawlana says that these did not reduce the weight of his sins.[72] In this section, Mawlana also condemns Mansūr al- Hallāj (killed in 922 AD). In another section, the author has castigated Mansur as a zindiq (believer in a Magi sect), an heretic and an infidel.[73] In the section dealing with Ghazāli, Mawlana says that he was a bigoted Sunnī whose life-mission was to strengthen enmity towards *Ahl-i bayt*. The author remarks that Ghazāli's defence of Yazīd was insanity and this shows that he had no respect for Imām Husayn.[74] Regarding Shaykh 'Abdu'l Qadir Jilāni (d. 1166 AD), Mawlana says that he hated the Shī'īs even more deeply than his predecessors. The Shaykh fervently believed that the tenth of Muharram was not a day of mourning but of rejoicing for before the advent of Islam, it had proved an auspicious day for some of the early prophets. According to Shaykh, 'Āishā was superior to all other women and the Shī'ī beliefs resembled those of the Jews.'[75]

Mawlana Sayyid Dildār Ali, in the section of Rumi, quotes verses from his Masnawi to show that Rumi did not discriminate between

Islam and Infidelity and that his similes and metaphors were blasphemy. The author also writes that the poetry of Attār, Sanā'i and other Sufi poets was heretical and irreligious.[76]

In the last but one chapter, Mawlana condemns the mystical practices of Sufis and accuses them of violating the basic principles of Islamic teachings. The Sufi meditational postures, music, ascetic exercises and love affairs with young boys are according to the author, unlawful. The author also says that their practices of wearing woolen garments and loud and silent zikr, the system of *bay'a* and the presentation of *khirqa* (Sufi robes) are acts of perversion and apostasy.[77] The last chapter of the book deals with various Sufi orders which in Mawlana's opinion, are totally profane, blasphemous and inculcate materialism and licentiousness.[78]

Sufis also retaliated by writing against Mawlana Sayyid Dildār Ali. They said that the mystical knowledge referred in Imāmi oral reports were nothing but Sufi path. They cited that many Shi'a Ulama did not like to criticize Sufism. They defended the listening of music and bestowal of cloack of initiation. They charged Sayyid Dildār Ali for associating himself with notables and to accept grants from them. These charges were not accepted and were explained by Sayyid Dildār Ali. J.R.I. Cole writes, "Sufis replied vigorously to Nasirabadi, writing in Persian. An anonymous manuscript survives by a Sufi in rebuttal of Lucknow's prayer leader".[79] Cole has given the main points of the manuscript.[80] He also mentions that, in 1803 AD, an Iranian Sufi named Mawlavi Sami came into conflict with Lucknow's Usūlīs. Mawlavi Sami sent a list of questions to Mawlana Sayyid Daldār Ali and on one point he put him to go defensive.[81] However, by 1816 AD, the attempts made by Mawlana to displace Sufi leaders from positions of influence took place successfully. The Sufi meetings declined among Awadh's Shī'īs to such an extent that both the high and the low opposed Sufism.[82] Mawlana declared that, "Sufis are unclean (najis) so that no one should drink and eat with them".[83] His followers (Usūlīs) verbally abused Sufis in public and shunned them. They successfully eroded the Shia custom of visiting Sufi tombs and samā (music). But they were unable to undermine the appreciation of Sufi poetry.[84]

Mawlana Sayyid Dildār Ali toed the line of Safavid ulama in fiercely opposing Sufism. It is difficult for anybody to say for sure, that the polemics of Usūlīs towards Sufism was purely for power-sake to dislodge them from the position of power or it was derived by religious fervor and force filled with which Mawlana Sayyid Dildār Ali had returned from Usūlī Iraq and Iran. Since he was the first Indian to return to India as a recognized Mujtahid (1785 AD). Before him, there was no one effectively competent to oppose Sufism on doctrinal grounds. Also, never before the environment was so conducive for a Shia ālim in India to oppose Sufism. Moreover, his attack on Sufism was largely retaliatory because some leading Sufis, both in Lucknow and Delhi, had declared war on Shia beliefs, Shia heroes, martyrs and Shia practices, particularly the tā'ziā rituals.

The Sunnī scholars were also deeply concerned with the rising tide of Shi'a popularity in northern India[85] in the second half the eighteenth century and wished to stem it. They intensely wrote against Shī'ī faith and many writings appeared against them. These writings specially, the *Tuhfa-i Isnā 'Ashariyya* by Shāh Abdul Aziz Dehlavi (completed in 1204 Hijri / AD 1789-90) provoked many Shi'a scholars to write rebuttal of it because Shāh Abdul Aziz considered it irrefutable and the last word on the truth of Sunnīsm.[85] Mawlana Sayyid Dildār Ali was one of them who wrote several tracts in refutation of views expressed by Shāh Abdul Aziz Dehlavi in *Tuhfa-i Isnā Ashariyya*. The Mawlana produced the *Zulfiqar* which is the refutation of eighth chapter, relating to Tawallā (devotion) and Tabarrā (dissociation). In this book Mawlana highlights the Shāh's distortion of Shī'ī evidences. The work demonstrates that the corner stone of the Islamic faith is belief in the impeccability of the Imāms coupled with devotion to 'Ali and *Ahl-i bayt*. Those who deprived 'Ali of his rightful succession to the Caliphate and rejected Fatima's right to inherit her father's gift of Fadak, were not their friends. If the Prophet's wife, Āishā, who fought against 'Ali at Basra (Jamal), and Mu'awiya, who fought against him at Siffin, were given benefit of erring in ijtihad (reasoning), the same benefit must be granted to Khawārij who fought against 'Ali in the battle of Naharwān.[86] The author's analysis effectively proves that Tawallā (devotion) to *Ahl-i-bayt* cannot be demonstrated without Tabarrā (dissociation) from their enemies.[87]

Mawlana wrote the *Sawārim-Ilāhiyat* refuting Shāh 's presentation of Ilāhiyat (Divinity) in the fifth chapter of *Tuhfa*. The author claimed that he had not confined himself to refuting the Shāh but had also included a relevant discussion on Kalām in the Sawārim to serve as an eye-opener to the Shāh and others.[88] This work points out the role of reason, as understood by Shī'īs in obtaining divine ma'rifa in detail.[89]

Sayyid Dildār Ali also wrote a rebuttal of the sixth chapter of the *Tuhfa* dealing with Shī'ī beliefs concerning the prophethood. The book is called *Hisāmu'l-Islam*. It says that the Shī'ī belief in 'Ali's superiority over pre-Muhammad prophets was based on the Qur'ānic verses and the argument that since the Prophet Muhammad was superior to all preceding prophets, his true deputy 'Ali, was inevitably superior to them also. The Shī'ī belief in the Divine obligation to appoint a Deputy did not refer to any external orders but was based on His promise as a self-imposed obligation. The Mawlana remarks that the Shāh accuses the Shī'īs of considering 'Ali superior to the Prophet Muhammad. But according to Mawlana, the Shī'ī beliefs are based on the most reliable traditions of the Imāms themselves, whereas the contradictions in the Sunnī ahādis are innumerable and reduce Muslims to the position of heretics. Mawlana cites many examples and says that the 'ismat (impeccability) of the Prophet Muhammad is not undermined by Shī'ī traditions.[90]

In the *Risālā-i Ghaybat*, the Mawlana refuted the seventh chapter of the *Tuhfa*, which deals Imāmate. It contains a detailed discussion on the occultation of the twelfth Imām.[91] Mawlana also wrote the *Ihya al-Sunna* to counter Shāh Abdul Aziz's allegation against the

Shī'ī beliefs on *mā'ad* (bodily resurrection) in the eighth chapter of *Tuhfa*. According to the Mawlana, the Shāh had borrowed his account on non-Imāmiyya sects from the bigoted Nāsibi, al-Shahrastāni and did not quote any reliable authorities.[92]

The above mentioned account shows that Mawlana Sayyid Dildār Ali's tirade against Akhbārī faith, Sufism and Sunnīsm undoubtedly established the Usūlī Shi'a faith on firm ground not only in Awadh but all over India.

Mawlana Sayyid Dildār Ali faced the criticism of an Irani Shī'ī ālim, who was also an Usūlī, during his lifetime. J.R.I. Cole sees it as part of continuing rivalry between Indian and Iranian ulama.[93]Aqā Ahmad Bihbahānī, an Irani alim visited Lucknow in 1807 AD. He was in search of patronage but he did not get the favor of Nawab Sa'adat Ali Khan. So, he was annoyed. He narrates an incident of 1222 AH/1807 AD. According to him, "At the end of Ramazān in 1222 AH/1807AD, some believers came to Bihbahānī in Lucknow and stated that they had seen the moon a sign that the month of fasting was over. Aqā Ahmad gave a ruling that the next day was the first of Shawwāl and the Holy Day (Id al-Fitr) marking the breaking of the fast. He sent the ruling to Mawlana and Nawab Sa'adat Ali Khan who, according to him at first accepted it. Later the Nawab changed his mind and issued orders that the Holy Day would be celebrated a day later. The next day Sa'adat 'Ali Khan went to the mosque for the Holy Day prayers which Sayyid Dildār Ali led. Aqā Ahmad insisted that the Law forbade holding the prayers a day later, but the Lucknow ālim justified it on the grounds of pious dissimulation (taqiyyah)." Bihbahānī did not like the answer. He indirectly criticized the Mawlana.[94] He wrote that, "many in Lucknow thought that simply receiving a diploma (Ijāzā) does not make a scholar mujtahid." He cattily remarked, "In all north India, he never found any true Ulama".[95] These barbs were directed at Mawlana Sayyid Dildār Ali aimed at disputing his status as mujtahid. But his remarks carry no weight. Undoubtedly, Mawlana was a great Shi'a alim and undisputed Shi'a mujtahid.

Observance of Muharram in Awadh was the important paradigm of Shi'a culture. Nawabs his courtiers notables of the society and poors all sections of society actively participated in the mourning sessions (Majlises) and processions of Muharram. Mawlana Sayyid Dildār Ali supported rituals of Muharram such a, breast-beating (ma'tam), reading of marsiya (elegiac poetry), Mehndi procession and offering of Fātihā. But he disapproved of chanting of Nauha (elegiac lyrics) with remodulation as being too close to music. He introduced some changes also. During the Āshurā (first ten days of Muharram), a day was fixed for describing the life of a martyr of Karbala. In the mourning assemblies (Majlises) the Persian style of elegy recitation was introduced. In private houses also majlises were held and tāziās exhibited. Mawlana collected the reliable accounts regarding the Waqiat-i-Karbala and reproduced them in his book entitled *Asarat-ul-Ahzān*. He himself described the details from a pulpit on the 10th Muharram barefooted bareheaded, his garment open at the breast, sleeves raised upon elbow. This set an example for the succeeding Shi'a ulama and Zākirs (preachers).[96] Mawlana fixed days for the zikr of a specific martyr of Karbala. This more or less, became a tradition and the Zākirs still follow it. Relating to the procession of 10th Muharram, Mawlana told that beating of drums were a heretical innovation, but the using camels to evoke the caravan of the doomed Imām's family for the purpose of rendering hearts tender did not invite objections.[97] According to Cole, "In later years camels draped in black were brought during the month of Muharram to the Nasirābādi's Imāmbārah itself".[98] Mawlana Sayyid Dildār Ali also built two Imāmbāras and two mosques, one of each at Lucknow and other at his hometown (Nasirābad).[99]

Under the influence of Mawlana the customs of nikāh, talāq and burial etc. were also brought in line with Shi'a laws and customs.[100] Mawlana devoted his entire life to teaching and writing scholarly works. He wrote near about thirty or more books.[101] Most of them are written in Arabic language. He started a separate Shi'a madrasa of his own, where he imparted religious education.[102] He also deputed he also deputed nearly twenty nine of his pupils in different parts of the State for the propagation of Usūlī Shī'ī faith.[103] He raised the standard of Indian Shī'ī learning and tried to raise the standard of education similar to the facilities at Najaf, Karbala, Samra, Qum and Mashhad.

Mawlana Sayyid Dildār Ali was a pious man. His fatwas were accepted by the Shī'īs without hesitation. He was also a successful arbitrator in many complex disputes. Even longstanding disagreements between Shi'a and Sunnīs were resolved through his verdicts. He was deeply respected by all section of populace.[104] On his suggestion Nawab Āsaf'ud-Dawla built a canal in Karbala and financed the re-building of Imām's tomb there. The Nawab also spent liberal gifts to the seminaries, students and deserving people at Karbala, Najaf and other holy Shī'ī centers in Iraq.

After rendering great services to Shi'a community, Mawlana Sayyid Dildār Ali left this world in the night of 19 Rajab 1235 Hijri/ 2nd May 1820 AD in Lucknow and buried in his own Imāmbārh (on 3rd May).[105] He was given the title of "Ghufrān Ma'ab" (He, who has taken refuge in Divine forgiveness or the one who lives in heaven).[106]

Undoubtedly Mawlana Sayyid Didār Ali 'Ghufran Ma'ab' was a great Shi'a ālim and first Indian Shi'a mujtahid of Awadh. He was the sole and undisputed leader of the Shi'a community of his age and his contribution are of far-reaching significance and consequence.

Notes and References

1. The followers of 'sunna' or Tradition; The majority branch of Muslims, who recognizes four orthodox successors of Prophet and also takes a positive view of Muslim monarchies that thereafter arose. See, J. R. I. Cole, *Roots of North Indian Shī'īsm in Iran and Iraq*, p. 294, OUP, Delhi, 1989. (Hereafter mentioned as Cole).
2. Shi'a is an Arabic word which occurs in several Qur'ānic verses. See,

Qur'ān, xxviii,15, xxxvii, 83; According to Arabic lexicons, the friends or followers of a person are called his Shi'as. See, al-Qūmūs, Tāju'l-'arūs, Lisān'ul- Arab; The devotees of Prophet Muhammad and his *Ahl-i-bayt* (members of the family defined by the Prophet himself) or āl or Qurbā or Itrat are Shi'as. See, Rizvi, Saiyid Athar Abbas, *A Socio- Intellectual History of the Isnā' Ashari Shī'īs in India*, vol-I. pp. 8-10 (Hereafter as, Rizvi, S. A. A., vol.-I).

3. The calamities brought about by the Umayyads were so open and unveiled that the majority of the Sunnīs were forced to divide the caliphs into two groups. They came to distinguish between the "rightly guided caliphs" (khulafā' rāshidun) who are the first four caliphs after the death of the Holy Prophet, Muhammad, (Abū Bakr, Umar, Uthmān and Ali) and the others who began with Mu'awiyah and who did not possess by any means the religious virtues of the rightly guided caliphs. In the name of avenging the martyrdom of the family of Prophet the Abbasid caliphs massacred the Umayyads and very soon they began to follow unjust ways of Umayyads. The sixth Imām died from poisoning after much torture and pain. The descendants of the Holy Prophet were sometimes beheaded in groups, buried alive, or even placed within walls of Government buildings under construction. By the dissolution of Umayyad rule and the establishment of the Abbasids, Shī'īsm did not benefit in any way. Its repressive and unjust opponents merely changed their name. The Abbasid's rule ended in 1258 AD. For details, see, Allamah Sayyid Muhammad Husayn Tabātabāī (English translation by Sayyid Husayn Nasr), *SHI'A*, pp. 61-63, Qum, Iran, February, 1989. (Hereafter mentioned as *SHI'A*).
4. S. Husayn M. Jafri, *The Origins and Early Development of Shi'a Islam*, pp. 19-21, Second published by Ansariyān Publications, Qum (Iran), Feb 1989 AD. (Hereafter referred as Jafri); Momen, Moojan, *An Introduction to Shī'ī Islam, The History and Doctrines of Twelver Shī'īsm*, p. 15, Yale University Press, New Haven and London,1985. (Hereafter referred as Momen); Naqvi, Mawlana S. Ali Naqi, *History of Islam*, pp. 469-492, Imamia Mission (Hind) Aligarh, 2002. TAKIM, Liyakat Nathani, *Shī'īsm in America*, p.1, Newyork University Press, 2009 AD. (Hereafter mentioned as Takim); *SHI'A*, p. 40, chapter I,

reference no. 6; Richard, Yann, *SHI'ITE ISLAM* (English translation by Antonia Nevill.), p.16, Blackwell Publishers, Cambridge, 1995 (Hereafter referred as Richard, Yann); Hollister, John Norman, *The Shi'a of India*, pp. 18-19, Second Editon,1979, Oriental Book Reprint Corporation, New Delhi. (Hereafter mentioned as Hollister).

5. Jafri, op. cit., pp. 17-18; Momen, op. cit., p.14.
6. Naqvī, Mawlana S. Ali Naqvi, op. cit., pp. 497-504; Takim, op. cit., pp.1-2., *Tārikh- i Tabari*, vol. II, p. 436; *SHI'A*, Chapter I, Notes, no.11.
7. Takim, op. cit., p. 2.
8. Ibid.
9. Ibid., pp. 2-4.
10. Richard, Yann, op. cit., pp. 34-38; *SHI'A*, op. cit., chapter II, *Divisions within Shī'īsm*, pp. 74-81; Momen, op. cit., pp.49-50; 53, 56; Hollister, For Kaisanis, see, pp. 66-67, 72; For Zaidis, pp. 68, 185-86, For Ismailis, 195-214, For, Isnā Asharis, pp. 58-99.
11. Richard, Yann, op. cit., pp. 69-70; Hollister, op. cit., p. 40. According to him, the Akhbārī school almost excludes esoteric and allegorical interpretations which are characteristic of Shī'īsm. See, p.41.
12. Richard, Yann, op. cit., p. 69; Hollister, op. cit., p. 41; Cole, op. cit., p. 17.
13. Cole, op. cit., p.18; Mujtahid (Arabic word), translated as Jurist, is a person who has the ability to deduce the jurisprudential rulings from reliable sources. There are different types of Mujtahids: absolute (mutlaq) and partial (mutajāzzi); actual and potential the most. See, Wikishia; Sayyid Dildār Ali described the two sorts of mujtahid, absolute and partial. For details, see, Cole, op. cit., pp. 161-162.; Hollister, op. cit., pp. 40-41.
14. Kamāluddin Haider, *Sawānihāt-i-Salātin-i-Awadh*, vol-I, p. 113; Umar, Mohammad, *Islam in Northern India, During the Eighteenth Century*, Reference no., 316, p. 245. New Delhi, 1993. (Hereafter referred as Umar, Muhammad)
15. Mirzā Qatil, *Haft-Tamāshā* (Lucknow,1875), pp.148-49; Umar, Muhammad, op. cit., Reference no. 316 on p. 245.
16. Sayyid Ali Naqi Naqvi, *Janāb, Ghufran Ma'ab*, (in Urdu) published by Imāmia Mission, Lucknow, Number-259,1378 Hijri/1958 AD, pp. 5-6.

17. Sibte Muhammad Naqvi, *'Awadh ke chand Mumtāz Ulama'* in *'Naya Daur'*, Awadh-Number (Urdu), Feb.-March, 1994, p. 59 (Publication Division, Lucknow, U.P. Govt.); Sayyid Ali Naqi Naqvi, "Hazrat Ghufran Ma'ab" in *Khāndān-i-Ijtihād*, Number (Urdu), p. 14, (Edited by Sayyid Mustafa Husayn Naqvi Asif Jaisi, for Noor-i-Hidāyat Foundation Imāmbārah, Ghufran Ma'ab, Lucknow. 1425 Hijri/ December, 2004.)
18. Rizvi, S.A. A., op. cit., vol. II, p. 128.
19. Ibid.
20. Ibid., pp. 128-29.
21. Cole, op. cit., p.77.
22. Ibid.
23. Ibid., p.78.
24. Rizvi, S.A. A., op. cit., volume -II, p. 129.
25. Ibid.
26. Ibid.
27. Cole, op. cit., p. 61.
28. Ibid., p. 62.
29. Ibid.
30. Ibid., For another example, see, p.62
31. Ibid.
32. Rizvi, S. A. A. vol-II, op. cit., p. 129.
33. Ibid.
34. Ibid., p. 129-30.
35. Ibid., p. 130.
36. Ibid.
37. Ibid., p. 159. Even, in nineteenth century also the Akhbārīs were dominating in Awadh, see, p.165.
38. Hollister, op. cit., p. 41; Richard, Yann, op. cit., p. 69; Cole, op. cit., pp. 21, 128, 160.
39. Cole, op. cit., pp. 18-19, 124.; Richard, Yann, op. cit., p. 69.
40. Cole, op. cit., pp. 27, 124, 128; Richard, Yann, op. cit., p.69.
41. Asāsu'l-Usūl, Aligarh University MS; *Āīna- i Haqq numā'* ff. 54b-59b. cf., Rizvi, S. A.A., vol. II, op. cit., p.132.
42. Ibid.
43. Cole, op. cit., p. 160.

44. Ibid., p. 128; Rizvi, S. A. A., vol.-ii., op. cit., p. 130.
45. Ibid., Rizvi, S. A. A., vol.-II, op. cit., pp. 130-31; It is said that a Sufi Shaykh Khwājā Sayyid Ali Akbar Maududi, who was attached to Bahu Begum in Faizabad also advised Hasan Raza Khan to arrange for Shi'a Friday prayer. See, Cole, op. cit., p. 129; It seems that the congregational prayers among the Shi'as had already begun at Faizabad (AD 1785). The credit goes to Jawahar 'Ali Khan. He had to plead hard, as Shi'as were not accustomed to congregational prayers. So, he employed 10 to 20 persons on condition that they would regularly offer their prayers in Imperial mosque. He also introduced the Friday prayers. Mawlana Mazhar 'Ali led the first prayers in 1785. See, Umar, Muhammad, op. cit., p. 197, and Reference no. 236 on p.241.
46. Ibid., pp. 128-29; Syed Ali Naqi Naqvi, *Hazrat Ghufran Ma'ab*, p. 13. (Hereafter, referred as Hazrat Ghufran Ma'ab).
47. Cole, op. cit., p.129; *Hazrat Ghufran Ma'ab*, p.14.
48. Cole, op. cit., p.129.
49. Ibid., pp. 129-30.
50. Ibid., p. 130.
51. Ibid.
52. Mawlana Dildār 'Ali, *Fawāid-i Āsafiyya wa Mawā'iz-i Husayniyya* (Aligarh University MS.) f. 3b-4a, c.f. Rizvi, S. A. A., vol. II, p. 131.
53. *Fawāid-i Āsafiyya*, ff.13b-14a, cf, Rizvi, S. A. A, vol-ii, p. 131.
54. Ibid., ff. 18b-25b., cf Rizvi, S. A. A. vol. II, p. 131.
55. Cole, op. cit., p. 137.
56. Ibid., pp. 163-65.
57. Ibid., p. 166.
58. *Imādu'l-Islam*, Lucknow, MS. pp. 2-5 cf. Rizvi, S. A. A., vol-ii, op. cit., p. 132; *Hazrat Ghufran Ma'ab*, op. cit., pp. 19-22; Naqvi, Sayyid 'Ali Naqi, *Janāb Ghufran Ma'ab*, pp. 11-12. (Hereafter mentioned as, Janāb Ghufran Ma'ab.)
59. Qatil, Mirzā, *Haft Tamasha*, pp. 148-49, cf. Umar, Muhammad, op. cit., Reference no. 316, p. 245.
60. *Āina-i Haqq-numā* f.63b, cf Rizvi, S. A. A., vol. II, op. cit., pp. 132-33.; *'Hazrat Ghufran Ma'ab'*, pp. 23-24; *Janāb Ghufran Ma'ab.*, pp. 13-14.
61. Rizvi, S. A. A, vol. II, op. cit., p. 133; *Hazrat Ghufran Ma'ab*, p. 28; *'Janāb Ghufran Ma'ab'*, p. 14.

62. Rizvi, S. A. A., vol. II, op. cit., p. 133.
63. Ibid., *Hazrat Ghufran Ma'ab*, p. 23.
64. Ibid., *Hazrat Ghufran Ma'ab*, p. 28.
65. Ibid., *Hazrat Ghufran Ma'ab.*, p. 28
66. Ibid., *Hazrat Ghufran Ma'ab*, p. 27.
67. Cole, op. cit., pp. 147, 149-151.
68. Ibid., pp. 149, 152-53.
69. Rizvi, S. A. A. vol. II, op. cit., pp. 133-34; *Hazrat Ghufran Ma'ab*, pp. 22-23; *Janāb Ghufran Ma'ab*, p. 12.
70. Rizvi, S. A. A. vol. II, p. 134.
71. *Shihāb- Sāqib*, (Aligarh University, MS.) f. 46b., cf. Rizvi, S.A.A., vol. II, p. 134.
72. Rizvi, S. A. A., vol. II, op. cit., p. 134.
73. Ibid., p. 135.
74. *Shihāb- Sāqib*, ff. 56b-57a, cf. Rizvi, S. A. A. vol. II, op. cit.,, p. 135.
75. Ibid., ff.58b-59a., cf Rizvi, S. A. A., vol. II, op. cit., p. 135.
76. Ibid., ff. 60a-61a., cf Rizvi, S. A. A., vol. II, op. cit., p. 135; Cole, op. cit., pp. 152-53.
77. Ibid., ff. 83b-85a. cf Rizvi, S. A. A., vol. II, op. cit., p. 135.
78. Rizvi, S. A, A., vol. II, op. cit., p. 135.
79. Cole, op. cit., p. 153.
80. Ibid., pp. 153-54.
81. Ibid., pp. 154-55.
82. Ibid., p. 157.
83. Ibid., p. 156.
84. Rizvi, S. A. A., vol. II, op. cit., 136.
85. Writing about the popularity of Shī'īsm, Shāh Abdul Aziz Dehlavi remarks: "*The mazhab-i-Asnā -i Āshariyā* is so popular and famous that in the cities where we live hardly there will be a house in which two or three persons converted to this faith or have leanings towards it, are not found." *Tuhfa-i Asnā-i 'Āshariyā;* p. 1, cf. Umar, Muhammad, op. cit., reference no.103 on p. 234.
86. Rizvi, S. A. A., vol. II, op. cit., p. 136; For details, see: Saiyid Athar Abbas Rizvi, *SHĀH 'ABD'AL-'AZIZ*, Canberra, 1982. (Hereafter referred as, Shah Abdul Aziz.)
87. Rizvi, S. A. A., vol. II, op. cit., pp. 136-37.

88. Ibid., p. 137.
89. Ibid., pp.137-38.; *Shah Abdul Aziz*, op. cit., pp. 388-92.
90. Ibid., p. 138; *Shah Abdul Aziz*, op. cit., pp. 392-996.
91. Ibid., *Shah Abdul Aziz*, op. cit., pp. 396-99.
92. Ibid., *Shah Abdul Aziz*, op. cit., pp. 410-13.
93. Cole, op. cit., p.141.
94. For details, see, Ahmad Bihbahānī, *Mirāt-ul-Ahwāl-i Jahān Numā* (Khuda Bakhsh Oriental Public Library, Patna, Bahar Collection, MS. No.96), ff.166b,168a-168b., (English translation by Prof. A.F. Haider as India in the Early 19th century, *An Iranian's Travel Account*), Patna, 1996, pp. 165-71; Cole, op. cit., p.141.
95. Cole, op. cit., p. 141.
96. Lucknowi, Saiyid Bāqar Shams, *Hindustan Mein Shi'at ki Tārikh*, pp. 23-24; Umar, Muhammad, op. cit., p.197.
97. Cole, op. cit., pp.113-14.
98. Ibid., p. 114.
99. Rizvi, S. A. A., vol. II, op. cit., p. 139.
100. Umar, Muhammad, op. cit., p. 197.
101. Rizvi, S. A. A., vol. II, op. cit., p. 139.
102. Lucknowi, Saiyid Bāqar Shams, op. cit., p. 14; Umar, Muhammad, op. cit., p. 196.
103. Umar, Muhammad, op. cit., p. 196; Mawlana Mufti Muhammad Quli Kintūrī, Mawlana Mirzā Muhammad Khalīl, Fakhru'd-Din Ahmad Khan alias Mirzā Jafar, MawlanaYād'Ali Naqwi, Mawlana 'Abdu'l-'Ali of Dawekhattā in Ghāzipur and his two sons, Sayyid Muhammad and Sayyid Kalb-i'Ali Fyzabadi, Mawlana Sayyid Ahmad 'Ali bin Ināyat Haydar of Muhammadābād (Azamgarh), Mawlana Ashraf Ali, Mawlana Sayyid Muhammad 'Ibādat bin Muhammad Najābat (Amroha), Mawlana Mirzā Muhammad 'Ali and many other Shi'a scholars were his famous disciples. See, Rizvi, S.A. A., vol. II, op. cit., pp. 152-55.
104. Rizvi, S. A. A., vol. II, op. cit., p. 139.
105. Ibid. For details of his Imāmbārah Ghufran Ma'ab, see, Allama Farogh, Kāzmi, *Shāhān-e Awadh Aur Shi'at*. (Hindi translation by Ali Imām Zaidi Gauhar, Lucknowi), pp. 217-19, Delhi, 1999.
106. Rizvi, S. A. A., vol. II, op. cit., p. 139.

Section 3: Education

Shi'a Madarīs of Awadh

Among all the religions, Islam stands on a higher pedestal for its concern for the instruction or education of the masses. The very first communication received by Prophet Muhammad through arch angel Gabriel was, "Iqrā: Bisme Rabbika-I-Iazee Khalaq....Al lazi Allamā bil Qalam."[1]. (Read: In the name of the lord who createth,...who teacheth by the pen). It may be mentioned here that the major emphasis of Islam has been on the oneness of God, the oneness which is indivisible (Ahad) and not the oneness which is divisible (Wāhid).[2] Yet the first revelation of communication to Prophet Muhammad was not about the 'Concept of God', but it was about reading, knowledge and writing (pen). It shows that the root cause of a stagnant society is ignorance and as such education deserves greatest attention so that the society does not become inhuman in due course.

It is interesting to see how the Prophet expressed his vision. The Prophet is attributed with the number of Ahādith on knowledge and education. The Prophet advised to seek knowledge even if one has to travel to China (a distant and difficult destination). He said, "knowledge is the hidden treasure for a momin (righteous person) and he should pick it up wherever he finds it". On another occasion, the Prophet advised his followers to seek knowledge from 'the cradle to the grave'. In Islam, seeking knowledge is mandatory and obligatory on every Muslim without any gender discrimination (*Talabul ilm faridatūn alā kullī Muslamīn.*).[3] The text of Holy Qur'ān is replete with verse inviting man to use his intellect, to ponder, to think and to know for the goal of human life. In Qur'ān the word 'Ilm' is frequently used next to the word 'God'. By 'ilm' it is meant that a man has to know about his surrounding and to ponder over life and the phenomena of nature. Thus, life and nature become objects of learning. Without learning, man and his society cannot progress. Unfortunately owing to various historical and social realities, the Muslim society has not been as progressive in education as desired by the Prophet.

A system of formal education is an instrument of progress for the civilized society. Though the literacy percentage is low but the tradition of learning right from the beginning has been there and is still surviving. Like, Gurukul among Hindus, Seminary among Christians, Madrasas have come up as an institution of learning including higher education in Muslim society.

Short History of Shī'ī Educational System and the Development of Madrasas in Islamic Society

The process of learning and dissemination of knowledge started in Islamic society from the mosques. In earlier days, a mosque was the center of all social activities. Prophet Muhammad used to address his fellow companions in the mosque. It was the mosque only where the assemblage used to memorize the verses of the Holy Qur'ān with explanatory interpretation offered to them by the Prophet.[4] In due course of time these mosques apart from being a place for congregational prayers began to serve the purpose of seminaries. However, the subjects taught were religion centered. Islamic (re jurisprudence (Fiqh), tradition (Ahādith), Qur'ān, interpretation of Qur'ān and laws, based on Sunnah formed the syllabus.[5] However, Hellenistic sciences such as logic, philosophy, mathematics, astronomy, medicine and alchemy were not parts of the syllabus.[6] For the study of these subjects, then academies and institutions were founded by a few rulers, scholars or wealthy men and were in a very small number. For example, al-'Ma'mun (198-202 AH/813-

818 AD) founded an academy *Bayt-al'-Hikma* in Baghdad. Besides, serving as a translation bureau the institute functioned as an academy and public library and also had an observatory.[7] Somewhat similar institution was established much later by al-Muta'did (279-289 AH/892-903 AD). In the west, Fatimids established their renowned institutes. In the year 395 AH/1005 AD, al Hakīm laid foundation of his famous academy *Dar-al-ilm* or *Dar-al-Hikma* in Cairo to impart knowledge of Maliki jurisprudence and Ahādith. This was a residential institution named as madrasa .[8] It may be kept in mind that though there were mosques and madrasas for imparting knowledge, but the mosques were public places for offering prayers in the first place and education was a subsidiary activity. The mosque was open to the masses while madrasas were private institutions even though the public was admitted in liberal way, but everyone could not enter it without obtaining formal permission.[9]

The most accepted date for the beginning of madrasa system is 1066 AD, when the Saljuq Wazir Nizamul Mulk founded the Nizamiyya Madrasa in Baghdad. The students boarded in this academy and many of them held endowed scholarships. The Nizamiyya Madrasa of Baghdad was recognized by the State. The purpose of this madrasa was to strengthen Sunnī-Islam. Nizam-ul-Mulk also founded many madrasas in other towns of the Empire. In Islam Founding a madrasa was always considered a noble charitable act. Therefore, many madrasas were established and a great number of them were raised in Iraq and in the Eastern countries. In all these higher institutions of theology, traditional sciences lay at the basis of the curriculum, and memory work was specially stressed.[10] Thus, by the beginning of fifth century AH/1009AD, a number of Sunnī-madrasa blossomed and this growth process continued onward.

The development of the madrasa as a stronghold of Sunnī doctrine makes it understandable why they did not gain much importance among the Shī'ītes (i.e. the followers of 'Ali and his descendants) in their formative period. Instead, they were guided by their a'imma [sg.: Imām] in its denomination of the Ithnā 'ashariyya (Twelver Shi'a) until the death of the eleventh Imām Hasan al-'Askari (d. 873/4). The first Imām 'Alī b. Abi Tālib is believed by Shī'ītes to have been the originator of Arabic grammar and algebra. His sermons dealt with theological, philosophical and ethical matters.[11] The a'imma succeeding' Ali continued these traditions but are believed to have not been able to get enough time for the dissemination of their teachings, due to the strong political opposition from the ruling Sunnītes and related to this their own untimely demise. However, the fifth Imām Muhammad al-Bāqir (d. 733) and the sixth Imām Ja'far as-Sādiq (d.765) were able to get at least some time to concentrate on imparting education to the community. This might have become possible since the Umayyads did not pay a lot of attention as they were occupied with the intrigues and fights for survival in the last legs of their reign. The schools of Islamic jurisprudence [fiqh], 'ulūm al-Hadīth, and Islamic philosophy [Hikma], set up by Muhammad al-Bāqir and Ja'far as-Sādiq, were declared open to all seekers of knowledge. Among those who benefited from these schools were the founders of the Hanafī and the Shafi'i Schools of Sunnī fiqh. Alchemy was given a new turn by Jābir b. Hayyan (d. 815), who is referred to as 'Geber' in the Western world and is considered the father of chemistry. He is said to have been a disciple of Imām Muhammad al-Bāqir (a. s.)[12] and has expressed his indebtedness to Jā'far as Sādiq in a number of his treatises. These scholars in turn used to transmit knowledge in their own spheres.

The Shī'ītes fared no better under the Abbasids. Though the Abbasid caliph al-Ma'mun went to the extent of declaring the eighth Imām Ali ar-Ridā (a. s.) (d. 818 A.D.) as his heir apparent, this proved of no permanent avail. The caliph al-Mutawakkil resumed the early practice of persecuting the Shī'ītes. The general hostility led the Shī'ītes to the adoption of the principle of dissimulation [taqiyya].[13] However, Shī'ītes were guided by their a'imma up to

941 AD when the twelfth and last infallible Imām Muhammad al-Mahdi disappeared into the 'Great Occultation' [*al-ghayba al-kubra*]. Afterwards Shī'ītes had to depend for guidance upon persons who did not share the privilege of the a'imma of being infallible. They were called 'deputy of the Imām [na'ib al-Imām] or 'authorized instance' [marja at-taqlīd] and made Baghdad their center. Due to their activities Shī'īsm was becoming popular in around Baghdad The sixth na'ib al-Imām or marja at-taqlīd, the 'Shaykh at-Taifa' Abu Ja'far Muhammad b. Hasan b. 'Ali at-Tusi (d. 1067), established a Shi'a madrasa in Baghdad. However, this madrasa was burned down by Sunnītes during a clash with the Shī'ītes soon after, and at-Tusi was forced to leave Baghdad. In an-Najaf, where he took shelter,[14] he founded a new juridical, seminary, the *Hawza al- ilmiyya*, which soon became the most famous center of Shi'a learning in the world.[15] Apart from Baghdad and an-Najaf, another center soon to become established as a Shi'a center of learning was Qom, situated in central Iran.[16]

During the Shī'ītes Buyid dynasty in Iraq and Iran, which lasted from 932 to 1055 AD, Shī'ītes- scholars developed a theology [Kalām] and principles of jurisprudence [usūl al-fiqh] on their own and considerably challenged the so-far dominating traditionalism. The elaboration of the concept of ijtihād (independent reasoning) on a rational basis in opposition to the idea of taqlīd [i.e. following of an established opinion] started a process that finally led to the division of the Shī'ītes learned community into two groups: the mujtahidūn and the muqallidun. Those who were formally trained in Islamic jurisprudence based on rational judgment were called mujtahidun. Muqallidun were those scholars who allotted the primacy in legal matters to the authority of the Hadīth or commoners without any proper training in legal matters.

The above-mentioned Madrasa at an-Najaf established by the 'Shaykh at Ta'ifa,' which was and still is considered the major center of Shī'ītes religious education acquired special significance for the development of the principle of ijtihād whereby the scholar is able to interpret and deduce religious precepts from three sources—the Qur'ān, the Ahādīth of the Prophet and the Shī'ītes a'imma, and their respective sunna. Such a scholar [mujtahid] expounds the application of Islam to the changing conditions of his times. Every member of the Shi'a sect is required to follow the teaching of a living mujtahid whose teachings lose authority after his death.[17] Thus, the Shī'ītes must always have a living mujtahid who is in theory, an embodiment of deep scholarship, original thinking and training in the thorough examination and analysis of religious precepts. Mujtahidūn also came to be known as usūliyān, a name applied for the first time to scholars in the legacy of Muhammad b. an Numān al-Hārithī—commonly known as 'Shaykh al-mufīd' (d. 1022 AD)– who pleaded against the overestimation of the handed-down word and for the dialectical method based on rational judgment. However, there remained a sizable number of Shī'ītes-scholars who stoutly rejected the idea of a mujtahid as a source of religious authority and would interpret the Islamic laws as per the description in Qur'ān, the Prophetic and Imāmite ahādith, and the oral reports from the Shī'ītes a'imma [akhbar/sg: Khabar]. This section of the Shi'a scholarship became known as Akhbārī.[18]

During the Safavid period between the 16th and 18th century, when Twelver Shī'īsm was proclaimed the official religion in Iran, large numbers of eminent Shī'īte 'ulamā' from the centers of religious learning in Southern Lebanon and Iraq came to Iran where they were very instrumental in the establishment of Shi'a Madrasas that became famous centers of higher religious learning. In this regard we only mention the so-called 'School of Isfahān,' which revolved around the personalities of Mīr Damad Astarābadi (d. 1631) and his pupil Sadr ud-Din Shirāzi (d.1640) commonly known as 'Mullā Sadra. This must be considered as a turning point in the history of Islamic philosophy. However, the position of the Iraqi madāris which are centered about the most venerated sanctuaries of an-Najaf and Karbala, remained superior in the eyes of the Shi'a community.

The History of Shi'a Madāris in North India (Awadh)

The history of Shi'a madaris in India is of recent origin. It is well known that the atmosphere during the medieval period was not congenial for the Shi'a faith. The correspondence between Mīr Yūsūf Ali Astarābadi and Qādi Nūrullāh Shustari (d. 1610) show that, even in the reign of Akbar, Shī'ītes were not in a position to abandon taqiyya.[19] Qādi Nūrullāh Shustari was killed during the reign of Jahangir because of his writings.[20] Thus, there was no question of establishing separate Shi'a madāris in India. With the death of Aurangzeb, however, the Shī'ītes acquired a position that more and more allowed them to express their faith openly. Finally, the establishment of Shi'a rule in the princely state of Awadh in the 18th century made it possible to establish Shi'a madāris. The first two nawabs of Awadh did not take interest in the field of education. Therefore, religious education was imparted by the Farangi Mahall, the school of theology of Sunnī 'ulamā'. Kamāl ad-Din Haydar writes in his *Sawānihāt-i-salātin-i* Awadh [The Auspices of the Rulers of Awadh], "Muslims in Lucknow were Shī'ītes only for name's sake. Due to their ignorance, they acted against the teachings of their faith. They did not appreciate the importance of their faith. Those who were familiar with it, owing to their education, did not openly offer their prayers in congregation and deliver sermons."[21] There was no Shī'īte mujtahid, nor a separate Shi'a madrasa and mosque in Lucknow. During the reign of Nawab Ās afud-Daula (reigned 1775-1797), Sayyid Dildār 'Ali' Ghufran Ma 'ab' (d. 1820) financed by Mirzā Hasan Riza Khan (the Deputy of the Nawab; d. 1801) went for higher studies to Iraq and Iran. He studied in an-Najaf and Karbala and in Mashhad in Eastern Iran. From Mashhad he returned home with certificates [ijazāt] from one Sayyid Mahdi Tabātabāī and one Mirzā Mahdi Isfahāni to practice ijtihād. He was the first Shī'īte mujtahid, who established separate congregational prayers for Shī'ītes with the approval of Nawab Āsaf ud-Daula and his deputy Hasan Rida Khan. He was appointed as the first leader of prayers [pesh-namāz].[22] Sayyid Dildār Ali also started a separate madrasa of his own where he imparted religious education. Nawab Āsaf ud-Daula had given him Rs. 1,50,000 to purchase books of Shī'īte theology during his educational travels.[23] Sayyid Dildār 'Ali also sent his pupils, numbering about 29 to different parts of the state for the propagation of the Shi'a faith. Under his guidance, his eldest son, the 'Mujtahid-i 'asr' Sayyid Muhammad (d. 1867) developed exceptional talents in the sciences of Hadīth, Qurānic exegesis [tafsīr], scholastic theology [Kalām], principles of jurisprudence [Usūl al-fiqh], jurisprudence [fiqh], the science of biography [ilm ar-rijal] and grammar [qawā'id]. Therefore, at the age of 19, Sayyid Muhammad was granted ijazāt from his father and was entrusted with teaching responsibilities. His lectures on fiqh and other branches of learning aroused considerable interest in academic circles.[24] Sayyid Murtada Akhbārī (d. 1860), Mawlana Mirzā Muhammad Khalil (d.-1805/1806), Fakhr ad-Din Ahmad Khan alias Mirzā Ja'far (d. 1815), Mawlana Yād 'Ali Naqwi (d. 1837), Mawlana 'Abd al-'Ali of Dewakhatta in Ghazipur (d. 1827) and his sons, Sayyid Ahmad 'Ali b. Inayat Haydar (d. 1878) of Muhammadabad, Mawlana Ashraf 'Ali of Bilgram (d. 1854), Mawlana Sayyid Ibādat b. Muhammad Najābat of Amroha (d.-1816), Sayyid Abul-Hasan Abbu Sahib Kashmiri (d. 1895) and Sayyid Muhammad's son Sayyid Muhammad Quli were other famous disciples of Ghufran Ma'ab, who rendered great services in the field of Shī'īte religious- education.[25]

Ghufran Ma'ab's sons and grandsons also trained a large number of 'ulama' and mujtahidun. They increased the standard of higher Shī'īte religious learning in India and tried to raise their standard of education to a similar level of an-Najaf, Karbala, Qom and Mashhad In 1812, Mirzā Qatil wrote in his *Haft Tamasha* [Seven Pleasures]:

"There had been scholars of fiqh in India, but they were not Shi'a scholars. Now with the grace of God, they are also to be found. It was the result of the efforts of some those scholars, who went to the countries of the wilāyat [a generic name for journey abroad, here meaning Iraq and Iran] and studied the religious sciences under the guidance of the 'ulama' of those places. After they came back, they made these sciences popular in their native country. Some of those scholars, who appeared to be inferior in their erudition, were said to have been hundred times better than those who flourished during the reign of Shujā-ud-Dawla and made tall claims of their scholarship in religious sciences".[26]

Sayyid Muhammad, the successor of Ghufran Ma'ab, persuaded King Amjad 'Ali Shāh of Awadh (reigned 1842-1847) to establish a madrasa. The King is said to have been a devout Shī'īte and an ardent follower of the religious leaders of this community. Therefore, he set up an institution of Shī'īte theology called 'Jāmi-i sultāniyya', or madrasa-yi Sultāniyya, or Shāhi madrasa, in 1843. The institution was originally accommodated in the mausoleum of Nawab Sa'adat 'Ali Khan in Khāss Bazār (later known as Qaysar Bagh). It was under the management of Ghufran Ma'ab's son Sayyid Muhammad, whose nephew Mawlana Sayyid Muhammad Taqī, alias Miran Sahib (d. 1872), was appointed principal [mudarris-i a'la] on a salary of Rs. 150 per month. Two posts of assistant principals [na'ib mudarris-i a'la] were also created and the above-mentioned Sayyid Ahmad 'Ali Muhammadabadi, a middle -class landholder [zamindar] and a leader of the small town of A'zamgarh in the south of Awadh was appointed senior assistant principal. The post of the second assistant principal was given to Muhammad b. Ali Faydābādi, a close student of Lucknow's chief mujtahid Sayyid Muhammad Nasirābadi (d. 1867). Besides these three administrators, 14 primary teachers, seven intermediate teachers and five advanced instructors were appointed to run the school. The pay scale for the teachers ranged from Rs. 20 for the junior teachers of primary classes to Rs. 40 for the intermediate teachers, and Rs. 70 for the advanced instructors. Students were also given monthly scholarship ranging from Rs. 4 to Rs. 10. Twenty advanced students received Rs. 10 per month each, 50 intermediate pupils were given Rs. 6 per month each, and 125 beginners had to try to live on Rs. 4 per month. The total expenses of this madrasa amounted to Rs. 31,200 per annum. Of the five advanced teachers, only a few can be identified from the biographical dictionaries. Their names are Sayyid Muhammad Siyādat Amrohawi (d. 1849) and Sayyid Muhammad 'Abbas Shushtari (d. 1888).[27]

Historical research provides evidence that the madrasa went through some important changes. For access to more and better facilities, in 1846 the government moved it to the Āsaf ud-Dawla's Badā Imāmbārah situated in the old part of the town. The faculty expanded from 29 to 38, though the number of students stayed around 200. The Madrasa had a boarding house consisting of 10 rooms under the charge of Mufti Muhammad 'Abbas. There is no list of the students who passed out from the Madrasa and the existing list of teachers often gives only the first name. The information available indicates that the Madrasa functioned for upper and middle-class Shī'ītes. Many of the teachers were small or medium landholders and others derived from high services families clustered around the court in Lucknow.[28]

Some information is available regarding the teaching method and syllabus of the Madrasa. Typical text books included an early Safawid period Usūlī work on the principles of jurisprudence, a standard work on metaphysics in Arabic, Mullā Sadrā's commentary on an early philosophical handbook a work by 'Sayyid al-'ulama' Sayyid Husayn Nasirābādi (d. 1856) on law, and a late 18th century usūlī commentary on law from Karbala. The syllabus mixed works incorporated in the dars-i Nizami the teaching canon developed in the Farangi Mahall in the 18th century with the central textbooks favored by or produced by the usulī revival in Iraq as well as in Lucknow. The works mentioned in the autobiography (ya'ni), sawānih-i 'umrī of Sayyid Ghulām Husayn Kintūri, an eminent Shī'īte scholar of that period very much concerned with reforms of the Madrasa syllabi, are 'Ma'ālim al-Usūl [The Abodes of the Principles], ash-Shams al-bāzigha [The Rising Sun], Mullā

Sadrā's *Sharh hidāyāt al-Hikma* [Commentary on The Guidance of Wisdom] which is a commentary on a philosophical hand book, Sayyid Husayn Nasirbādi's *Manahij-al-tahqiq* [The Methods of Investigation] on prayers and Sayyid 'Ali Tabātabāī's *Sharh al-Kabir* [The Great Commentary].[29] Thus, it is not surprising that quite a number of Shī'ītes were to be found during nawwābi times among the students at the otherwise Sunnīte Farangi Mahall.

Development after 1857

In 1857 that Shāhi madrasa was abolished by the British after the annexation of Awadh. As a consequence, the Shi'a studies in Awadh declined. The abolition marked a very important point in the history of Shī'ītes because of its historical significance and because it had also put an end to the study of Shī'īte students at the Farangi Mahall,[30] thus opening up the opportunity for the increase of tension between Sunnītes and Shī'ītes in Lucknow, which culminated for the first time in the violent riots in 1911. Thus, the learned Shī'īte establishment was forced to work out alternatives in order to maintain religious education for their community after 1857.

The Madrasa-yi nāzimiyya

After the shutdown of the Madrasa-yi sultāniyya, the Shī'īte ulama first continued religious teaching through private tutorage. Around 1872, Mawlana Sayyid Abū Al-Hasan, Abbū Sahib, the above-mentioned son of Sayyid Muhammad b. Ali Shāh Kashmiri had founded the madrasa-yi imāniyya as a center of higher learning. It turned out a failure and its founder became so disappointed that he wanted to move permanently to Iraq. Nevertheless, he eventually changed his mind.[31] In February 1890, he founded the Madrasa-yi nāzimiyya and made Mawlana Najm al-Hasan the director of the Madrasa.[32] Mawlana Najm al-Hasan was born in 1863. He was the son of Sayyid Akbar Husayn of Amroha and the favorite disciple and son-in-law of Mufti Muhammad 'Abbas. After completing his higher education under these teachers, he was teaching Qur'ānic exegesis, 'ulūm al-hadīth, fiqh, usūl al-fiqh, literature and astronomy to higher level students. As director, the Mawlana made the college famous and Shī'īte 'ulama' from all parts of India came there for higher religious learning. He even built a new building for the Madrasa on Victoria Street, Lucknow.[33] After his demise Mufti Sayyid Ahmad 'Ali became its director. He was followed by Mawlana Sayyid Hamid al-Hasan. After the latter's retirement, his son Sayyid Farid al-Hasan became principal and is presently running the madrasa very successfully. Today the madrasa is financially aided by the Uttar Pradesh government. The principal, 16 teachers, one clerk and three other people involved, in running the madrasa are getting their salaries from the state government. About 150 students are studying in the Madrasa. However, the higher section, which is run by Mawlana Hamid al-Hasan is unaided. The sources of income for the maintenance of the institution are traditional Shī'īte means, such as the 'share of the Imām' [sahm -i Imām], or naturalia [fitra]. Admission is restricted to students belonging to the Twelver branch of the Shi'a sect. There is also a boarding house attached to it providing free boarding to deserving students. It also boasts a well-equipped library.

The Madrasa consists of two sections—[tahtāniyya and fawqaniyya], secondary and higher education. The secondary education career offers a nine-year course in the fundamentals of religion and elementary knowledge in arithmetic, geography, etc., whereas the latter is of 11 years duration, instructing students in Islamic sciences like Qur'ānic exegesis, ulūm al-hadīth, Shī'īte jurisprudence, dogmatics, grammar and syntax, logic and philosophy, Arabic Literature, Islamic history, etc. The higher course prepares students for the degree of qābil, fādil and mumtāz al-afadil, corresponding to Intermediate, Graduate and Post-Graduate degrees respectively of the U.P. State education system.[34] Earlier the articles for examinations were set by the 'ulama' of Iraq (but later on, it was not possible to continue the tradition for a number of reasons which we do not have time and space to elaborate), and now the articles are set by the Indian 'ulamā'. Many eminent Shī'īte scholars—Mawlana Maqbul Ahmad of Delhi (d. 1921), Sayyid Farman Ali, Mawlana Muhammad Bāqir (killed 1857), Mawlana Sādiq, Mawlana Sayyid 'Ali Naqi, alias Naqqan Sahib who later became chairman of Shī'īte theology at Aligarh Muslim University, Mawlana Jawwādi, and Mawlana Ghulām Askari were student of this Madrasa at one point in their lives.

The Sultan al-madāris

In 1889, Mawlana Sayyid Abū l-Hasan, Abbū Sahib also established the Sultan al-madāris with the assistance of the Husaynabād Trust originally brought to life by the late Nawab Muhammad 'Ali Shāh in 1839 to replace the Shāhi Madrasa which was founded by King Amjad 'Ali Shāh but was closed in 1857.[35] Abbū Sahib was the chief patron of this institution.[36]

Sayyid Muhammad Bāqir Ridwi Kashmiri, known as 'Bāqir al-ulūm', was appointed head of the madrasa. He took keen interest in its development. In the initial phase, classes were run in the corridors attached to the Rūmi Darwāzā of the Barā Imāmbārah complex in Lucknow. In 1911, the Husaynabād Trust had developed the present site of the new venue the foundation stone for the building of Sultan al-madāis was laid by the then British Lieutenant Governor of United Provinces, Sir John Prescott Hewett. The imposing double-story building with a large hall in its center with rooms and galleries all-around was formally inaugurated by the Lieutenant Governor on May 21, 1913 AD, on the day of Nawruz, the ancient Persian New Year festival which is nowadays celebrated by Shī'ītes too. The building was constructed with the financial support of the Nawab Mirzā Mahdi Hasan Khan (b. 1854), whose contribution had been due to the efforts of Sayyid Muhammad Bāqir Ridwi, the principal of the institution.[37] Another two-storeyed building designed on the lines of the main building was later built just behind it.[38] Bāqir Sahib, who died on February

9th 1928, put much effort, into raising the standard of teaching.[39] After his demise Mawlana Muhammad Hādi Sahib became the principal and taught a number of famous 20th century 'ulama'. He died on April 2nd 1938, during a visit to Karbala.[40] After him the headship of the Madrasa devolved upon his successor Sayyid Muhammad Sahib and was then passed on to Mawlana Sayyid Ali Sahib who died in 1985. Finally, Sayyid Muhammad J'afar Sahib became principal. Some information regarding the madāris syllabus, teachers, teaching method and changes made in the term period to acquire certificates [sanad] have also been provided during a number of interviews with officials of the madāris under investigation. According to Mawlana Yūsūf Sahib (d. 1940), a previous student of Sultan al-madāris in the beginning a teacher used to teach two classes but all the books were taught completely. A student used to get the sanad of sadr al-afadil, after completing five years study. Sayyid Hādi, Mufti Muhammad Husayan and Mawlana Sayyid Muhammad Ja'far were the teachers for the classes of sadr al-afadil. Wajāhat Husayn and Nāzim Sahib were appointed as teachers after the retirement of Ja'far Sahib. In the first class Ibn al-Hājib's syntax work Kāfiyya fī n-nahw [The Sufficient in Syntex], 'Abd Allāh Yazdi's logical commentary Sharh at-tahdhib fī ilm al-mantiq [The commentary on 'The Instruction in the Science of Logic], al-Abhāri's *Hidāyāt al-Hikma* [The Guidance of Wisdom], and Muhammad 'Ali Shirwani work on Literature *Nafāhat al-yaman* [The Scents of Yemen] were taught among others by Nāzim Sahib. In the second class, 'Abdar-Rahmān's *Jāmi Sharh Jāmi* on the Kāfiyya: the Qutbi, a gloss on Katibi's logical treatise *ar-Risālā ash-shamsiyya* by Qutb ad-Din at-Tahtāni (d. 1365); the *Dūrūs al-balāghā* [Lessons in Rhetorics]; and the *Mukhtasar Nāfi* and *Sharh Babi*, two works on dogmatic ['Aqā'id], were taught by Hādi 'Asr Sāhib, Mawlana 'Ali Ābid, in turn, used to teach the grammatical work *Mizan as-sarf* [The Measure of Morphology] by Siraj ad-Din al-Awadhi (d. 1357); Mullā Hamza Bada'uni's *Munsha'ib* [Ramification]; and 'Abd al-

Qādir *Jurjāni's Nahw-i Mīr* [The Syntax of Mīr] and *Sarf-i Mīr* (The Morphology of Mīr); while another old teacher taught the *Hidāyāt an-nahw* [Guidance in Syntax], believed to be a revision of the Kāfiyya.

Later, the study was divided into nine classes and teachers were appointed for each class. It was decided that the certificate of sadr al-afadil would be awarded after two years study. (Earlier, a student would get this sanad after completing a three-years course). What we have given above is the description of the personnel and syllabi of the year 1921-1922.[41] Notable among the teachers in this Madrasa were Wali Muhammad, Sayyid 'Ali, 'Ali Ābid, Wajāhat Husayn, Mufti Muhammad Husayn, Shāh 'Abd al-Husayn, and Shāh Ghulām Haydar. Sultan al-madāris was recognized by the British government in 1922. In 1972, it was affiliated to the Board of Arabic and Persian Studies in Allahabad. The U.P. government handed out a grant to the Institution in the same year. The higher section remains unaided.

Sayyid Ahsan Mahdi Ridwi, who in 1982 took admission in class five of the Sultan al-madāris and passed the examination of sadr al-afadil in 1992, told me in a personal interview that each student of class five used to get Rs. 30 per month as subsistence allowance [wazifa], dependent, however, on his attendance. There was a fine of one rupee per day for being absent. Lodging in the hostel was free but the student had to arrange his personal bedding. In summer a cloth [gārhā] was provided to each student by the Madrasa. Three students were put in one room. The allowance in class six was Rs. 40, in class seven Rs. 45 and in class eight Rs. 50 per month. In 1986, when he took admission for the sanad of a mawlawi, the stipend was substituted by free food. After passing the mawlawi stage he entered the class of 'ālim in 1988. He passed the examination to obtain the title of an 'ālim, which was conducted by the Allāhabad Board. Then he passed the three-years course for the sanad of sadr al-afadil in only two years, because there was a provision that a student may pass a two years course in one year. In

1992 he passed the examination of sadr al-afadil, which was conducted by the Madrasa itself. The number of students who successfully passed this last examination were seven. Four among them passed in the first division and three in the second.[42]

Today the Sultan al-madāris is an outstanding Shi'a madrasa of Lucknow which is imparting Shi'a religious education to the community under the able guidance of Mawlana Sayyid Muhammad Ja'far Sahib and his sons.

The madrasāt al-wai'zin

In 1919-1920 Sir Muhammad 'Ali Muhammad Khan, the late Raja of Mahmūdabad and his younger brother, the late Sāhibzādā Muhammad Ali Ahmad Khan established the Madrasāt al-wa'izin in order to train Shī'īte preachers for missionary work. This institution specializes in and provides selective training to post-graduate or holders of diplomas in higher learning from the Shi'a madāris like the Nāzimiyya and the Sultan al-madāris. It offers instruction in practical training as preacher (wa'iz) for which all such students as have acquired higher degree of religious knowledge, have flair for writing, possess a gift of expression and have some knowledge of fundamentals of rhetoric are eligible. The training is of three years duration, split into three grades, each of which contains quarterly, half yearly and annual examinations. The candidates who qualify themselves with honors at the final-year's examinations and complete two years practical experience while preaching become eligible for the degree of a wa'iz. There is a hostel attached to the madrasa which provides modern amenities and food subsidy. The Madrasa also has a fine library attached to it, which is called *Dhakhirat al-wa'izin*.[43] Its missionaries took Shī'īsm to Tibet, Burma and Africa and even some places in Europe. The Madrasa has a publication department with its own press producing a monthly Urdu journal, *al-Wa'iz* and an English magazine called, *The Muslim Review*. The major work translated into English and published by the Madrasa are the Qur'ān, the

Sahifā-yi kāmilā [The Perfect Page] and a section of the *Majālis al-mu' minin* [The Gatherings of the Faithful].

Mawlana Najm 'al-'Hasan was its first principal. He guided the multifarious programs of the Madrasa. In recognition of his services, the government awarded him the title of a 'Shams al-'ulama'.[44] Among the prominent teachers of this madrasa were Mawlana Sayyid Sibt-i Hasan Lakhnawi, Mawlana Sayyid 'Abū Āl-Hasan Lakhnawi, Mawlana Mufti Sayyid Ahmad' Ali Lakhnawi, Mawlana Sayyid Rahat Husayan Gopalpuri, Mawlana Sayyid Mumtaz Husayn, Mawlana Sayyid Diya al-Hasan, etc.[45] At present Mawlana Warith Hasan is the principal and about 10 students are studying there.

The disciples of 'Ghufran Ma'ab' and his sons carried the torch of knowledge to different parts of the country by establishing madāris. Mawlana Mirzā Muhammad'Ali (d. 1872) set up a major Shi'a Madrasa in Calcutta. His family originated from Kashmir but they settled in Lucknow in the 18th century. However, he moved to Calcutta (then capital of India) with Wajid 'Ali Shāh , the last king of Awadh, who was a captive there.[46] Similarly, Jāmi'a mansabiyya in Meerut,[47] the Shi'a Arabic College in Lucknow, Wathīqa Arabic College in Faydabad (Faizabad), Jāmi'a Imāmiyya and Jawwadiyya Arabic College in Benares, Madrasa-yi Nāsiriyya in Jawnpur, and the girl's college Jāmi'at az-zahra in Lucknow were established in the 19th and 20th centuries. However, this list is by no means complete but only illustrative one.

Present Developments

Even today, the Shi'a madāris award the highest certificate of *a-fadil*. The change took place in the shape of attaching an identifying prefix before fadil. The certificate of *fakhr al-afadil* is awarded by Madrasa-yi Jawwādiyya in Benares, while *sadr al-afādil* is awarded by the Sultan al-madāris. The Madrasa-yi nāzimiyya awards the *Mumtāz al-afādil*. However, there are no provision for studying dars-i-khārij in India which poses an important problem since an ālim has to go to Iraq and Iran for the study of *dars-i khārij* in order to be able to become a mujtahid. Thus, there is no mujtahid in India in present time. Most Shī'ītes are the followers of Sayyid Ali Husayn al Husayni Sistānī (b. 1930) of an-Najaf in Iraq even though there are some akhābārīs in Southern India, particularly in Hyderabad.

The course content and methodology of imparting religious education and training is the same everywhere. All the madāris may show some independence and impart extra information, but after the God, all of them are accountable for the community. This is true even for those madāris that have not accepted government aid. Grammar [Qawā'id], jurisprudence [fiqh], logic [mantiq], philosophy [Hikma], astronomy ['ilm al-hay'at], psychology ['ilm-al nafsiyat], linguistics [lughat], rhetorics ['ilm al-balaghā], mathematics, tafsir al-Qur'ān and the history of Islam are the main subjects. Teaching of foreign languages is not included in the new syllabus of higher-classes.[48]

The financial burdens of the Shi'a madāris are borne entirely by the community in the form of Khums Fitra, alms and charity. There is a provision in Shī'īte law that every Shi'a has to pay Khums (20 per cent of the savings) yearly, out of which the share of the Imām [sahm-i-Imām] is 50 per cent. This share goes to Shi'a madāris and other social institutions with the permission of the mujtahid. At present most of the Shi'a madāris, except the Madrasa-yi Jawwādiyya in Benares are government aided. Their syllabi are recognized by the government. They award certificate for every class. The teaching hours of these madāris are from 8 a.m. to 12 p.m. But they also claim the share of sahm-i Imām for the expenses of boarding and lodging of the students.

However, this account is of little relevance if we do not outline the place of madāris in modern times. Certain changes bear witness to the changing role of Madrasa education in general and for Shī'ītes in particular. Shī'īte 'ulama' do accept that the worldly sciences [ulūm-iduniya] are also essential for the survival and the instruction of the young generation. Therefore, Mawlana Kalb-e Sādiq, Mawlana Kalb-e-Jawwād and many others are trying to establish English schools, along with engineering and medical colleges. Mawlana Kalb-e Sādiq has founded the Unity Public School and the Era Medical College in Lucknow, Mawlana Kalb-e Jawwād, the guardian of the Shi'a orphanage [yatim-khana] in Lucknow has permitted the students to study in the English schools which are governed by the Central Board of Secondary Education (C.B.S.E.) and Council for the Indian School Certificate Examination (I.C.S.E.), New Delhi. Mirzā Jafar Abbas, Joint Secretary and Manager of Jame-Atot-Tableegh, Musahabganj, Lucknow (established in 1974 AD), informs us that, the *Hauza-e-Ilmia* has also launched a "Computer Faculty" and English-speaking course. Students are learning computer courses like, DOS, MS-Office, Internet, ctt, DTP, etc. This Idārā has also launched a girls' madrasa in the residence of Maulana Mirzā Mohd. Alīm Sahib. 200 girls are getting religious knowledge and acquaintance with the essential principles and basic laws of Islam. A brief awareness of Hindi and Urdu language is also being given, so that illiteracy amongst girls can be eradicated.[49] Similar attempts also have been made in other parts of the country.[50] The efforts made by the late Mawlana Ghulām 'Askari are also commendable. On August 15, 1968 he founded the Tanzim al-makātib with the prime object of religious awakening among the members of the Shi'a community. This organization started opening makātib (sg: maktab) and, madāris, publishing religious Litarature, particularly Diniyyat books in different language. Diniyyat books in Urdu, Hindi, Gujarati and Bengali were published during the life time of the founder of the institution but yet English versions could not printed. The reason for that is the unavailability of the proper translators for the time being. However, Dr. Sayyid Manzur Naqi, who obtained his M.D. in New Jersey, (USA) came forward to help and translated some Diniyyat-books of the primary level into English.[51] The institution has requested him to take the trouble of translating the remaining diniyyat-books into English. Thus, the

Tanzīm al-makātib is rendering great services to the community according to the need of the hour.

Conclusion

The foregoing description has shown that the Shi'a Madrasa education system developed in India only after the establishment of Shi'a state of Awadh. It has come to an age by now owing to the fact that many reputed Shī'īte 'ulama' have been trained in India. Religious education, to be brought to the majority of the Shī'ītes with the help of the State was never a reality in Awadh. The first Madrasa established in 1843 already faced closure in 1857; this also ended the independent Shī'īte state of Awadh as it was now taken over by the British Crown. However, the trend and attention generated in this field with the emergence of Dildār 'Ali did not subside. The attention of past Shī'īte rulers and influential Shī'īte ta'alluqdars, like Raja of Mahmūdabad kept in spirit of Shi'a madāris alive. The inbuilt system of khums among Shī'ītes was also responsible for significant financial support in running the madāris. In those days, the students in madāris were from the middle and upper middle classes; now the students in madāris have started to come from the economically very weak strata of the Shi'a society, including orphans who have no other way to get education. Thus, the mass appeal has increased. This has caused a deterioration in the condition and standard of the Shi'a madāris with respect to the number of staff, student and infrastructure such as buildings and libraries.

Recently, Madrasa education in India in general has been under attack for two reasons. Primarily, for its orthodox syllabus, which is deemed unfit for keeping pace with modern developments and demands of contemporary societies. Secondly due to the alleged links between Madrasa education and the spread of orthodoxy and terrorism. As far as Shī'īte Madrasa education in India is concerned, there has not been much of a revision in the religious subjects and their syllabi, because there is no need to revise subjects like fiqh'ulūm al-Hadith, theology and History of Islam—the source book for all these subjects as the text of the revelation will essentially remain the same. However, the requirement is the introduction of certain subjects which are very essential in the contemporary world and life. In addition to the teaching of religious knowledge, the syllabus should be designed so that it enable the graduates of a madrasa to find jobs in the public and private sectors, in order to be able to earn their livelihood. For this, subjects like natural sciences, modern mathematics, English and Hindi and computer applications[52] should be included, along with the traditional subjects. Work in this regard should be taken up by the board-members and advisory committees of madāris. Both parts of the syllabus can co-exist. However, the non-revision of the syllabus and its lack of relevance to contemporary society in terms of earning livelihood through madrasa education is at least to some extent responsible for the present conditions of Shi'a madāris in Awadh. Furthermore, the Shī'ītes of India still have to depend upon the institutions of an-Najaf, Karbala, Qom and Mashhad for *dars-i-Khārij*, the research level course, as none of the Shi'a madāris in India are yet equipped with these facility. At present, most Shī'īte students are continuing their studies in Iran after doing the initial and lower courses in India even though some of those courses are perfectly available in India too, simply because the necessary placement services are not available in India. The large number of Shī'ītes living in India, do indeed require a better educational system for their religious needs as well as for their social needs and should not be forced to depend on foreign madāris. Moreover, the Indian perspective in the development of the Shi'a faith as such can only be properly assessed if the Shī'ītes have at least an indigenous Madrasa of higher learning of the level of dars-i-khārij or doctoral research. Such an indigenous institution of Shī'īte higher learning is thus required in India and efforts should be made in this direction to design courses with emphasis on the contribution of Indian Shī'ītes in the field of education.

APPENDIX-I

Current syllabus of the Madrasa-yi nāzimiyya, Victoria Street, Lucknow.[53]

Āliyyā (10 Years)

Tahtāniyyā (Duration: 6 years)

Qur'ān, Diniyyat, Amadnama of an anonymous author, Gulzar-i dabistan-basic (of Siva-Narayana), Hisāb-i basic, Geography of the Province, General Science, Basic Hindi, Basic Urdu, English Reader.

Fawqāniyyā (Duration: 3 years)

Islamic Jurisprudence [Fiqh];

- *Bidāyat al-hidāyā* (Arabic) of Muhammad b. al-Hasan al-Hurr al- Āmilī (d. 1688).
- *Tawdih al-masa'il* (Persian) of Sayyid Abū I-Qāsim Khu'ī (d. 1992).

Logic [Mantiq]

- *ar-Risālā al-Kubrā fī l-mantiq* (Arabic) of Sharīf al-Jurjānī (d. 1413).

Grammar (Sarf wa nahw)

- *Sharh mi'at amil* (Arabic) of Husayn an-Nawqānī (d. 1520)
- *Dastūr al-mubtā dī* (Persian) of Safī d-Din b. Nāsir Rudawlī (d, 1416).

Literature (Adab)

- *Nisāb-i fārsi* (Persian) of Dr. Ghulām Sarwar (b. 1926)
- *al-Qir ā'at ar-rashīda* (Arabic) of 'Abd al-Fattah Sābiri and 'Umar Beg.

Essay Writing

- *Riyahin-i inshā* (Persian) of an unknown author.

World Geography ['alamgir]

- No particular text.

Mathematics [riyāddiyyat]

- *Iritmatik* (Urdu)
- *Aljibra* (Urdu).

Hindi (Compulsory)

- No particular text mentioned.

English (Compulsory)

- English Reader for Class 8 of an unknown author.

Mawlavi (Duration: 2 years)

Islamic Jurisprudence [Fiqh]

- *Tabsirāt al-mutā'allimīn fi ahkam ad-dīn* (Arabic) of 'al-' Allamā' Ibn al-Mutahhar al-Hillī (d. 1325)
- *Irshād al-ma'rid* (Urdu) of Sayyid 'Ali Taqi Tabassura.

Principles of Islamic Jurisprudence (usul al-fiqh)

- *Mabadi' al-Usūl la 'ilm al-Usūl* (Arabic) of 'al-'Allamā' Ibn al-Mutahhar al-Hillī.

Logic (Mantiq)

- *Sharh tahdhib fi ilm al-mantiq* (Arabic) of 'Abdallāh al-Yazdī (d. 1574).

Philosophy (Hikma)

- *Hidāyat al-Hikma* (Arabic) of Athir ad-Din al-Abhārī (d.1265).

Grammar [Sarf wa nahw]

- *al-Kāfiyya fi n-nahw* (Arabic) of Jamāl ad-Din b. al-Hājib (d.1249)
- *Fusūl-i akbari* (Arabic) of Muhammad Hādi 'Ali Akbar Illahabadi (d.1680).

Literature [Adab]

- *Azhar al-arab* (Arabic) of 'Abd allāh Muhammad b. Yusuf.

Sciences of Hadīth ['ulūm al-Hadīth]

- *Jāmi al-akhbār, or Ma'ānī l-akhbār* (Arabic) of Muhammad b. 'Ali b. Babūya as-Sadūq (d. 991)
- *Ma'rūf al-akhbār* (Urdu) of Sayyid Dhu l-Fiqār Husayn (d. 1960).

Science of Exegesis ['ilm at-tafsīr]

- *Tafsīr Āsafi* (Arabic) of Muhammad b. Murtadā Muhsin Fayd Kāshānī (d. 1679).

Rhetorics ['ilm al-balāghā]

- *Durūs al-balāghā* (Arabic) by a collective of authors from the *Jāmi'at al-Azhar* (Cairo), edited by 'Abd al-Afdāl Muhammad Fadl-i Haqq, Rampuri.

History [Tārīkh]

- *Kitāb al-Irshād* (Arabic) of Muhammad b. an-Nu'man 'Shaykh al-Mufid
- *Maqātil Yā'qūbī* (Arabic) of Muhammad b. Ya'qūb (translated into Urdu by Mujtaba Hasan Kanpuri)

National Languages: Hindi or English (optional)

- No particular texts mentioned.

Ālimiyya (Duration: 2 years)

Islamic Jurisprudence (Fiqh)

- *Kitāb sharā 'i' al-Islam* (Arabic) of Najm ad-Din Ja'far al-Hillī al-Muhaqqiq al-awwal' (d. 1277).

Principles of Islamic Jurisprudence [usul al-fiqh]

- *Mā'alim ad-din wa-malādh al-mujtahidīn fī Usūl ad-dīn* (Arabic) of Mansur Hasan b. Zayn ad-Din al-Āmili (d. 1602).

Logic [Mantiq]

- *Sullam al-'ulūm of Muhibballāh Bihārī* (d. 1707)
- *Qawā id al-mantiqiyyā fī sharh ar-risālā ash-shamsiyyā*, or *Qutbi* of Qutb ad-Din Tahtānī (d. 1365)
- *al-Hādiyya as-sa 'idiyya fī l-Hikma at-tabi'iyyā* of Fadl-i Haqq Khayrābādī (d. 1862)

Philosophy (Hikmā)

- *Sharh hidāyat al-hikma of 'Abd al-Haqq Khayrābādī* (d. 1900).

Grammar (Sarf wa nahw)

- *al-Fawā'id ad-diyā' iyya, or Sharh Jāmī*, of 'Abd ar-Rahmān Jāmī (d. 1492)
- *ash-Shāfiyyā* of Jamāl ad-Din b. al-Hājib.

Literature [Adab]

- *Diwān Mutanabbī* of Abū Tayyib Ahmad al-Kindī 'al-Mutanabbī (d.1655).

Sciences of Hadīth ['ulūm al-Hadīth]

- *Wajīza* (Arabic) of Baha'ad-Din Muhammad b. 'Abd as-Samad al-Harīthī (d. 1622)
- *Usūl al-Kāfī* of Abū Jā'far Muhammad al-Kulaynī (d. 940).

Science of Exegesis ['ilm at-tafsīr]

- *Tafsīr Āsafī* (Arabic) of Muhammad b. Murtadā Muhsin Fayd Kāshānī.

History [Tārīkh]

- *Duwāl al-arab* of Muhammad Muhyi d-Din al-Ja'far 'Tal'at-i Hazm'.

Rhetorics ['ilm al-balāghā]

- *Talkhis al-miftāh* of Muhammad b. 'Abd ar-Rahmān 'al-Khatib' Qazwīnī (d. 1338).

National Languages: Hindi (Intermediate) or English (Intermediate)

- Books issued by the U.P. Government, Allahabad.

Qābil (Duration: 1 year)

Islamic Jurisprudence [Fiqh]

- *ar-Rawdā al-bahiyya sharh al-luma' ad-Dimashqiyya* (Arabic) of Zayn ad-Din al-'Āmilī 'Shahid ath-thānī' (killed 1558).

Principles of Islamic Jurisprudence [Usūl al-fiqh]

- *Usūl al-Muzaffar* (Arabic) of Muhammad Ridā al-Muzaffar (b. 1904).

Logic [Mantiq]

- *Sharh tahdhīb al-mantiq*, or *Mullā Jalāl* (Arabic), of Jalāl ad-Dīn ad-Dawānī (d. 1502).

Theology [Kalām]

- *al-Jawhar an-nadid fī sharh Kitāb at-tajrīd* (Arabic) of 'al-'Allamā' ibn al-Mutahhar al-Hillī.
- *al-Bāb al-Hādī 'ashar* (Arabic) of 'al- 'Allamā' ibn al-Mutahhar al-Hillī.

Literature [Adab]

- *Maqāmat al-Harīrī* (Arabic) of Abū Muhammad al-Qāsim b. 'Ali al-Harīrī (d. 1122)

Rhetorics ['ilm al-balāghā]

- *Nahj al-balāghā* (Arabic) of Muhammad b. at-Tāhir al-Husayn ar-Rādī (d.1016).

Astronomy ['ilm-I hay' at]

- *Sharh tashrīh al-aflāk* (Arabic) of Imām ad-Din b. Lutfallāh Muhaddīth Lahawrī.

Philosophy (Hikma)

- *Ifādat al-qudsiyyā* (Arabic) of Hakīm Muhammad Sharif Mustafābadī.

Essay-Writing

- No particular work mentioned.

Fādil: (Duration: 2 years)

Islamic Jurisprudence [Fiqh]

- *ar-Rawdā al-bahiyya sharh al-luma' ad-Dimashqiyya* (Arabic) of Zayn ad-Dīn al-'Āmilī 'Shahīd ath-thānī' (chapters on marriage and property).

Principles of Islamic Jurisprudence [Usūl al-flqh]

- *Qawānin al-usūl* (Arabic) of Mirzā al-Qāsim b. Muhammad b. Husayn al-Qummī (d. 1816).

Logic [Mantiq]

- *Sharh bāsit 'alā sullam al-ulūm*, or *Hamdallāh* (Arabic), of Hamdallah Sandīlawī (d. 1746-1747).
- *Sharh Sullam ul-ulūm*, or *Qādī Mubārak* (Arabic) of Muhammad Mubārak b. Muhammad Da'im Gopāmawī (d. 1748).

Litarature [Adab]

- *Hamāsat at-Tammām* (Arabic) of Abū Tammām Habib b. Aws at Ta'i (d. 846) (marāthī and nasīb).

Sciences of Hadīth ['ulūm al-Hadīth]

- *Ghurar al-fāwā id wa-durar al-qalā'id bi-l-muhādarāt*, or *al-Āmalī* (Arabic), of Abū- l-Qāsim 'Ali ash-Sharif al-Murtadā (d. 1044) (10 Majālis [lectures])

Rhetorics ['ilm al-balāghā]

- *Nahj al-balāghā* (Arabic) of Muhammad b. at-Tāhir al-Husayn ar Rādī (from lesson 21 to the end).

Essay Writing

- No particular work mentioned.

Mumtāz al-afādil (Duration: 2 years)

Islamic Jurisprudence [Fiqh]

- *Riyād al-masa il al-mā'ruf bi-sharh al-kabir* (Arabic) of 'Ali b.Muhammad b. 'Ali Bahr al-'ulūm Tabātabāī (d. 1815)
- *Farā'id al-Usūl* (Arabic) of Murtadā b. Muhammad Amīn al-Ansārī; (d. 1864)
- *Bahth az-zann* of an unknown author.
- *Kitāb al-makāsib* (Arabic) of Murtadā b. Muhammad Amin Ansārī.

Sciences of hadīth ['ulūm al-Hadīth]

- *al-Istibsār fi ma 'khatutlifa min al-akhbār* (Arabic) of Abū Ja' far Muhammad b. al-Hasan at-Tūsi 'Shaykh at-Ta'ifā' (d. 1067)
- *Furū al-kāfi* (Arabic) of Abū Ja'far Muhammad al-Kulaynī.

APPENDIX-II

Current Syllabus of the Sultan al-madāris, Arabic College, Lucknow[54]

Tahtāniyya: (Duration: 5 years)

Year 1 : Hindi: *Gyān Bharati* (Vol. 1); Basic English Reader (Vol.I), Hisāb (Vol. 1); Urdu; Diniyyāt; Qur'ān.

Year 2 : Qur'ān; Diniyyāt; Urdu; Hindi; Hisāb; General Science.

Year 3 : Qur'ān; *Diniyyāt*; Urdu; Hindi; Hisāb; *Mashārit-i 'ulūm; Mālumat-i a'immā*; Sports: P.T.: Natural Science.

Year 4 : *Gulzār-yi dabistān* (Vol. 1); *Minhāj al-arabiyya* of Sayyid Nabil-Haydar Haydarabadī (Vol.1); *Āmadnāmā* of an unknown author; urdu; Qur'ān; Diniyyāt; Hindi; P.T., Mizān.

Year 5 : Qur'ān; Diniyyāt; Urdu; Hindi; Persian; Arabic; English; Hisāb; Samāj-i 'ilm; General Science; P.T.; Arabic Grammar: Munsha 'ib of Mullā Hamzā Badāuni.

Fawqāniyya: (Duration: 3 years)

Year 1

Literature [Adab]

- *Minhāj al-arabiyyā* (Arabic) of Sayyid Nabī-Haydar Haydarābādī (Vol. 2)
- *Ta'līm al-lugha al-arabiyyā* (Arabic) of Dr. Muhammad Amin Misrī (Vol. 1)
- *Gulistān* (Persian) of Sā'dī Shīrāzī

Grammar [Sarf wa nahw]

- *Nahw Mīr* of Sharīf al-Jurjānī

Isamic Jurisprudence [Fiqh]

- *Tawdīh al-masā'il* (Persian) of Sayyid Abū l-Qāsim Khu'ī (Vol. I)

Year 2

Literature (Adab)

- *Minhāj al-arabiyyā* (Arabic) of Sayyid Nabi-Haydar Haydarābādī (Vol. 3)
- *Tā'līm al-lughāt al-'arabiyya* (Arabic) by Dr. Muhammad Amīn Misri (Vol. 2)
- *Afsānā-yi bāstān* (Persian) of Yūsūf Husayn Musāwī (d. 1972)

Grammar [Sarf wa nahw]

- *Nahw Mīr* of Sharif al-Jurjānī (Vol. 3)
- *Panj Ganj* (Persian) by an unknown author

Islamic Jurisprudence [Fiqh]

* *Tawdīh al-masa'il* (Persian) of Sayyid Abū l-Qāsim Khu'i (Vol.2)

Logic [Mantiq]

- *ar-Risālā al-Kubrā fi l-mantiq* (Persian translation) of Sharif al Jurjānī

Year 3

Literature (Adab)

- *Tā'lim al-lughāt al-arabiyyā* (Arabic) by Dr. Muhammad Amin Misrī (Vol.3)
- *Afsānā-yi bastān* (Persian) of Yūsūf Husayn Musāwī

Grammar [Sarf wa nahw]

- *Hidāyāt an-nahw* (Arabic) of Anwar 'Ali (commentary on al-Kāfiyyā fi n-nahw of Jamāl ad-Din b. al-Hājib)
- *Sharh mi'at āmil* (Arabic) of 'Abd ar-Rahmān Jāmi (on the Mi'at amil of Abū Bakr' Abd al-Qahir Jurjānī [d. 1078].
- *Kitāb at-tasrīf, or al-Izzī,* or *Mabādī at-tasrīf* (Arabic) of 'Izz ad-Din Abū Fada'il Zanjāni (d. 1257)

Islamic Jurisprudence [Fiqh]

- *Tawdīh al-masa'il* (Persian) of Sayyid Abū I-Qāsim Khu'i (Vol. 3)
- *Ahkām al-Islam* (Persian) of Sayyid Abū I-Qāsim Khu'i

Logic [mantiq]

- *al-Mantiq wa-manahij al-bahth* (Arabic) of Muhammad Ridā Muzaffar.

Mawlawiyya: (Duration: 2 Years)

Year 1

Literature (Adab)

- *Majānī l-adab* (Arabic) published from al-Majma 'al-ilm al-Islami, Lajnat at-tanzīm ad-darsiyya, Qom.

Grammar [sarf wa nahw]

- *al-Kāfiyyā fi n-nahw* (Arabic) of Jamāl ad Dīn b. al-Hājib
- *Fūsūl-ī akbari* (Arabic) of Muhammad Hādi 'Ali Akbar llāhābādī.

Islamic Jurisprudence [fiqh]

- *Tabsirāt al-mutā allimin fi ahkām ad-dīn* (Arabic) of' al-'Allamā' ibn al-Mutahhar al-Hillī.

Philosophy (Hikmā)

- *Hidāyat al-hikma* (Arabic) of Waqār 'Ali Ashrafi

Logic (Mantiq)

- *Matn al-kāfi* (Arabic) of Muhammad Husayn Shamsī

Rhetorics ['ilm al-balāghā]

- *Durūs al-balāghā* (Arabic) of Taht al-Muhammad Zaki Bāshā.

Year 2

Literature [Adab]

- *Azhār al-'arab* (Arabic) of 'Abdallāh Muhammad b. Yūsūf.

Grammar [sarf wa nahw]

- *al-Kāfiyya fi n-nahw* (Arabic) of Jamāl ad-Din b. al-Hājib.

Islamic Jurisprudence [Fiqh]

- *Tabsirāt al-mutā 'allimin fi ahkāmad-dīn* (Arabic) of 'al-'Allamā' ibn al-Mutahhar al-Hillī.

Sciences of hadīth ['ulūm al-hadīh]

- *Jāmi al-akhbār*, or *Ma'ani i-akhbār* (Arabic) of Muhammad b. 'Ali b. Babūyā as-Sadūq

Ālimiyya (Duration: 2 years)

Year 1

Islamic Jurisprudence [Fiqh]

- *Kitāb sharā'i' al-Islam* (Arabic) of Najm ad-Din Ja'far al-Hillī 'al- Muhaqqiq al-awwal'

Principles of Islamic Jurisprudence [Usūl al-fiqh]

- *Ma'ālim ad-din wa-malādh al-mujtahidīn fi Usūlad-din* (Arabic) of Mansur Hasan b. Zayn ad-Din al-'Āmilī.
- *Sharh al-wajizā* (Arabic) of Bahā' ad-Din Muhammad b. 'Abd as-Samad al-Hārithī (d. 1622).

Literature [Adab]

- *Mansūrat* of 'Abd al-Mājid Nadwī.

Logic [Mantiq]

- *Sharh shamsiyyā*, or *Qutbī*, of Qutb ad-Din Tahtānī.

Philosophy [Hikma]

- *al-Hādiyyā as-sa 'idiyya fi I-hikma at-tabī'iyya* of Fādl-i Haqq Khayrābādī.

Science of Exegesis ['ilm at-tafsīr]

- *Tafsīr Āsafi* (Arabic) of Muhammad b. Murtad a Mushin Fayd Kāshānī.

Science of Hadīth ['ulūm al-hadīth]

- *Usūl al-kāfi* of Abū Jā'far Muhammad al-Kulaynī

Year 2

Islamic Jurisprudence [Fiqh]

- *Kitāb sharā'i al-Islam* (Arabic) of Najm ad-Din Ja'far al-Hillī 'al- Muhaqqiq al-awwal'.

Principles of Islamic Jurisprudence [Usūl al-fiqh]

- *Ma'ālim ad-din wa-malādh al-mujtahidīn fi Usūl ad-din* (Arabic of Mansur Hasan b. Zayn ad-Din al-'Āmilī).

Litrature [Adab]

- *Diwān Mutanabbī* of Abū Tayyib Ahmad al-Kindi 'al-Mutanabbī.
- *Mansīurāt* of 'Abd al-Mājid Nadwī.

Logic [Mantiq]

- *Sullam al-'ulūm* of Muhibballāh Bihārī (d. 1707).

Philosophy (Hikma)

- *Sharh hidāyat al-hikmā* of Mīr Husayn al-Maybudhī (d. 1498).

Science of Exegesis ['ilm at-tafsīr]

- *Tafsīr Āsafi* (Arabic) of Muhammad b. Murtadā Muhsin Fayd Kāshānī.

Science of Hadīth [Ulūm al-Hadīth]

- *Usūl al-kāfi* of Abū Jā'far Muhammad al-Kulaynī.

Rhetorics ['ilm al-balāghā]

- *Talkhis al-miftāh* of Abū Ya'qub b. Yūsūf as-Saqqāqī (d. 1229).

Sanadallāh fādil (Duration: 3 Years)

Year 1

Islamic Jurisprudence (Fiqh)

- *al-Kitāb tajrīd al-'Aqā'id* of Nāsir ad-Din at-Tūsī (d. 1274).

- *ar-Rawdā al-bahiyya sharh al-lumā ad-Dimashqiyya* (Arabic) of Zayn ad-Din al-'Āmili 'Shāhīd ath-thānī'

Principles of Islāmic Jurisprudence (Usūl al-fiqh)

- *Usūl al-Muzaffar* (Arabic) of Muhammad Ridā al- Muzaffar (Vol. I)

Literature [Adab)

- *Nahj al-balāghā* (Arabic) of Muhammad b. at-Tāhir al- Husayn ar-Radī (Vol. 3)

Logic [Mantiq]

- *Sharh mutālā al-anwār* (Arabic) of Muhammad b. Muhammad Rādi 'Mullā Qutb Ranawi' (Synopsis of the L awami' al-asrar of Siraj ad-Din Mahmūd al-'Urmawi (d. 1283)

Year 2

Islamic Jurisprudence [Fiqh]

- *al- Kitāb tajrīd al-Aqā'id* of Nāsir ad-Din at-Tūsī (d. 1274)
- *ar-Rawdā al-bahiyya sharh al-lumā' ad-Dimashqiyya* (Arabic) of Zayn ad-Din al-Āmili 'Shāhīd ath-thānī')

Principles of Islamic Jurisprudence [Usūl al-fiqh]

- *Usūl al-Muzaffar* (Arabic) of Muhammad Ridā al-Muzaffar (Vol-2)

Literature [Adab]

- *Nahj al-balāghā* (Arabic) of Muhammad b. at-Tāhir al-Husaynar-Radī (Vol.3).

Logic [Mantiq]

- *Sharh basīt 'ala sullam al-'ulūm*, or *Hamdallāh* (Arabic) of Hamdallāh Sandilawī

Year 3

Islamic Jurisprudence [Fiqh]

- *ar-Rawdā al-bahiyā sharh al-lumā' ad-Dimashqiyyā* (Arabic) of Zayn ad-Din al-'Āmili' Shāhīd ath-thāni'.

Principles of Islamic Jurisprudence [Usūl al-fiqh]

- *Usūl al-Muzaffar* (Arabic) of Muhammad Ridā al-Muzaffar

(Vol. 3)

Literature [Adab]

- *Nahj al-balāghā* (Arabic) of Muhammad b. at-Tahir al-Husayn ar-Radī (Vol. 3)

Sciences of hadīth ['ulūm al-Hadīth]

- *Usūl al-kāfi* of Abū Ja'far Muhammad al-Kulaynī.

Sadr al-afadil (Duration: 2 years)

Year 1

Islamic Jurisprudence [Fiqh]

- *Riyād al-masa'il al-ma 'rūf bi-sharh al-kabir* (Arabic) of 'Ali b. Muhammad b. 'Ali 'Bahr al-'ulūm' Tabātabā'ī.

Principles of Islamic Jurisprudence [Usūl al-fiqh]

- *al-Kifāyā fī Usūl al-fiqh* (Arabic) of Muhammad kāzim Khurāsānī (d. 1911) (Vol. 1)

Year 2

Islamic Jurisprudence [Fiqh]

- *Kitāb al-makāsib* (Arabic) of Murtadā b. Muhammad Amin al Ansārī.
- *ar-Rasā'il al-arba'a*, or *Farā'id al-usūl* (Arabic) of Murtadā b Muhammad Amin al-Ansārī.

(The abovementioned syllabus of both madrasas were applicable up to 2004 A.D. . At present, there may be some changes in it.)

Notes and References

1. Qur'ān, surah, Al-Alaq., 96/1 and 4.
2. Qur'ān, surah, Al-Ikhlas.112 (Qul Ho wal lāho Ahad)
3. Shaykh Abū Ja'far Muhammad Kulayni, *Usūl -e- Kafi*, vol.-I (Urdu translation as, Ashshafi, by Sayyid Zafar Naqvi, Nāzimabad, Karachi-2) p. 67; *Tauhid-4, Madinat ul -Ilm*, Number (Hindi), 1406 Hijri/ November 1986, [Editor- Sibte Mohd. Naqvi], Lucknow, pp. 92,

110-111, 116, 125, 131; B. Aisha Lamu, Fatima Heeren, *Women in Islam*, pp. 14-15, New Crescent Publicity, Co. Delhi, Reprint, 2001.

4. Pedersen, J, "Some Aspects of the History of Madrasa", in *Encyclopaedic Survey of Islamic Culture* [Edited by Mohamed Taher], New Delhi, p. 9.
5. Ibid., p.5; Hitti, Philip K., *History of the Arabs*, Tenth Edition, Reprint,1977, pp. 412-13.
6. Pedersen, J, op. cit., p.5.
7. Ibid., Hitti, Philip K., op. cit., p. 410.
8. Pedersen, J, op. cit., p. 8.
9. Ibid., p. 9.
10. Hitti, Philip K, op. cit., p. 412.
11. Khan, M.M. Taqui, 'Islamic Education and Modern Challenges' in '*The Noor*', An Islamic Research Journal, vol,1, Issue no-II, 1994-95, p. 3, [Editor: Dr. Sādiq Naqvī], HyderabAD
12. Ibid., pp. 3-4.; *Usūl-i-Kafi* (Urdu translation), op. cit., p. 5; Jafri, S.H.M., *The Origins and Early Development of Shi'a Islam*, pp. 254, 260, 292, Qum (Iran),1989; *The Great Muslim Scientist, Imām Ja'far ibn Muhammad as-Sādiq* (a.s.), translated by Kaukab Ali Mirzā, 2nd. Revised Edition, 2002, Mumbai.
13. Hitti, Philip K., op. cit., pp. 439-40; Rizvi, Saiyid Athar Abbas, *A Socio-Intellectual History of Isnā 'Ashari Shī'īs in India*, vol.1. pp. 61-65, New Delhi, 1986.; Arjmand, Sayyid Saeed, Imām Reza (a. s.), *The Eighth Imām of the Shī'īte*, pp. 18-47, 60-78, 84-88, fourth-edition, Mashhad, Islamic Research Foundation of Āstān-Quds Razavi, 2004.
14. Naqwi, Mujtahid Mawlana Sayyid Ali Naqi, *Shi'a Itihas ki Sanchhipt Rooprekha*,(Hindi translation by Sayyid Muhibb ul Hasan Rizvi), pp. 12-13, second edition,1413 Hijri/1992 AD, Imāmiya Mission Aligarh.
15. Fischer, Michael M.J., *IRAN: From Religious Dispute to Revolution*, p. 252, Appendix-I, Harward University, London, 1980.
16. Naqvi, Mujtahid Mawlana, Sayyid Ali Naqi, op. cit., p.12.
17. Jamāli, Mohamed Fahdil, "The Theological Colleges of Najaf", in *Encyclopaedic Survey of Islamic Culture*, vol.-III, pp. 196-97, [Editor: Mohamed Taher], New Delhi.
18. Cole, J.R.I., *Roots of North Indian Shī'īsm in Iran and Iraq*, OUP. Delhi,

1989; pp.17-18, Momen, Moojan, *An Introduction to Shī'ī Islam*, New Haven, Yale University Press, 1985, pp. 223-25.

19. Rizvi, Saiyid Athar Abbas, op. cit., pp. 358-63.
20. Ibid., pp. 376-83.
21. Haider, Kamāl-ud-Din, *Sawanihat-i-salatin-i Awadh*, vol. I, p. 113, Lucknow, 1896.
22. Cole, J.R.I., op. cit., pp. 61-65,127-30; Rizvi, Saiyid Athar Abbas, op. cit., pp. 128-31.
23. Lucknowi, Saiyid Bāqar Shams, *Hindūstān mein Shi'at kī Tārīkh aur Shī'ī Aqāid ki Tafsil*, p. 14.
24. Rizvi, Saiyid Athar Abbas, vol-II, op. cit., p.139-40.
25. Ibid., pp. 146-56.
26. 'Qatil', Mirzā Muhammad Hasan, *Haft Tamāshā*, pp. 148-49, Lucknow, 1875.
27. Cole, J.R.I., op. cit., pp. 204-06, foot-note, no. 24; Hasan, Amir, *Palace Culture of Lucknow*, pp. 21-22, Delhi, 1983.; Rs. 20, the minimum salary of a teacher, seems to have been quite enough in those days. Moreover, for these teachers the salaries were more of perquisite than an income because they had landed property around their Qasbat; Naqvī, Sibte Muhammad, *Amjad Ali Shah* (Urdu), pp. 119-20.
28. Cole, J.R.I., op. cit., pp. 207-08.
29. Ibid., p. 208, foot-note no. 36.
30. Hasan, Amir, op. cit., pp. 22, 176.
31. Fāzil, Mawlana Murtazā Husayn, *Noor- ain Anwār ul Mataleh*, pp. 47-48, Lahore; Rizvi, Saiyid Athar Abbas, op. cit., vol. II., p. 155.;For details about Sayid Abul Hasan (1844-1895AD), see, Jones, Justin,op. cit., p. 248.
32. Rizvi, Sayyid Athar Abbas, op. cit., vol. II. pp.155,157.; According to Justin Jones, Mirzā Muhammad 'Abbas (1809-1889 AD) is credited as the co- founder of madrasa nāzimiyya in 1889. See, *Shi'a Islam in Colonial India*, p. 248.
33. Ibid., p. 157.; About, Sayyid Nazm ul Hasan (1862-1938 AD), see, Jones, Justin, op. cit., p. 249.
34. Desai. Ziyaud-Din, Abdul Hayy, *Centres of Islamic Learning in India*, Govt. of India Publication, New Delhi,1978; p. 30, For present

syllabus, see, Appendix-I. (Hereafter referred as, Desai, Z.A.)

35. Rizvi, Saiyid Athar Abbas, op. cit., vol. II. pp. 155-56.; However, according to Mawlana Muhammad Ja'far Rizvi, the present principal and manager, it was founded in 1892. Cf. *The Hindustan Times*, Lucknow, Edition, February, 4. 1998.
36. Rizvi, Saiyid Athar Abbas, op. cit., vol. II., p. 156.
37. *The Hindustan Times*, Lucknow, Wednesday, February, 4, 1998, p. 11.
38. Ibid.
39. Rizvi, Saiyid Athar Abbas, op. cit., vol. II., p. 156; Rizvi, Dr. Syed Mohd. Raza, *Farisht-i gan-i Iahān*, p. 10, (Bāqar Uloom Foundation, Lucknow), 18 Shaban, 1424 Hijri/11, October 2003 AD.
40. Ibid., p. 156; *Farisht i gan- i Jahān*, op. cit., p. 26.
41. Husayn, (Late) Allamā Saiyyid Murtazā, "Tafsara Mawlana SayyidAli Haydar Sāhib", 1340 Hijri/1921-22 AD, in *Islah-Sadi*, Number, 1999.
42. Interview conducted on June 20, 2004 in Gorakhpur.
43. Desai, Z.A., op. cit., p. 29.
44. Rizvi, Saiyid Athar Abbas, op. cit., vol. II, p. 157-58.
45. Desai, Z.A., op. cit., p. 30.
46. Rizvi, Saiyid Athar Abbas, op. cit., vol-II, pp. 158-59.
47. For details, see, Desai, Z.A. op. cit., p. 31.
48. For present syllabi of the Jāmi'-i Nāzimmiyya and of the Sultan al - madāris, both in Lucknow, c.f, the appendices of the present chapter.
49. For details, see, Mirzā, Aghā Muhammad Sultan, *The Caliphate, Its Conception and Consequences*, pp. 3-5; Idaarā-e-Āliā-Tableegh-O-Ishaat, Rustam Nagar, Lucknow, 1988.
50. Naqwi, Dr. Sādiq, *'The Noor'*, vol. XI, pp. 37-38, 1992,
51. Haider, Syed Safi, (Secretary of the Tanzim al-makatib), Imāmiyya Diniyyat, Books for class 3, Lucknow, June, 1990.
52. Mawlana Kalb-i Sādiq (1938-Nov. 2020), one of the Vice-Presidents of the All-India Muslim Personal Law Board and eminent Shī'īte cleric, suggested that Indian Muslims should not be guided solely by religious teaching in educating their children, but should impart worldly education to enable them to raise the standard of Muslim society. He said in a majlis, that, "Computers are the need of hour and Muslim society should encourage their children into pursuing

this line". *The Times of India*, Lucknow Edition, August, 4. 2004 AD, p. 4.

53. I am thankful to Janab Shakir Sahib, the senior-most and aged teacher of the Madrasa-yi nāzimiyya, for his help in preparation of the present syllabus. Peter Hartung of Erfurt University, has also provided me many informations regarding the authors and publication place of the books. He made many spelling corrections also. Therefore, I am grateful to both of them.
54. For the preparation of Sultan al madāris, syllabus, I got help from Mawlana Muhammad Sādiq Rizvi Sahib of the Madrasa. I express my gratitude to him for his co-operation.

Section 4: Culture

Nauroz—A Festival of Cultural Integration*

We have entered a new millennium, where the future of mankind looks uncertain. Yet while we wonder what the future may hold, there are many questions to be answered about our past. Learning about the past is the best way to understand the present and the future– but only if we succeed in interpreting its mysteries with a human and realistic touch. This article attempts a historical reconstruction of the Iranian National Festival of Nauroz which celebrates the arrival of spring in the context with the Medieval Indian Civilization. Culture knows no boundaries and this Iranian affiliation with India has survived up till now. We have tried to reinterpret this 'new day' in our search of a new future.

A festival of renewal, hope and happiness, Nauroz begins on the first day of Farvardin, the first month of the Iranian solar calendar at the spring equinox, and continues for twelve days.[1] Ehsan Yarshater specifies that "it is the most widely celebrated, the longest, and the most colorful of Iranian festivals, and though inherited from Zoroastrian Persia, it is the only festival that is not confined to a single religious group"[2]

---

* This was the joint article. Mrs. Poonam Pant, was my colleague, had presented this papers in the session of Indian History Congress, Amritsar. Now she is no more, May God place her in Heaven.

The origins of Nauroz remain an enigma. A survey of the rites and rituals of the festival confirms our belief that it was pastoral in nature and can be identified with fertility and renovation. According to Iranian legend, Nauroz is associated with the illusory King Jamshed of Iranian myth.[3] Firdausi's epic *Shāh-namah* offers the mystical explanation that Jamshed ascended the skies in a chariot built by demons, defeated by him. Nauroz commemorates this event.[4] Persian Prophet Zarathustra's mystical vision of Ahurā Mazadā led to the theory of individual accountability and reconsecration of Nauroz more than 2500 years ago. In Zoroastrian Iran, Nauroz proper began at dawn as the fravishes (the spirits of the departed) withdrew and the old year faded away.[5]

Nauroz or "Naugroz"[6] as the Sassanids called it, seems to have been secularized to some extent under them. The Muslim rulers of Iran continued the Sassanid tradition of celebrating Nauroz lavishly with colourful ceremonies.[7] Siraji Khurāsāni's quasidas which were written to eulogise Nusrat ud-din, the brother of Sultan Tajuddin Abul Makarim emphasizes the revelry and enthusiasm in the celebration of Nauroz in Makran.[8] It was a non-Muslim festival adopted by Muslims in Iran and Central Asia. The poet describes the gaiety with which the festival was celebrated in 1207 AD despite its occurrence in the month of Ramzan, a time of fasting and offering prayers to God.[9] The Ilbari Tūrks to which all the Sultans of India from Iltutmish to Kaiqubad, belonged were racially Turks but culturally they were Iranians.[10] Their obsession with Iran led them to claim their descent from Afrā Siyāb a formidable warrior and enemy of Iran.[11].

Yarshater opines that, the Turks themselves cultivated the legend of Afrā Siyāb as a Turkish hero, after they had come into contact with the Iranians.[12] The Sultans of Delhi identified respectability and dignity with Iran. Greatness, glory, grandeur were co-related with Iran.[13] Customs, ceremonies, feasts, festivals completely modelled on Iranian pattern overwhelmed the atmosphere of the court. Somewhere, their tribal origin culturally in the shadow of Iran bestowed respectability on itself by adopting the festival of Nauroz and the customs of pābos, zaminbos.[14] Balban introduced the festival of Nauroz in India.[15] It was celebrated on a grand scale at the court by all the succeeding Sultans. Amir Khusrau has given graphic details of its celebration by Sultan Miuzuddin Kaiqubad In the Qirān us Sādain, he speaks about beautiful arches, curtains of Zarbaft (gold embroidered), chatrs of five colors, artificial trees with birds on them, which added to the charm and attraction of celebrations.[16]

Nauroz, which fell on 21st and 22nd of March[17] was celebrated for nineteen days[18] in India and was ordained the status of a National Festival with the advent of the Mughals. Under Akbar assuming spectacular proportions, it no longer remained confined to the upper classes but penetrated each and every strata of society. An occasion of happiness reflected in the new clothes, decorated houses of the general public, it seemed to envelop all the cities, towns and villages of the Empire. Father Monserrate[19] calls it a nine-day festival. Here it would be interesting to note Alberuni's account of the celebration in Persia where it appears festivities were held for five days. Alberuni says "In these five days it was the custom of the Kisrās (Persian Kings) that the king opened the Nawruz and then proclaimed to all that he would hold a session for them and bestow benefits upon them. On the second day the session was for men of high rank and for the members of the great families. On the third day the session was for his warriors and for the highest Maubadhas (priests). On the fourth day it was for his family, his relatives and domestics and on the fifth day it was for his children and clients. When the sixth day came and he had done justice to all of them, he celebrated Nawruz for himself and conversed only with his special friends and those who were admitted into his privacy."[20] Monserrate speaks of games and pegeants being held and distribution of gifts to Akbar's generals. "Instructions were issued that all citizens should enjoy the festival by singing and dancing. He welcomed all who came to see the festival. At this particular occasion a group of *jogis* delighted the king with their dance. Women were allowed to visit the palace and see its magnificent appointments".[21] Badaoni speaks of the 17th of March on which day entered..."the earth illuminating sun, which is the greatest heavenly body and the light giver of the world, into the constellation of Aries".[22] Badaoni observes that a grand feast in ancient fashion was held during which the Emperor distributed a lac of rupees to every class of person present at the assembly.[23] Badaoni terms the festival 'Nou-roz-i-Jalali'.[24] This terminology was used by Minhaj-us-Siraj in his *Tabquat-i-Nasiri* wherein he affirms that confusion existed with regard to the lunar months and that calculations had fallen into disorder and that the zodiacal signs in the almanac had become involved in error. Hence Sultan Malik Shāh Saljuki had the calendar reformed and so the 'first day of spring, which is the first degree of the sign Aries became named, after that monarch, the *No-roz-i-Jalāli*'.[25] Badaoni's virulent denunciation of the festival as being both Hindu and Zoroastrian in nature is an expose of either his confusion or misconceptions. Here we can also draw the inference that celebrated enthusiastically by the general public Nauroz emerged predominantly as a cultural festival rather than sectarian. It is indeed strange that neither Badaoni nor Abul Fazl and none of the contemporary travelers have mentioned the Shī'īte religious beliefs attached to Nauroz. Shia Muslims believe that it was on Nauroz that Adam was created, that God made a covenant with humankind, that Abraham destroyed pagan idols, that Prophet Muhammad took his young son-in-law Ali on his shoulders to smash the idols in Mecca and he chose Ali as his rightful successor (Id-i-Ghadir).[26] The Shi'a community claims that their 6th Imām Ja'far-as-Sādiq (a.s.) whose teachings are recorded in *Fiqh-i-Jāfaria* has clarified the importance of this day.[27]

Badaoni accuses Birbal of persuading the emperor that since the sun is a giver of light as well as its supporter because all the products of the earth such as grain, fruits ripen due to its beneficence, hence it should be venerated. His polarization becomes all the more acute as he lashes out the Birbal convinced the emperor..."that the face should be turned towards the rising and not towards the setting sun, which is the west, that man should venerate fire, water, stones and trees, and all natural objects, even down to cows and their dung, that he should adopt the sectarian mark, and Brahmanical thread Several wise men at court confirmed what he said, by representing that the sun was "the greater light" of the world, and the benefactor of its inhabitants the patron of kings, and that kings are but his vice regents. This patron of kings, and the kings are but his vice-regents. This was the cause of the worship paid to the sun on the 'Nou-roz-i-Jalāli' and of his being induced to adopt that festival for the celebration of his accession to the throne.... He began also at midnight and early dawn to mutter the spells which Hindūs taught him for the purpose of subduing the sun to his wishes.[28] Badaoni also takes into cognizance the feminine influence of the Hindu wives of Akbar in his assault on Nauroz. He accuses Akbar of performing 'hom' within the female apartments. He attributes the derivation of this ceremony to sun worship.[29] Badaoni again comments "but on the New year of the 25th year after his accession he prostrated himself both before the sun and before the fire in public, and in the evening the whole court had to rise up respectfully when the lamps and candles were lighted."[30] Again at the same time he attributes Akbar's adaptation of Nauroz and sun worship to the followers of 'Zardusht'[31] who had come from Nousari in Gujarat and taught him the customs, rites, ordinances of the "Kaianians" an old Persian dynasty. Akbar's multi-cultural image surfaces upwards as Badaoni clarifies that Abul Fazl was entrusted with the safety of the sacred fire and ordained to ascertain that it was never extinguished..."and that after the manner of the kings of Persia, in whose temples blazed perpetual fires".[32]Abul Fazl has left a memorable account of the Feast of Nauroz. While attributing Zoroastrian influence for Akbar's acceptance of the Jashn, he clarifies that Akbar inquired about past customs and accepted those which he thought proper. He justifies his patrons' action on the ground that Akbar sought occasions to bestow gifts upon various classes of men. Hence "when His Majesty was informed of the feasts of the Jamsheds, and the festivals of the Parsi priests, he adopted them, and used them as opportunities of conferring benefits".[33] Abul Fazl insinuates that Akbar paid a high price of this. Defending Akbar's action of sun worship he says "there can be nothing improper in the veneration of that exalted element which is source of man's existence and of the duration of his life". He quotes Shaykh Sharf-ud-Din, the famous saint who died in the beginning of the fifteenth century, "what can be done with a man who is not satisfied with the lamp when the sun is down."[34] Abul Fazl is explicit in his explanation that without light and fire there would be poverty of food and medicine and lack of vision. He finally sums up beautifully, "the fire of the sun is the torch of God's sovereignty."[35] What finally emerges is not only Akbar's affinity towards all religious sects but his deliberate elevation of Nauroz as primarily a cultūral function, with no religious overtones ideally suited to India's multi-cultural and plural society. Giving details of the celebration he observes that a round, white shining stone called 'Suraj Krant' is raised to the rays of the sun and a piece of cotton is held near it and when it catches fire it is used by lamp lighters, torch bearers and cooks of the household.[36] After the passing of the year the fire is renewed. The vessel in which the fire is preserved was termed 'Agingir' in the *Ain*.[37] The celebration days have been given as nineteen in the *Ain*. Abul Fazl says "Two days of this period are considered great festivals, when much money and numerous other things are given away as present, the first day of month of Farwardin; and the nineteenth which is the time of the Sharaf."[38] The author of *Ain* also elaborates on Akbar's practice of holding banquets on those days the names of which coincided with the names of months. This was an ancient Parsee practice and as such 19th Farwardin, 3rd Urdibihsht, 6th Rhurdād, 13th Tir, 7th Amurdād, 4th Sahriwar, 16th Mihr, 10th Aban, 9th Azār, 5th Isfandarmuz.[39]

Nauroz continued to be celebrated on a lavish scale under Jahangir. William Hawkins[40] describes that within the fort, tents were pitched which were so rich that their like could not be found in the world. A shamianah occupying two acres of land was erected wherein silk and gold carpets were spread Both Hawkins and Roe[41] speak of bestowal of lavish gifts. Edward Terry appears amazed at the spectacular variety of gifts of incredible value exchanged between the Emperor and his nobles during the festival.[42] He too testifies to the feast being celebrated in camp. Jahangir describes the "The Great Feast of Nawruz"[43] in the *Tuzuk-i-Jahangiri* graphically, "on the night of Tuesday Zi-l-qa'da 11th AH 1014 (March 11th or 12th 1606) in the morning, which is the time of the blessing of light, his Eminence of Great Luminary passed from the Constellation of Ram. As this was the first New-Year's day after my auspicious accession I ordered them to decorate the porticoes of the private and public halls of the palace, as in the time of my revered father, with delicate stuffs, and to adorn them handsomely. From the first day of the Nawruz, to the 19th degree of the Ram (Aries) which is the day of culmination, the people gave themselves over to enjoyment and happiness. Players and singers of all bands and castes were gathered together. Dancing lulis and charmers of India whose caresses would captivate the hurts of angels, kept up the excitement of the assemblies."[44] Jahangir's orders that whoever desired to use intoxicating drinks and drugs should not be stopped is another evidence of the festival having no religious overtones in that period. Jahangir also speaks of elevating the ranks of state officials at the time.[45]

Under Shah Jahan Nauroz continued to be included amongst the court festivals. Descriptions of lavish and grand Jashns can be ascertained from the accounts of Bernier,[46] Manucci,[47] Tavernier,[48] Monrique.[49] The beginning of Aurangzeb's reign saw the complete suspension of the spring festival.[50] It offended his religious sentiments and he considered it un-Islamic. Nishāt Afroz Jashn, an Imperial Festival which began in the pious month of Ramzan and culminated on Id-ul-Fitr was initiated in place of Nauroz.[51] The later Mughal period, a time of political and economic decline saw the revival of the Nauroz Jashn in all its old splendour.[52] Shiv Das Lakhnavi, the author of *Shahnama Munawwar Kalām* informs that on 10th March 1722, Jashn-i-Nauroz was celebrated according to old practice.[53] He gives an account of the Jashn at Muhamad Shāh's court. In accordance with the instructions of His Majesty pearls and rubies (Yaqut) were scattered on all sides in charity and alms. The great nobles paid their respects and made their obeisance. Prostitutes sang and danced both on the right and left. A review was held of elephants and horses.[54] Syed Hasan Askari clarifies that Nauroz or the New Year Day according to the Persian calendar fell on the way when sun entered Aries. This was called Amma or general, and it initiated a week of festivities which terminated on the 6th or 7th after vernal equinox which was termed Khāssa or Nauroz-i-Buzurg. Both Amma and Khāssa days and those in between, were celebrated in Persia and India with feasts, enjoyment, conferment of rewards, presents and gifts.[55]

The widespread public participation in the festivities at the Imperial Court and the provincial capitals contributed to its popularity in the cities, towns and villages of the Empire. Nauroz Jashns were celebrated in Awadh and Bengal.[56]

Mrs. Meer Hassan Ali observes about Lucknow, "Nou- Roze" (New Year's Day) is a Festival or Eade of no mean importance in the estimation of Mussalmaun society. The exact period of commencing the Mussulmaun new year is the very moment of the sun's entering the sign Aries. This is calculated by practical astronomers, who are in the service of most great men in native cities; ... And according to the hour of the day or night when the sun passes into that particular sign. So are they directed in the choice of a colour to be worn in their garments on this Eade: if at midnight, the colour would be dark puce (a dark brown or brownish purple) almost a black; if at mid-day, the colour would be the brightest crimson. Thus, to the intermediate hours are given a shade of either colour applicable to the time of the night or the day when the sun enters the sign Aries; and whatever be the colour to suit the hour of Nou-Roze, all classes wear the day's livery, from the King to the meanest subject in the city".[57] Giving specific details of the Jashn, she observes that, "The King, on his throne, sits in state to receive the congratulations and 'Nuzzas' or nuzar from his nobles, courtiers and dependents. Exchange of greetings "Nou- Roze Mubarak!" (May the New Year be fortunate) are the terms of salutation exchanged by all classes of society, the King himself setting the example." The day was devoted to amusements. Sending presents, and exchanging visits among all classes of society, was observed by her.[58] She speaks of a public breakfast at the palace.[59] Relating to the occasion she speaks of a custom prevalent amongst the ladies to ascertain the exact moment of commencement of the year. A freshly plucked rose was placed into a basin of water, eye downwards. "They, say, this rose Turns over of itself towards the sun at the very moment of the luminary passing in to the sign Aries.[60] In the female apartment domenie performed dances.[61] Her narrative also draws our attention to the gradual identification of Nauroz with religion. She speaks of "pious men offering prayers so that the commencing year might be propitious for the family".[62]

With the association of religious overtones of Nauroz a gradual wane in its popularity was created. Elphinstone in his account of Kabul is very specific in the regard: "The Nauroz or Vernal Equinox, has always been a time of great rejoicing in these countries but the Persians having ingrafted some fable about Ali, the patron of their religious sect, upon this ancient festival, it has fallen into disrepute with the Mussalmuns of the opposite belief".[63]

Presently Nouroz is not entirely wiped out but has now it is localized to the Parsees and Shias.[64] In India, perhaps intolerance, bigotry and the communal traumas of colonial India which tore the fabric of her cultural life also played their part for its present sectarian look. The polarization of Hindu, Muslim and Sikh communities helped its identification with particular religious sects and as such it no longer remains the bearer of Culture.

We finally sum up with the thought, that let us introspect and remove the seeds of hatred within, for other communities, nations, people of a different castes or colour, by focusing not on the differences but what makes us alike, a common humanity leading to the dawn of a Global Civilization.

Notes and References

1. *The Encyclopedia of Religion*, Vol. 10, edited by Mircea Eliade, MacMillan, New York and Collier MacMillan Publishers, London, p. 341. Also see, Thomas Patrick Hughes, *Dictionary of Islam*, Reprint, 1995, New Delhi, p. 341.
2. Ibid.
3. Ibid., Allami Abul Fazl, *Ain-i-Akbari* (Eng. trans., Blochman), Vol. 1, p. 286; See also Jivanji Jamshedji, Modi, *Religious Ceremonies and Customs of the Parsees*, 2nd edition., Bombay, 1937; Josef Marquart's "Das Nawruz, Seine Gechichte Und Seine Be deutung" in Dr. Modi Memorial Volume, Bombay, 1930, pp. 709 & 765; translated by Manilel Patel as "The Navroz: its History and its Significance." *Journal of K.R. Cama Oriental Institute (Bombay)*, no. 31, (1937), pp. 1-51.
4. Firdausi, *The Shāh-Nāmāh of Fardausi* (Eng. trans. Alexander Rogers, New Delhi, 1989, pp. 19-20, "And many Divs would this great throne upbear, And, lift to the clouds in middle air". *The Encyclopedia of Religion*, Mircea Eliade, Vol. 10, p. 341.
5. Ibid., also see, Jivanji Jameshedji, op.cit., gives an account of the rites and ceremonies of the Farvardigan, the holidays for the remembrances of the dead among the Parsees of India.
6. *L'Iran Sons Les Sassanids; a Christansen* (Urdu translation M. Iqbal), pp. 225-26, cited by Khaliq Ahmad Nizāmi, *'Royalty in Medieval India'*, New Delhi, 1997, pp. 80, 83. Sassanid rulers (226 AD-651 AD) were contemporary of Gupta Emperors.
7. Mircea Eliade, op.cit., p. 341.
8. I.H. Siddique, *Perso-Arabic Sources of Information on Life and Conditions in Sultanate of Delhi*, 1992, Delhi., see, *"Thirteenth Century Divāns of the Persian Poets"*, p. 58.

9. Ibid.
10. Khaliq Ahmad Nizāmi, op. cit., p. XVII.
11. According to Persian legend, Kai-Khusrau son of Siyawash son of Kai Kaus overthrow Afrasiyab, The Turkish Emperor, see, *Fatawa-i-Jahāndarī* (Eng. trans. Mohd. Habib and Dr. Mrs. Afsar Umar, Salim Khan), Allāhabad, p. 22 fn. 1.
12. *Encyclopaedia Irānica*, p. 576; Ziauddin Barani, *Tarikh-i-Firuz Shāhī* p. 37; Fakhr-e Mudabbir, *Tarīkh-i- Mubarak Shāh* , p. 37.
13. Minhaj-us-Siraj links Iltutmish with the heroes of ancient Iran when he refers to the Sultan as "Faridun fur. Qubad Nibad Ka'os Namus Sikandar dault. Bahram Shaukat", see,*Tabqat-i-Nāsiri*, Vol. 1, p. 440.
14. Khaliq Ahmad Nizāmi, op. cit., p. XVII.
15. Ibid., p. 80, Barani says in the *Fatawa-i-Jahāndarī* that "O sons of Mahmood: Know well that Kingship is not possible without following the traditions of the Emperors of Iran, and it is known to all religious scholars that this tradition of are opposed to the traditions of the Prophet and to his mode of life and living", see *Fatawa-i-Jahāndarī* (Eng. trans.) p. 40.
16. *Qirān-us-Sādain*, pp. 74-86 or 67-68, S.A.A. Rizvi, *Ādi Turk Kalīn Bhārat* (Hindi), p. 289; Ferishtā (Eng. Translation Briggs, Cal, 1966). Vol. I, p. 140. Radhey Shyam, *Despotism on Trial*, Agra, 1992, p. 186.
17. Mīr Ghulām Husayn Khan Tabatabaī; *Siyar-ul-Mutakhkhīrīn* (English translation), vol-1, p. 192, fn. 3, 286.
18. Jahāngīr, *Tuzuk-i-Jahangirī* (Eng. trans. Rogers and Beveridge), New Delhi, 1978. Vol. I, p. 48; Mohd, Azhar Ansari, *Social Condition at the court of Akbar and its influence on Society, Encyclopaedic Survey of Islamic Culture*, Vol. 9, Edited by Mohamed Taher, New Delhi, 1997, p. 1.
19. *Monserrate S.J., Commentarius* tr. by J.S. Hoyland and annotated by S.N. Banerjee under the title "The Commentary of Father Monserrate, S.J." on his journey to the Court of Akbar, 1992, p. 176.
20. Alberuni as cited in *Encyclopaedia of Religion and Ethics*, Vol. V (edited by James Hastings). Edinburgh, 1914. p. 872.
21. Monserrate, *Commentarius Hoyland*, 1992, p. 176.
22. Al Badāonī, *Muntakhab-ut-Tawārīkh*, Patna, 1973, (Text, p. 172), English Translation, p. 175.
23. Ibid.

24. Ibid., p. 268.
25. Minhāj-us-Sirāj,*Tabkāt-i-Nāsirī* (Eng. trans. Raverty), Vol. 1, p. 137.
26. Ehsaan Yarshater in *The Encyclopaedia of Religion*, Vol. 10, p. 342.
27. See, *'Tohfat-ul Imām'*, Imām Jafar-as-Sādiq (a.s.) died in 148 Hijri (765 AD), Every Shia family keeps Tohfat-al-Imām for his religious guidance, See also. *Bahār-al-anwār*, Vol. 14, the Section on Nauroz, cited from *The Encyelopaedia of Religion*. p. 342.
28. Badaoni, op. cit., p. 268.
29. Ibid., p. 269.
30. Ibid.
31. Ibid., p. 268.
32. Ibid.
33. Ibid., pp. 268-269.
34. Abul Fazl Allāmī, *Āin-i-Akbarī* (Eng. trans. Blochmann) volume- I, New Delhi, Reprint 1989, p. 286 (A'in 22).
35. Ibid., p. 52 (A'in 18).
36. Ibid.
37. Ibid.
38. Ibid., p.286 (A'in 22)
39. Ibid.
40. Ibid.
41. Mohammad Azhar Ansari, *European Travellers Under the Mughals (1580-1627)*, Idarah-i-Adabiyāt-i-Delhi, First Published, 1975, p. 118.
42. Roe, Thomas, *The Embassy of Sir Thomas Roe to India (1615-1619)*, edited by William Foster, London, 1926, p. 29, Also see, Mohammad Azhar Ansari, op. cit., pp. 282-83.
43. Terry Edward, *A Voyage to East India*, published by J.Wilke (London, M.D.C.C.L. XXVII) p. 21.; Also see, Mohamad Azhar Ansari, op. cit., p. 376.
44. Jahangīr, *Tuzuk-i-Jahāngīrī* (Eng. trans. Roger and Beveridge) Vol. II, Delhi 1978, p. 48.
45. Ibid., pp. 48-49.
46. Ibid., p. 49.
47. Bernier Francois, *Travels in Mughal Empire (1656-68)*, translated by Archibald Constable, Westminster or DCC X CI., pp. 268-269.
48. Manucci, Niccolao, *Storia Do Mogor*, Vol. II (1653-1708), (trans. by

William Irvine), Calcutta, 1965-66, pp. 348-49.

49. Tavernier Baptiste Jean, *Travels in India* (Pub. MacMillan and Company, London, 1889); Tavernier's, *Travels in India*, published by Bangbasi Office, Calcutta, 1905, Part 1.
50. Monrique, *Travels of Sebastian Monrique (1629-1643 AD)*, Part-II, published by Hakluyt, Society, London, 1928.
51. Sāqī Mustaid, Khan, *Maasir-i-Alamgiri* (tr. J.N. Sarkar) published by Royal Asiatic Society of Bengal, Calcutta, 1947, p. 14.
52. Ibid., Also see, Mohammad Yasin, *A Social History of Islamic India* (1605-1748), Lucknow, 1958, p. 61.
53. *Tārikh -i-Farrukshiyar*, edited by Syed Hasan Askari, pp. 103-5; Shiv Daslakhnawi, *Shāhnāmā MunawwarKalām* (English Translation by S.H. Askari), p. 119, Patna, 1980, Khushal Chand *Tārīkh -i-Muhammad Shāhi*, 16a; Muhammad Qāsim, Aurangābādī, *Ahwāl-ul-Khawāqīn*, f. 59b; *Ibratnama*, ff. 546-56b; Khāfī Khan, *Muntakhab-ul-Lubāb* II, p. 806; *Siyar-ul-Mutākhīrīn III*, pp. 848, 852, 856, 857-859 (English translation, Vol-I, p. 237; For Jahāndar Shāh, see, an anonymous author, MS. Patna No. 142 ff, 48 ab; Muhammad Muin Jafarabadi Shaykh, *Farrukh-nāmā*, ff 123a-125a.; For Ahmad Shah, see, *Tārīkh -i-Ahmad Shahi*, ff 33a-b; For Shah Alam II, see, Tek Chand Rai, *Roz Nāmchā-i-Shāh Ālam I*, ff IIa, 108b-109b, 159a-160b, 189a-190ab, 220b-222a-b; II, ff 313b, 364b, 366a-b, 473a-b, 474a, 504b, see also for Shah Alam Sānī, *Āftāb Nādirat Shāhi*. For the last two Mughal Emperors, see, Faiyazddin, *Bazm-i-Akhir*, Delhi 1920, pp. 43-46, see, Mirzā Qatil, *Samrāt-ul-Badā'i* (Lucknow, 1261 AH) p. 9; for its celebration by the Nawab Alīvardi Khan, see, Yusuf Ali Khan bin Gulam-Ali Khan (edited by Abdus Subhan under the title, *Tārīkh -i-Bangālā-i-Mahābat Jangi*, 1969 (Extracts, English Translation, Sir Jadunath Sarkar), Bengal Nawabs, Calcutta,1952, p. 53.
54. Shiv Das Lakhnawi, *Shāhnāmā Munawwar Kalām*, (tr. in Eng.), by Syed Hasan Askari, Patna, 1980, p. 119; Footnote, no. 179, p. 192.
55. Ibid., p. 119.
56. Ibid., footnote, p. 192.
57. For celebration of Nauroz by Nawab Āsaf-ud-Daula of Awadh, see, Mirzā Qatīl, *Samrāt-ul- Badā'i*, Lucknow, p. 9; For the last two kings of Awadh, See, Knighton, William, *The Private life of An Eastern Queen*

pp. 71-76, London, 1865 and for Bengal's Nawab Ali Wardi Khan, see, *Tārīkh-i-Bengal*, p. 9.

58. Meer Hassan Ali (Mrs.), *Observations on the Mussalmauns of India* (ed., by W. Crooke), 1832, Reprint, Deep Publications, New Delhi, 1975, I, p. 152
59. Ibid., pp.153-54.
60. Ibid., pp.152,155, Mrs. Ali also describes about the presents prepared by women of Lucknow for their friends on the occasion of Nauroz. She writes, "The trays of presents...are tastefully set out, and the work of many days' previous arrangement. Eggs are boiled hard, some of these are stained in colours resembling our mottled articles; others are neatly painted in figures and devices; many are ornamented with gilding; every lady evincing her own peculiar taste in the prepared eggs for 'Nou-Roze'. All kinds of dried fruits and nuts, confectionary and cakes, are numbered amongst the necessary articles for this day's offering: they are set out in small earthen plates, lacquered over to resemble silver, on which is placed coloured article, cut out in curious devices (an excellent substitute for vine leaves) laid on the plate to receive the several articles forming 'Nou-Roze' presents.

    Amongst the young people these trays are looked forward to with child-like anxiety. The ladies rival each other in their display of novelty and good taste, both in the eatables and the manner of setting off with effect." See, op. cit., p.153.
61. Ibid., p. 153.
62. Ibid., p.154.
63. Ibid., p.153.
64. Elphinstone Hon. Mount Stuart, *An Account of the Kingdom of Caubul*, Vol. I, London, 1839, p. 183.
65. An interview with Mohd. Mehdi Advocate (66 yrs.), President of Shia Federation of Gorakhpur. He told me that "we celebrate Eid-i-Nauroz according to the directives of Imām-Jafar-as Sādiq(a.s.). Our forefathers also celebrated this festival."

Muharram in Awadh and Eastern Uttar Pradesh

The Shi'a community of India is the minority among minorities. The number of Shi'as in comparison to the total Indian Muslim population was most probably negligible about 1600 AD and not very significant around the 1700 AD. Shāh 'Abdul 'Aziz's estimate suggests that there had occurred enormous expansion of Shī'īsm in the eighteenth century. During the last decade of the 18th century only one-third were Shi'as of the Muslim population. The modern Shi'a community in India was the creation of the eighteenth century. In 1881 AD, the Shi'a numbered less than 2% of the total Muslim population of British India. Modern census reveal that the Shi'a population hardly reaches 10% of the Muslim population in any district of Northern India. Lucknow was an exception, where the Shi'as comprised 14% of the Muslim population of the district in 1922, while before partition in 1881 the Shi'a numbered 23% of the total Muslim population of Lucknow district.[1] According to the study of Hasnain, Nadeem and Abrar Husayn 10 to 15% of the Muslim in India is Shi'a,'of which 90% are Isnā' Ashari (Twelvers).[2] At present, according to Moojan Momen, whose book intitled, *Shī'ī Islam: A Beginner's Guide* published in 2016 AD a more neutral observer, puts the figure at around 25 million, which represents 14% of India's Muslims and 2% of the total population.[3] This article solely deals with the observance of Muharram by Shi'a community of the region of Awadh and Eastern Uttar Pradesh. It does not discuss those rulers or scholars who opposed Shī'īsm and their rituals, especially, observance of Muharram in the past.

A single thread links all the groups of Shi'a society of India—their love for the Prophet and his family. They share the essential rituals of Islam, including the performance of daily prayers, fasting and the pilgrimage to Mecca (Haj). But an inherent element in the Shi'a religion is the commemoration of the martyrdom of Husayn (the grandson of Prophet Muhammad). This experience is marked annually with a series of Majlises and the performance of various Muharram rituals and processions. Annual observance of the Muharram, according to Donaldson, is the most distinctive and the most widely known of all Shī'īte customs.[4] Muharram has always represented the center of the Shi'a religious calendar and so much attention has been given to it that it has sometimes been portrayed as virtually synonymous with the religion itself.[5] Generally the members of other religions in Eastern Uttar Pradesh recognize Shi'as as "mā'tam waale Musalmān."

Mrs. Meer Hassan 'Ali has described the principal causes for the observance of Muharram. She writes that, " Hasan and Husein were the two sons of Fatima and 'Ali, from whom the whole Saiyids race have generated; Hasan was poisoned by an emissary of the usurping Caliph's and Husayn, the last victim of the family to the King (Caliph) Yuzeed's fury, suffered a cruel death, after the most severe trials, on the plains of Karbala, on the tenth day of Arabian month Muharram; the anniversary of which catastrophe is solemnized with the most devoted zeal. This brief sketch constitutes the origin of festival."[6] Mrs. Ali also gives the details at some length the history of that period, which better explains the motives assigned by the Muslims for the deep grief exhibited every year, as the anniversary of Muharram returns to these faithful followers of their martyred leaders, Hasan and Husayn, who with their devoted families, suffered innocently by the hands of the guilty.[7] She further writes, "Yuzeed, the king of Shawm (Syria), it appears, was the person in power, amongst the followers of Mahumud (Muhammad), at that early period of Mussulmaun (Muslim) history. Of the Soonie (Sunnī, a traditionalist) sect, his hatred to the descendants of Mahumud was of the most inveterate kind; jealousy, it is supposed, aided by a very wicked heart, led him to desire, the extirpation of the whole race, particularly as he knew that, generally, the Mussulmaun people secretly desired the immediate descendants of their Prophet, to be their rulers. They were, however, intimidated by Yuzeed's authority; whilst he, ever fearing the possibility of the Syaads'(Saiyids') restoration to their rights, resolved, if possible, on sacrificing the whole family, to secure himself in his illegal power.

Ali had been treacherously murdered through the contrivances of the usurping Caliph; after his death, the whole family removed from Kūfā, the capital of Ali, to Medina, where they lived some years in tranquility, making many converts to their faith, and exercising themselves in the service of God and virtuous living. Unostentatious in their habits and manners, they enjoyed the affection of their neighbors, their own good name increasing daily, to the utter dismay of their subtle enemy.

In the course of time, the devout people of Kūfā, being heartily tired of Yuzeed's tyrannical rule, and fearing the true faith would be defamed by the excesses and abuses of power committed by him, they were desirous of calling to their aid a leader from the Prophet's family, who would secure, in its original purity, the performance of that religion which Mahumud (Muhammad) had taught. Some thousands of respectable Mussulmauns, it is related, signed a petition to Hosein, requesting his immediate presence at Kūfā, in order, as the petition stated,' that the religion his grandsire taught might be supported and promoted"; and declaring' the voluptuousness and infamy of Yuzeed's life to be so offensive and glaring, that the true faith was endangered by his vicious examples'; and entreating him to accept his lawful rights as 'Emaum' (Leader of the Faithful).

Hosein received the petition, but declined accepting the proposed restitution of his family's rights at that time; yet he held out hopes in his reply, that he might eventually listen to their entreaties, should he be convinced his presence was essential to their welfare; and as a prelude to this, he sent his cousin, Moslem (Muslim) on whom he could rely, to make personal observation of the real state of things at Kūfā; expecting to learn, from his matured knowledge, the real causes of complaint, and the wishes of the people, and by whose report he would be guided, as his final acceptance or rejection of the proposed measure for his becoming their leader.

Moslem (Muslim), accompanied by his two sons, mere youths, left Medina on this important mission, and having accomplished the tedious march without accident or interruption, he delivered Hosein's letters to those persons of consequence in Kūfā, who were at the head of the party petitioning his appearance there, and who proffered their influence and support for the recovery of the rights and privileges so long withheld from the descendants of Mahumud. (Prophet Muhammad).

Moslem (Muslim) was kindly greeted by them and multitudes flocked to his quarters, declaring Hosein the lawful leader of true Mussulmauns. Elated with these flattering indications, he too promptly dispatched his messengers to Hosein, urging his immediate return to Kūfā.

In the meantime, and long before the messengers could reach Madina, Yuzeed, learning the state of things in the capital, was seriously alarmed and greatly enraged; he issued orders for the seizure of Moslem and his children, and desiring to have them brought to his presence, offered immense sums of money for their capture. The friends of Moslem, however, succeeded for a time, in secreting his person from King Yuzeed's emissaries, trusting the darkness of night would enable him to escape. But the slaves and dependents of the tyrant being dispatched into all quarters of the city, Moslem's retreat was eventually discovered; and, through the influence of a purse of gold, his person was given up to the King's partisans.

The unfortunate agent of Hosein had confided the charge of his two sons to the Kauzy (Qāzi) of the city, when the first report reached him of the tyrant Yuzeed's furry. This faithful Kauzy, as the night advanced, intended to get the poor boys conveyed to the halting place of a Kaarawaun (carvān), which he knew was but a few miles off, on the route for Medina. The guide, to whom the youths were entrusted, either by design or mistake, took the wrong road; and, after wandering through the dreary night, and suffering many severe trials, they were taken prisoners by the cruel husband of a very amiable female, who had compassionately, at first, given them shelter as weary travelers only; but on discovering whose children they were, she had secreted them in her house. Her husband, however, having discovered the place of their concealment, and identified them as the sons of Moslem (Muslim), cruelly murdered the innocent boys for the sake of the reward offered for their heads. In his fury and thirst for gold, this wicked husband of the kind-hearted woman spared not his own wife and son, who strove by their united efforts, alternately pleading and resisting, to save the poor boys from his barbarous hands.

This tragic event is conveyed into pathetic verse, and as often as it repeated in the families of Mussulmauns, tears of fresh sympathy are evinced, and bewailing renewed. This forms the subject for one day's celebration during Mahurrum; the boys are described to have been most beautiful in person and amiable in disposition.

After enduring ignominy and torture, and without even being brought to trial, Moslem was cast from a precipice, by Yuzeed's orders, and his life speedily terminated, to glut the vengeance of the tyrant King.

As the disastrous conclusion of Moslem's mission had not reached the ear of Hosein, he elated with the favorable reception of his cousin, and the prospect of being received at Kūfā in peace and goodwill, had without delay commenced his journey, accompanied by the females of his family, his relations, and a few steady friends who had long devoted themselves to his person and cause. The written documents of that remarkable period notice, that the whole party of Hosein, travelling from Medina towards Kūfā, consisted only of seventy-two souls: Hosein having no intention to force his way to the post of leader, had not deemed it necessary to set out with an army to aid him, which he undoubtedly might have commanded by his influence with the people professing 'the Faith'.

Yuzeed, in the meantime, having by his power destroyed Moslem and the two youths, his sons, and receiving positive intelligence that Hosein had quitted Medina to march for Kūfā, as his fears suggested, with an army of some magnitude, he ordered out immense force to meet Hosein on the way, setting a price on his head, and proclaiming promises of honors and rewards, of the most tempting nature, to the fortunate man who should succeed in the arduous enterprise.

The first detachment of the Shawmies (as they are designated in the manuscript of Arabia) under a resolute chief named Hurrh, fell in with Hosein's camp, one day's march beyond the far-famed ground, amongst Mussulmauns, of Kraabaallāh (Karbala) or 'Hurth Maaree' (Mareea), as it was originally called.

Hurrh's heart was subdued when he entered the tent of the peaceable Hosein, in whose person he discovered the exact resemblance of the Prophet; and perceiving that his small camp indicated a quiet family party journeying on their way, instead of the formidable force. Yuzeed's fear had anticipated, this chief was surprised and confounded, confessed his shame to Hosein that he had been induced to accept the command of the force dispatched against the children of the Prophet, and urged, in mitigation of his offences, that he had long been in Yuzeed's service, whose commission he still bore; but his heart now yearning to aid, rather than persecute the Prophet's family, he resolved on giving them an opportunity to escape the threatened vengeance of their bitterest enemy. With this view, he advised Hosein to fall with his party into the rear of his force, until the main body of Shawmies had passed-by; and as they were then on the margin of a forest, there to separate and secret themselves till the road was again clear, and afterwards to take a different route from the proposed one to Shawm.

Hosein felt, as may be supposed, grateful to his preserver; and, following his directions, succeeded in reaching confines of Kraabaallāh (Karbala) unmolested."[8] Shia Zakirs provide different narration to this event.

After mentioning the prediction of Prophet Muhammad,[9] Mrs. Ali further writes that, "Hosein and his family having concluded their morning devotions, he first inquired and learned the name of the place on which their tents were pitched, and then imparted the subject of his last night's dream, 'that his grandsire had appeared to him, and pronounced that his soul would be at peace with him ere that day closed'. Again, he fell on his knees in devout prayer, from which he rose only to observe the first warnings of an approaching army, by the thick clouds of dust which darkened the horizon; and before the evening closed upon the scene, Hosein, with every mule of his small party capable of bearing arms, had been hurried to their final rest. One son of Hosein's, insensible from fever at the time, was spared from the sacrifice, and, with the females and young children, taken prisoners to the King's palace at Shawm.[10]

The account given by historians of this awful battle, describes the courage and intrepidity of Hosein's small band, in glowing terms of praise; having fought singly, and by their desperate bravery, 'each arm (they say) levelled his hundreds with their kindred dust ere his own gave way to the sway of death'.[11]

Amongst the number of Hosein's brave defenders was a nephew, the son of Hasan: this young man, named Cossum (Qāsim), was the affianced husband of Hosein's favourite daughter, Sakeena Koobraah; and previous to his going to the combat on that eventful day, Hosein read the marriage lines (nikah) between the young couple, in the tent of the females.[12]

During the whole of this terrible day, at Kraabaallāh (Karbala), the family party of Hosein had been entirely deprived of water; and the river Fraught (Euphrates) being blockaded by their enemies, they suffered exceedingly from thirst. The handsome Abbas, another cousin of Hosein, and his standard-bearer, made many efforts to procure water for the relief of the almost famishing females; he had, at one attempt, succeeded in filling the mushukh (mashk), when retreating from the river, he was discovered by the enemy, was pursued and severly wounded, the mushakh pierced by arrows, and the water entirely lost ere he could reach the camp. In remembrance of this privation of the sufferers at Kraabaallāh, every good Mussulmaun, at Muhurrum, distributes Sherbat in abundance to all persons who accept this.[13]

Hosein, say their historians, was the last of the party who suffered on the battle; he was surrounded in his own camp—where, by the usage of war, at that time, they had no right to enter—and when there was not one friendly arm left toward the blow. They relate 'that his body was literally mangled, before he was released from his unmerited sufferings'. He had mounted his favorite horse which, as well as himself, was pierced by arrows innumerable; together they sank on the earth from loss of blood, the cowardly spearmen piercing his wounded body as if in sport; and whilst, with his last breath, 'Hosein prayed for mercy on his destroyers, Shimeear (Shimar) ended his sufferings by severing the already prostrate head from the mutilated trunk'.- Thus they scaled (say those writers) the lasting disgrace of a people, who calling themselves Mussulmauns, were the murderers of their Prophet's descendnts."[14] According to Mrs. Ali, This slight sketch gives but the outline of those events which are every year commemorated amongst the zealous followers of Ali, the class denominated Sheahs (Shi'a)".[15]

Yann Richard, a French writer, has also described the battle of Karbala in brief, which also explains those events, where the heart of Shī'īsm lies. He writes that, "The situation bequeathed by Imām Hasan to the Family of 'Ali was not enviable. Hoseyn, born in 626, had looked on, powerless to act, at the pact of his brother Hasan with Mo'awiya. But on the latter's death in May 680, he refused to pledge allegiance to his son Yazīd, whose overt impiety and taste for feasting and wine are described by historical sources. Hoseyn, who was at Damascus, took refuge in Medina where he received an appeal from the inhabitants of Kūfā (a small town, situated on the Euphrates, not far from Medina and the capital of Hazrat 'Ali) urging him to head a rebellion. Ill-informed of the real danger, and especially of the counter measures taken by Yazīd, Hoseyn sent his cousin Moslem b. 'Aqil as a scout and set off after he had completed the "little pilgrimage" ('omra'). To the objections of his supporters who were frightened to see him run headlong into so senseless an enterprise, Hoseyn answered: "God does as He pleases...I leave Him to choose what is best...He is not inimical to the man who proposes what is right and good (al-haqq)".

Prevented from getting to Kūfā by Omayyad troops sent to head him off, on October, 2, 680 AD (2 Moharram 61 Hijri) Hoseyn find himself obliged to bivouac at Karbala, a tiny spot in the desert. Access to the water of the Euphrates was cut off by the enemy. 'Abbas, Hoseyn's half-brother, managed to fill a few pitiful goatskins to give a sip to the 72 companions, who had camped for several days in the torrid heat. Among them was Zeynab, the Imām's sister, and 'Ali, his son, who was still a child and the future fourth Imām, both of whom would survive.

Having refused invitations to surrender, the Imām prepared for the final battle and warned his friends of the dangers of staying with him: "I praise God who has honored us with the Prophecy and has taught the Korān and religion.... I know of no companions more worthy ... than mine, or any family more pious than mine ... May God reward you all. I think tomorrow will be the end of us...Go, all of you. I will not keep you. The night will cover you. Use it as your steed..." After a final vigil of prayer came the last combat and massacre: on the morning of 10 Moharram, Hoseyn addressed his enemies to ask them to reflect before attacking the one whom the

Prophet had cherished and to let him depart with dignity. But others demanded submission. Hesitant assailants, held back by last-minute scruples, set fire to the tents and tried to seize the women. Among the first victims that the Imām gathered in his arms were his son 'Ali-Akbar, Qāsim the son of Hasan, and Abo'l-Fazal al-'Abbas his brother. Heart-rending scenes are recorded by tradition and magnified by the mournful piety of the Shī'ītes. Thus, when Hoseyn was holding a new born baby (of six months) in his arms, an arrow pierced the baby's neck and Imām shed the blood on the ground invoking God against the wicked.

Shemr b' Sa'd (known to the Sunnīs as Shamer) advanced at the head of a group and attacked Hoseyn, who was decapitated. His head would be taken to Kūfā, then to Damascus. His body, trampled by horses, was buried on the spot, where today is a great mausoleum."[16] The author further writes, "The impact of the massacre of Karbala is out of all proportion to the event itself, a small battle between rival clans which lasted only a day and resulted in no more than a few dozen dead. But Muslim consciousness was shaken by the tragic fate of the grandson of the Prophet Mohammad and his determination to fight to the very end a government that held up to ridicule the ethics and principles of earliest Islam. The martyrdom of Hoseyn has become the prototype of every struggle for justice, every suffering."[17]

Observance of Muharrram started after the Karbala. According to Shi'a tradition, after the release of prisoners of Husyan's family from Yazid's prison in Syria, Zainab, the sister of Husayn organized a majlis to pay homage (pursa) to the martyrs of Karbala. Saiyid Athar Abbas Rizvi mentions this event in following words, "When Yazid ordered Imām Husayn's family to return to Medina from Damascus, he transferred them from the dungeon to a separate apartment in his palace. The ladies of the Umayyad palace called on Imām Husayn's family to offer their condolences. Several meetings were held in the precincts of Yazid's palace at which tears were shed by his family. These may be regarded as the first free assemblies commemorating the Karbala tragedy."[18] During the period of Imāms, how the Shi'as paid homage to the martyrs, is not known. But it is sure that they continued it, though not publicly. According to S.A.A. Rizvi, "When Husayn's family returned to Medina, the entire city was filled with wailing and lamentations. Imām Zaynu'l-'Abidin, his successors and friends never, for a single moment, forgot the tragedy. Imām Ja'far as-Sādiq reminds us 'Every day is 'Āshūrā' (10th Muharram) and every land is Karbala'."[19] Umayyad and Abbasid Caliphs discouraged it[20] for their survival. But, as early as AH 352/963 AD, during the supremacy of the Buwaihids (Buyids), at Baghdad, Muizz-al-Daula publicly introduced the custom, commemorating the events of Muharram with a period of mourning.[21] S. Khuda Bakhsh (a Sunnī historian) writes, "The bazaars were closed; the butchers suspended their business; cooks ceased cooking; the cisterns were emptied of their contents; pitchers were placed with felt coverings on the streets; women walked about with fallen tresses, blackened faces, torn dresses, striking their faces and wailing for Husayn."[22] Muhammad 'Ali, in his 'Burhān'l Futuh', writes that, "At that time too, elegies and lamentations were read."[23]

In India, the observance of Muharram was discouraged by the orthodox Sunnī Sultans of Sultanate period. Sometimes the Shi'as were severely crushed by the Sultans. But after the disintegration of the Bahmani kingdom several Shi'a dynasties came to power in southern India and the Shi'as got the permission for observance of Muharram.[24] Similarly, in the north India, Chak- family of Kashmir accepted Shī'īsm. This family ruled over Kashmir from 1561 AD to 1586 AD. Shī'īsm flourished during their rule and Shi'as observed Muharram freely.[25]

During the Mughal period, a large number of Iranis came to India and they (Irani-Shi'as) got the opportunities of appointments to the administrative and military posts. But they followed taqaiyyah (The Shī'ī doctrine that a believer must lie about his branch of Islam should he feel his life to be in danger.) and did not openly declare themselves as the follower of Shī'īsm, though there were many exceptions also.

From the early eighteenth century, the Shi'as began to participate in the mourning ceremonies without any inhibition. But the number of Shi'as was so minuscule that they did not form any separate community. Prior to the appointment of Sa'adat Khan Burhān-ul Mulk Nishāpuri as the governor of Awadh in 1722 AD, there is no evidence of a Shia community assertion. We also do not get any evidence that the first Nawab of Awadh popularized his sect in the Subah (province). But his successor, Safdar Jung openly patronized Iranian scholars and immigrants.[26] Shujā-ud Daula followed the tradition of the Shi'as. He was magnanimous and open-hearted towards the Saiyids. The Nawab took keen interest in the observance of Shi'a-rituals, the most important of which was the observance of Muharram. Separate building for mourning ceremonies, known as Imāmbārah was constructed. In 1767 AD, the Nawab himself shouldered the tā'ziyās and helped to carry them to the Imāmbārah with all pomp and show. Charity was profusely distributed among the Saiyids and Faqīrs. We find that, there was so much rush of the spectators on the fourth of the Muharram that near about seventy persons among the pilgrims were trampled to death.[27]

Shujā-ud Daula never neglected the observance of Muharram. When he went to Pānipat in 1761 AD, the month of Muharram occurred. Shujā-ud Daula clothed himself in black garments, and with his followers in similar dress, barefooted and bare-headed, passed before the encampment of Ahmad Shah Abdali, beating his chest. He and his followers loudly uttered the words of lamentation, though the 'tabarra' (the curse on the enemies of the Prophet's house) was not recited aloud.[28]

Nawab Āsaf-ud Daula, the successor of Shujā'-ud Daula, transferred the seat of his government from Faizabad to Lucknow. His generosity attracted all kinds of people to Lucknow and it became the most populous city in India and outdistanced Delhi. Many of the immigrants changed their faith while settling down at Lucknow.

Scholars and artisans accepted Shia faith. During his reign outside Lucknow, Bilgram, Jaunpur, Sandila, Benares and Allahabad also became the Shi'a centers. In these places Shi'as could be seen as a small community.

Āsaf-ud Daula was very enthusiastic in the observance of Muharram. He felt the need of Imāmbārah for organizing the Majlises and remembering the Imām. Therefore, he built a magnificent Imāmbārah along with a mosque in Lucknow, known as Āsafi Imāmbārah. After completion of Imāmbārah, he spent four to five lakhs rupees per year on its decoration. Hundreds of Tāziās were constructed of gold and silver.[29] According to Abū Talib, "When Dr. Blane was going to England, he gave him an order for two glass Tāziās with chandeliers and shades and other appointments, one to be green and the other red. The price was fixed at a lakh of rupees. In 1211 AH/1796 AD one arrived, and the other was promised for the next year."[30] Two volumes of selected news-bulletins from Āsaf-ud Daula (1775-1797AD) court, entitled, *'Intikha'b akhbār-i- Nawwāb Waziru'l- mamālik Bahadur wa intikhāb-i-darbar-i mu'alla wa atraf,* indicate that the Āsafiyya, or Bada Imāmbārah, was the center for the mourning ceremonies organized by the Nawab. His visits to Imāmbārahs, belonging to the Begums, the dignitaries at the court and the poor citizens, had made the Āshūrā mourning rituals popular with all sections of the society.[31] The Nawab, as a devout Shi'a, participated in the mā'tam (Flagellation) and beat his chest with an iron- chain during the Muharram. According to J.R.I. Cole, "Extravagance marked the observance of the month of ritual mourning, Muharram, during the Āsaf-ud Daula period. In 1784 AD the Nawab beat himself so violently on the tenth of that month that he bled profusely, falling seriously ill after accompanying representations of Imām's tomb to the river, into which they were thrown at the end of the day."[32]

In the reign of Nawab Āsaf-ud Daula, the Shrine of Hazrat Abbas (Hazurat Abbas ki Durgah), at Rustam Nagar in Lucknow also became the center for mourning rites of Muharram. In the late eighteenth century this shrine came into existence. One Mirzā Faqir Beg brought a relic from the shrine city of Karbala. He said that a dream helped him unearth the metal crest that had surmounted the banner of Hazrat Abbas. He kept the crest at his home in Rustam Nagar, where people began bringing offerings (nazr). The building at first consisted of four bare walls, an unadorned roof and a small courtyard. Nawab Āsaf-ud Daula built a dome for the Darvish's house, rendering it a proper shrine. His successor, Nawab Sa'adat Ali Khan in 1803 AD ordered that a new edifice, with an impressive gilded dome be raised on the site. He also established a fund to cover the shrine's expenses, and people began gathering there regularly on Thursday evenings. Finally, the shrine was integrated into the mourning rites of Muharram.[33]

Nawab Āsaf-ud Daula also built an Imāmbārah at Gorakhpur in 1782 AD. A document, dated 1796 AD, testifies that Rs. 10,000 along with gold and silver Tāziās were presented to the Sufi's Imāmbārah by Nawab Āsaf-ud Daula. At that time, Roshan Ali, an eremite mendicant, was the custodian of the Imāmbārah. He was a native of Persia. Nawab requested him to conduct Azādari in Muharram on his behalf. Roshan Ali agreed to this and his descendants are still keeping the promise that he had made to the Nawab. These, two tāziyas—one of pure gold and another of silver – are still in the Imāmbārah. Besides, many alams (Imitation of the standard given by Imām Husayn to his cousin Hazrat Abbas in Karbala) of gold and silver are also there. Even today, during the Muharram days (ashrā), the Imāmbārah is open for public. The Imāmbārah and its property are under the custodian of the Imāmbārah. The custodian is from Sufi (Sunnī)-family. The Imāmbārah always have a fire (*dhooni*) burning inside it, which, as per source, is still on.[34]

During the reigns of Āsaf-ud Daula's successors the Muharram ceremonies became more formalized. Sa'adat 'Ali Khan (1798-1814), the British-imposed successor of Āsaf-ud Daula spent far less on Muharram due to his territorial cuts and hence financial losses. But he maintained the Azādari. He also established the Karbala of Talkatora in Lucknow.[35] Next ruler of Awadh, who assumed the title of King in 1818 AD, Ghāzi-ud Din Haider built the Imāmbārah of Shāh Najaf in Lucknow, which is, the replica of the tomb of Hazrat 'Ali at Najaf (Iraq).[36] His wife, known as Badshāh Begum extended the days of mourning (*ayyam-e Azā*) till 8th Rabi- ul-Awwal.[37] Even today, most of the people by their own choice, avoid celebrations during the *ayyam- e Azā*. According to Knighton, Badshāh spent "upwards of three hundred thousand pounds" on Muharram rituals".[38]

The next ruler of Awadh was Nasiruddin Haider (1827-37 AD). He constructed a 'Karbala', known by his name, near Daliganj, across the Gomti river. During his reign, there was much terror in the month of Muharram that even the way farers could not smile, the people wept day and night, slept on the ground, wore black garments, and much amount was distributed by the Nawab in charity.[39]

Badshah Muhammad 'Ali Shāh (1837-1842) built an Imāmbārah at Husaynabād in 1839 AD which still exists.[40] He himself carried Tāziā on his head from his house to Imāmbārah on first of Muharram. While carrying Tāziā, he walked barefooted for a few miles on uneven road. He also established a trust for the maintenance of the Imāmbārah.[41]

Amjad 'Ali Shāh (1842-1847) built another Imāmbārah in Hazratganj and continued Azādāri with enthusiasm.[42] His successor and the last king of Awadh, was Wajid Ali Shāh . He was pious and religious man. He built an Imāmbārah at Qaiser Bagh also. He also wrote marsiya during the Muharram.[43]

The nobles of Awadh also took keen interest in observing Muharram. Many Imāmbārahs were built in the cities of Faizabad and Lucknow. Nawab Begum, the mother of Shujā-ud Daula and Bahu Begam, the mother of Asaf-ud-Daula who lived at Faizabad fostered the development of Muharram rituals and Shī'ī Culture there. Bahu Begam built a mosque and an Imāmbārah near the Moti

Bagh.[44] Jawahar 'Ali Khan used to observe Muharram rituals and had constructed a mosque and an Imāmbārah in Faizabad.[45] Darab'Ali Khan, a, eunuch of Shuja-ud Daula, constructed a big and lofty Imāmbārah of brick in place of the old wooden structure built by Jawahar 'Ali Khan.[46] In the same way, an Imāmbārah was constructed by Mirzā Husayn, son of Shafiq 'Ali Khan.[47] In the Imāmbārah, built by Darab 'Ali Khan, cooked food was distributed during Muharram. Bahar 'Ali Khan, a eunuch, continued to stay in Faizabad with Bahu-Begum, the mother of Āsaf-ud Daula. A large number of men were employed at his residence, every year, on the 7th of Muharram, to construct the Tāziās. In the majlis, the crowd was immense and when the reading of marsia and Hadis-khwāni (by an ālim) was over the people rose up for m'atam (Flagellation).[48]

Āghā Bāqar Mirzā constructed an Imāmbārah at Lucknow, which is very near to the present Imāmbārah of Ghufran Ma'ab. Another Imāmbārah was constructed by Āghā Abū Tālib Khan. Sarfaraz-ud Daula Mirzā Hasan Riza Khan and Mirzā Ali Akbar 'Munis', a native of Isfahān, also built their own Imāmbārahs.[49] Several Imāmbārahs were constructed in Awadh during the period of Shia rulers. The list is non-exhaustive here. This is enough to say that, "Under Āsaf-ud Daula and his successors, Lucknow became the city of Imāmbārahs although Faizabad was not neglected. The Shī'ī noblemen and dignitaries of Awadh built Imāmbārahs, introduced Muharram rituals and tāzāiyā processions into the headquarters of their jagirs."[50]

The 'Imāmbārah', according to Mrs. Meer Hassan Ali, is a sacred place, erected for the express purpose of commemorating Muharram. Literally, 'Imāmbārah', means, 'enclosure of the Imām' or the place where the Muharram rites are performed as contrasted to masjid or Idgah.[51] "An Imāmbārah is a square building, generally erected with a cupola top, the dimensions guided by the circumstances of the founder. The floor is matted with the date-leaf mats, in common use in India, on which is spread a shutteringhie (shatranji, a chequered cloth from shatrang, the game of chess), on which the assembled party are seated, during the several periods of collecting together to remember their leaders: these meetings are termed Mudgelluss (majlis or mourning assemblies)."[52] According to Mrs. Ali "It would be esteemed in decorous or disrespectful to the Emaums, if any one in error called these assemblies Moollakhaut (Mulāqāt), the usual term for mere worldly visiting."[53] Imāmbārah is not a Maqbara (mausoleum)".[54] It is also noteworthy that no part of the Shī'īte commemoration is at a mosque. That is set apart for the prayer. In many places Imāmbārahs have been erected solely for the purpose of majlis, for remembering the Imāms. Some of these are seldom used except at Muharram. "The remarkable plainness of the mosque contrasted with the superb decoration of an Emaumbarah may be seen as the mosque is devoted only to the service of God, while Emaumbarah is erected for the purpose of doing honor to the memory of Emaums."[55]

"The word 'Tāziā' signifies grief. The term is applied to a representation of the mausoleum at Karbala, erected by their friends and followers, over the remains of Hasan and Husayn. It is formed of every variety of material, according to the wealth, rank, or preference, of the person exhibiting, from the purest silver down to bamboo and article, strict attention being always paid to preserve the model of Karbala, in the exact pattern with the original building. Some people have them of ivory, ebony, sandal-wood etc.——The expensive Tāziās were fixtures, but there were temporary ones required for the outdoor processions. The middle class and poor's Tāziās were composed of bamboo frames, over which was fixed colored ubrak (talc); these were made in bazaar, of various sizes and qualities, to suit the views of purchasers, from two rupees to two hundred each"[56] in 1832 AD. This tradition is still dominately in practice. But now the prices of Tāziās are in thousands and lakhs.

Mrs. 'Ali, further writes, that, "The more common Tāziās are conveyed in the procession on the tenth day of Muharram and finally deposited with funeral rites in the public burial place, Karbala, situated outside the town.[57] In some places these Tāziās are drowned in the water of the river."[58]

The use of Tāziās, (miniature tombs) is said to date from the time of Amir Taimur (AD 1336-1405), who on his return from Karbala, made a model of Husayn's tomb.[59]

In Imāmbārah, according to Mrs. 'Ali "the Tāziā is placed against the wall on the side facing Mecca, under the canopy of rich embroidery. A pulpit (Mimbar) is placed in a convenient situation, for a Ālim or Zakir to face Mecca, and his voice to be heard by the whole assembly of people. It is constructed of silver, ivory, ebony, & etc. to correspond with the Tāziā, if possible. The steps of Mimbar are covered sometimes with gold-cloth or broad-cloth of black or green. The shape of a Mimbar is flight of steps with a flat top, without any railing or enclosed place. The Zakir or reader sat on the steps of the Mimbar during his taqreer (reciting)."[60] The sozkhwans do not mount the pulpit but sit with other members of the assembly and chant their dirge and elegies.[61] Those who recite marsiyas or Salaam (a genre of poetry of greeting which praises holy personalities including members of the Prophet's family) might sit or stand, as per their convenience.

On the walls of many Imāmbārahs, mirrors and looking- glasses are fixed in suitable positions to give effect to the brilliant display of light, from the magnificent chandeliers suspended from the cupola and cornices. The nobles and the wealthy are excited with a desire to emulate each other in the splendor of their display on these occasions; all the mirrors, glass, lustres, chandeliers etc. are brought together to this place, from their several stations in the mansion; and it is due to them to admit the effect to be often imposingly grand, and the blaze of light splendid.[62]

On each side of the Tāziā—the whole length of the wall—banners are ranged in great variety of color and fabric; some of them are costly and splendid. Mrs. Meer Hassan Ali had seen many "constructed of the richest embroidery, on silk grounds of gold and silver, with massy gold fringes, cords and tassels; the staff is cased with gold or silver, worked into figures of birds and other animals, in every variety; the top of which has a crest, in some a spread hand, in others a sort of plume, and not unfrequently a crest resembling a grenade, formed of the precious metals, and set with stones of great value."[63] The spread hand designates the Shī'īs sect and five spread fingers represent the "five souls"—Muhammad (The Prophet), Fatimah, 'Ali, Hasan and Husayn.[64]

"On the base of the Tāziā, several articles are placed conceived likely to have been used by Husayn at Karbala; a turban of gold or silver tissue, a splendid sword and belt, the handle and hilt set with precious stones, a shield, the Arabian bow and arrows. These ancient emblems of royalty are indispensable in order to do honor to Husayn, in the view they take of his sovereign right to be the head or leader of the true Mussulmauns. Wax lights—red and green—are also placed in great numbers about its base, in silver or glass candlesticks; and censers of gold and silver, burning incense perpetually during Muharram. Many other minor tributes to the Emaums are discovered near the Tāziā, as choice fruits and garlands of sweet-scented flowers, the offerings of ladies of the family to their relative's Tāziā."[65]

"Amongst the poorer classes of the people an equal proportion of zealous spirit is evinced; and according to their several abilities, so they commemorate the period, interesting alike to all. Those who cannot compass the real splendor of an Imāmbārah, are satisfied with an imitative one in the best hall their inhabitation affords; and where mirrors and chandeliers are not available, they are content to do honor to the Emaums with lamps of uberuck (Abrak), which in truth are pleasing substitutes at a small price: these lamps are made in a variety of pretty shapes, curiously painted, and ingeniously ornamented with cut article; they burn oil in them, and, when well arranged, and diversified with their wonted taste, produce a good light, and pleasing effect."[66]

Mrs. Meer Hassan Ali further writes, "The banners of Husein, in the houses of the poor, are formed of materials according to their humble means, from tinsel imitations down to dyed muslin; and a similar difference is to be perceived in their selection of the metal of which their crests are made."[67]

In early nineteenth century Awadh, notables held mourning-session in their Imāmbārahs, twice a day during the first ten days of Muharram. Regarding the Majlises of those days, Mrs. Meer Hassan Ali provides the details in her own words. She writes, "Mourning assemblies are held in the Emaum-barahs twice every day during Muhurrum; those of the evening, however, are the most attractive, and have the fullest attendance of visitors. The master of the house, at the appointed hour, takes his seat on the floor near the pulpit, surrounded by the males of his family and intimate friends, and the crowd of strangers arrange themselves—wherever there is sitting room—without impending the view of the Tāziā."[68] The host hired a maulvi to read that day's passage from a Persian prose text that described the sufferings of the Imām Husayn and his supporters and family in their struggle against the Yuzeed's army. Among the Persian-educated notable class in Awadh, such readings could be extremely effective, particularly if the maulvi wept and groaned with great sincerity from his mimber. Mrs. Meer Hassan Ali notes, "One of the most popular Maulvees of the age is engaged to recite the particular portion appointed for each day from the manuscript documents, called, 'Dhie Mudgellus' (ten Majlises) in the Persian language. This work is in ten parts, and contains a subject for each day's service, descriptive of the life and sufferings of the Emaum, friends and children, particularly as regards the eventful period of Mahurrum in which they were engaged. It is, I am assured, a pathetic, fine composition, and a faithful narrative of each particular circumstance in the history of their leaders, the heroic bravery of their friends, &c. They are particularly anxious to engage an eloquent reader for this part of the performance, who by his impressive manner compels his hearers to sympathize in the effecting incidents which are recited by him."[69] Mrs. Ali was present in a majlis, when the effect produced by the superior oratory and gestures of a Maulvi had terrified her, the profound grief, evinced in his tears and groans, being piercing and apparently sincere.[70]

Since the role of a Maulvi, required some Persian education, he could be one of the subaltern ulama or even relatively untrained in specialized religious sciences. High ulama often held their own sessions, where they tie their recitation of the martyr's sufferings more closely to Arabic oral reports from the Imāms, a style known as Hadīs-khwani. One of the students of Sayyid Muhammad Nasirabadi, the chief mujtahid of Lucknow, described that, "reciting oral reports from the Imāms with translation, he found him on the tenth of Muharram in the mourning-session mentioning the calamities that befell the Martyr at Karbala, weeping violently, as was his audience. Then he descended from the mimber, barefoot, bareheaded, tears streaming from his ruddy cheeks. This was always his wont on such days. He thereafter went home and people gathered there."[71]

After Persian reading, came an intermission during which servants handed around sweetened rose water to the mourners. Devout Shī'īs refrained from chewing betel leaves during Muharram, so servants passed about an assortment of spices on small silver trays. The highest -ranking members of the assembly, smoked huqqa (water-pipes), during the intermission, though the rest of the guests, of even slightly lower rank, dared not to join them.[72]

When the process terminated, the marsiya (An elegiac poem with a six-line verse form having anywhere from eight to over a hundred verses. It is distinguished by having a rhyming scheme of aaaa bb.) was chanted, by several well-practiced voices, with good effect. This part of the majlis was, perhaps the most impressive, as the very ignorant, even can comprehend every word—the 'Murseeah' (eulogies) being in the Hindustani tongue, a poetical composition of great merit, and embracing all the subjects they meet to commemorate.[73] Sayyid Dildār Ali Ghufran Ma'ab, the first mujtahid of Awadh disapproved of chanting marsiya with remodulation. Other ulama also favored the straight forward reading of the poetry (taht al-lafz-khwani),while readers presented verse works commemorating the martyrdom of Imām Husayn in various rhetorical styles.[74] Cole mentions the newly developed style of suz-khwani of elegies.[75]

The whole assembly rose up afterwards, and as with one voice, recount the names of the lawful leaders after Prophet Muhammad, entreating blessings and peace to their souls. Then, they read the 'tabarra' (curse to the hated usurpers), which in earlier times, was not the part of the Majlises in Awadh.[76] It seems that, after writing the *Zulfiqar* by Ghufran Ma'ab, the Shi'as were encouraged to recite 'tabarra'.

After all the aforementioned process the m'atam follows. Mrs. Ali writes, "I have even witnessed blood coming from the breast of sturdy men, who beat themselves simultaneously as they shouted the name 'Hasan!' 'Husein!' for ten minutes, and occasionally during a longer period, in that part of the service called, Mortem (Ma'tam)."[77] This performance concluded each day's majlis, either of the morning or evening. But the evening sessions, with their dazzling lightings derived from myriads of candles, mirrors and chandeliers, were best attended.[78]

The ulama disapproved of flagellation (ma'tam). According to Mrs. Ali, "Maulvees, Moolahs, and devoutly religious persons never joined in beating their breasts, although they were present in the audience, while others thus violently expressed their grief. The ulamā carried on their own mourning practices for longer than most believers in the 1820s, for a full forty days. They apparently did not participate in the mourning processions."[79] Sayyid Muhammad Nasirabādi, the chief mujtahid of Lucknow, asked about self- flagellation in the 1820s or 1830s, replied that wailing and beating one's chest over the calamities that befell the family of the Prophet was only permissible if one lost control of one's self.[80]

Thus, the Hadīs-khwani, mersiya and ma'tam were the main part of a majlis. Majlises were held in popular or common language. In the earlier period, Persian was the language. But in the beginning of the 18th century, the common people could not understand it.

Therefore, in order to satisfy such people, Fazl Ali, 'Fazli' wrote, *Karbal Katha* in Urdu. The work was written during the reign of Muhammad Shāh (1732-33) and revised in 1748-49. Fazli writes in his introduction, that "Nawab Sharaf 'Ali KhanYamin-ud Daula, used to organize in closed doors the majlis-i azā at his residence during the month of Muharram with full devotion and sincerity, used to read the abridged account based upon the 'Rauzat-ush Shuhada' (in Persian), but the meaning of the text could not be understood by those present and they could not weep, though every sentence was heart-rending."[81] Hence, he felt the need for compiling *Karbal-Katha*. Perhaps, this was the first work in Urdu. Another work was *Ahzan-us Sudur*, written by Sadr-ud din Muhammad Khan 'Faiz' Dehlavi, in 1722 AD. It was written in the style of Dah Majālis to read in the majlis-i azā.[82] Mrs. Ali mentions that, "Dhie-Mudgellus' written in Persian was in practice." But one should keep in his or her mind that, she was from a high-class family and she attended the majlis organized by the upper class of the Shi'a society. They could understand the Persian. In my opinion, the *Karbal-Katha* was more popular amongst common people. Mrs. Ali, too, writes that, 'the marsiya was recited in Hindustani (Urdu)'. This evidence shows the popularity of Urdu-marsiya in Awadh. Sauda, who had composed several marsiya in Delhi, set the tradition of marsiyacomposition and recitation at Faizabad and Lucknow. Mīr Hasan Dehlawi and several other eminent marsiya composers came to Lucknow and within a short-time, a separate school of marsiya- composition and recitation developed there under the leadership of Mīr Anis and Mīr Dabir. Afterwards, Mīr Atish and Mīr Nasikh competed with each other in this art. Mīr Anis promoted the art of recitation. Sweetman praises him stating that, "The Marthiya (lamentation or elegy on the death of Hasan and Husayn) is frequently great literature. The Marthiya of Mīr Anis in spite of its extraordinary length, its manifest anachronisms and its hyperbole, is a piece of literature which, when recited during the ten days, stirs the deepest emotions and rouses the strongest feelings. Its descriptive power is great and its appeal moves the strongest to tears. The taunts of the warriors in battle and description of the tiny babe, which was slain so young that it was 'not able to open its little hands,' the depicting of the fierce heat of strife and the equally moving and tender narrative of the calmness and courage and the affection of the family of Husayn are such as to affect not merely the Shi'a whose faith inclines him to take these things to heart, but the Sunnī also."[83] The marsiya became the medium of expression of feelings and this art developed till the Urdu language was dominant among the Muslims. In the nineteenth century, especially in the later half, medium of expression was Urdu. But, now, after 1950, the mixed Urdu-Hindi is used. Now in nauhas, Hindi-words are frequently used and sometimes the zakir or Hadis-khwan (orator) also use the typical Hindi words, in his sermon from the mimber.

Shi'as do not restrict the people of any religion and sections, from visiting their assemblies (Majlises). Free admission granted when the Imāmbārah is first lighted up, until the hour of performing the service, After it the strangers, that is the multitude, are civilly requested to retire. Mrs. Ali also mentions about the practice to which every visitor had to comply in order to maintain the sanctity of Imāmbārah. The vistors are expected to leave their shoes outside before entering the place. This is already being followed by the Asian people, but the Europeans were required to be reminded of the same. It was the duty of the servant of Imāmbārah to oversee and maintain this practice of respecting the place.[84] Mrs. Ali narrates an incident when some gentlemen of cantonment, with bad intention, tried to enter Imāmbārah, without removing their shoes, but were checked.[85]

It will not be wrong to say that Shi'a women are the custodian of their religious rituals, specially, the Muharram. They strictly follow the rituals, not only themselves, but also train their children or future generation to observe them. Sometimes, they chide their children for not attending the Majlises, because, in their eyes, these Majlises are the best educational centers of religion. Their ideals are Bibi Fatima, the daughter of Prophet (whose importance may be seen at the time of the incident of Mubāhila. Hadīth-e-Kisā also mentions her importance) and Bibi Zainab, the daughter of Ali and sister of Husayn, known as Sāni e Zehra. I have heard a nauha in Ghāzipur district from the maternal grand-mother of my late wife, who was leading the ma'tam of women in a ladies (zanani) majlis. The nauha begins: "*ye m'atam kabhi na rukne paaye, Zehra ki du'a hai, ye m'atam kabhi na rukne paaye.*" The 'Nauha (dirge) gives the massage that, "with the blessings of Bibi Fatima, this m'atam is continuing and it is our duty to continue it." It is also said that the Shi'a qaum is born to commemorate the Muharram and to weep on the martyrs of Karbala. The Shi'a women know that, the Zainab, (Sāni-e Zehra) was the first lady who organized the majlis, first- time, in commemoration of the martyrs of Karbala; the lady who sacrificed her two sons for the right cause of her brother, Imām Husayn; who was the custodian of the family after Karbala and saved the future generation of Imāms. Bibi Zainab is the ideal for the Shi'a women. The deep impact of her leading role, specially of her duties, is more visible on women. They trace their identity with Bibi Fatima and Bibi Zainab. If by chance, a Shi'a girl marries with the boy of other sects of Islam or other religion, she tries to maintain her identity through commemoration of the Muharram. I have seen many such cases in Gorakhpur and other parts of India. It seems that the women are more determined to continue the commemoration of Karbala for the well-being of their future generation and for establishing an ideal society, where love and affection should prevail and justice should be for everyone. Hence, Mrs. Meer Hassan Ali said in 1832 AD that, "in commemorating the Muharram, the expression of grief, manifested by the ladies, are far greater and more lasting than with other sex (men)".[86] She further writes ,"In sorrowing for the martyred Emaums, they seem to forget their private griefs; the bereavement of a beloved object even is almost overlooked in the dutiful remembrance of Hasan and Husein at this period; and I have had opportunities of observing this triumph of religious feeling in women, who are remarkable for their affectionate attachment to their children, husbands and parents; they tell me, 'We must not indulge selfish sorrows of our own, whilst the Prophet's family alone have a right to our tears'.————Everything which constitutes, comfort, luxury or even convenience at other times, on these occasions are rigidly laid aside. The *pallungh* and the *charpoy* or cot, on which the females love to lounge for some hours in the day and night, are removed from their standings, and, in lieu of this comfort, they take their rest on a common date mat, on the floor. The musnud (masnad) and all its cushioned luxuries, give place, on this occasion, to the simply matted floor. The indulgence in choice dainties, at other times so necessary to their happiness, is now forgone, and their meal limited, throughout Mahurrum, to the coarsest food, such as barley bread, rice and peas boiled together (called *Kutcher* or *Khichar*) without even the usual additions to make it palatable *khichri* as ghee, salt, pepper and spices; these ingredients being considered by the zealous females too indulgent and luxurious for humble mourners during Mahurrum."[87]

"The pawn leaf, another luxury of no small moment to Asiatic tastes, was now banished for ten days' mourning."[88] A very poor substitute, the mixture of tobacco leaf, lime and a bitter gum (*Kattha*), called, 'Gota', was consumed by them. But it was only allowed for the health's sake. When visitors call on ladies at Muharram, the 'Gota' (mixture) was presented on trays, accompanied by bags, called, Batua (small bag)."[89] Variety of ornaments were entirely laid aside from the first hour of Muharram, until the period for mourning concluded.[90] The hair, were unloosed from its usual confinement and were allowed to flow in disorder. The dyeing of hairs and garbing were not allowed. The colored *pyjaamahs* (leg clothing or drawers) and *dupattahs* were removed, with every other article of their usual costume, for a suit that, with them, constituted mourning. Some chose black, others grey, slate or green and the widows wore white from the day her husband died. The widow never altered her style of dress. Many of rigidly zealous, among the females, mortified themselves by wearing their suit of mourning, during the ten days, without changing.[91] Mrs. Ali's serving-maid went the entire time without drinking water during the day. Mrs. Ali's maid-servant used to say that, "Her Emaum Husein and his family, suffered from thirst at Kraabaalah, why should such a creature as she is be indulged with water?"[92] Every evening the ladies gathered about the cenotaph they had set up, with female friends, slaves and servants surrounding the hostess.[93] The educated Shi'a women presided at these distaff sessions. These were from Saiyid families. Hostesses hired them for the first ten days of Muharram. They read both the ten sessions in Persian and the elegiac poetry in Urdu.[94] The mourning-sessions organized for ladies were generally held in homes during Muharram because there were very few separate Imāmbārah for ladies.[95]

Zohra Mahmud, in her article, published in *The Stateman*, on 25th February1940, writes, "When the Moon of Muharram is seen the women assemble in grave solemnity and break their glass bangles. In ordinary days no woman with her husband alive would deliberately do so as arms without bangles are a sign of widowhood. Not a vestige of any other ornament should remain on the body after the moon is seen. No woman may comb her hair, wear red, yellow, gold or any other color. Green and black are the only colors are allowed. Laughter is strictly forbidden and no music except sad tunes of compositions called 'nawha' (dirge) may pass the lips. The couplets which are sung describe the woes and sufferings of the Prophet's family in all their terrible details. The words are often put in the mouth of a mother weeping for her young one or a sister mourning the loss of her brother. Very often the poem (nawha or dirge) describes the agonies of children writhing in thirst for a drop of water, holding empty glasses in their hands, looking wistfully in the direction of river".[96]

The above description shows that after 110 years, there was no change in the style of the observance of Muharram by the Shi'a women. After 155 years, I saw the same tradition in my own family and in the Shi'a- community of Gorakhpur and other parts of India. In 2020 AD I was in Hyderabad during the Chehllum and there I saw the ladies in the same position as Mrs. Ali or Zohra Mahmud has described. Even the Shi'as, who migrated from India and Pakistan to United States, follow the above stated tradition. From early July till the end of October in 2018 AD. I was in U.S.A. and attended the Majlises of first twelve days and of other important days at a Shi'a center during the month of Muharram and also the procession of arbayin (Chehllum) at Boston. Most of the Zakirs (Mawlana or Preacher) were from undivided India and their religious taqreer (lectures) were of high standard.

The rituals of first ten days of Muharram, in Lucknow are described by Mrs. Meer Hassan Ali in details. She writes , "The first day of Mahurrum invariably brings to my recollection, the strongly impressed ideas of 'The Deserted Village'. The profound quiet and solemn stillness of an extensively populated native city, contrasted with the incessant bustle usual at all other times, are too striking to Europeans to pass by unheeded. This cessation of the animated scene, however, is not of long duration."[97] In other words, the first day of Muharram, witnessed, no activity, but an eerie quiet as shops closed and families began mourning at home.[98] According to Mrs. Ali, "The second day presents to the view vast multitudes of people parading backwards and forwards, on horseback, in *palkies*, and on foot, through the broad streets and roadways, arrayed in their several mourning garbs, speeding their way to Emaum-baarahs of the great men, and the houses of friends, to pay the visit of respect (zeearut), wherever a Tāziā is set up to remembrance of Hasan and Husein."[99] Further she writes, "After the Tāziā is brought home (as the temporary ones are from the bāzār on the eve of Mahurrum, attended by a ceremonious display of persons, music, flags, flambeaux, & c.), there is little to remark of outdoor parade beyond the continual activity of the multitude making the sacred visits to their several Emaum-baarahs, until the fifth day, when the banners are conveyed from each of them in solemn procession, to be consecrated at the Durgah (of Hazārut Abbas)."[100]

Mrs. Ali witnessed a notable's entourage undertaking the trip. She described the procession in following words "The order of procession, appointed by each noble proprietor of banners, to be consecrated at the Durgah, forms a grand spectacle. There is no material differences in their countless numbers; the most wealthy and the meanest subject of the province make displays commensurate with their ability, whilst those persons who make the most costly exhibitions enjoy the greatest share of popular favor, as it is considered a proof of their desire to do honor to the memory of Hosein and Hasan, their venerate Emaums."[101]

She further mentions, "A description of one, just passing my house, will give you a general idea of these processions." She notes the following:

"A guard of soldiers surrounds four elephants, on which several men are seated, on pads or cushions, supporting the banners; the staffs of several are of silver, they spread hand, and other crests, are formed of the same metal, set with precious stones. Each banner—they all resemble—is in the shape of a long scarf of rich silk, of bright florid colors, embroidered very deep at the ends, which are finished with gold and silver bullion fringes; it is caught together near the middle, and tied with rich gold and silver cords and tassels to the top of the staff, just under the hand or crest. The silks, I observe, are of many different colors, forming an agreeable variety, some blue, purple green, yellow, & c. Red is not used; being the Soonies' distinguished color at Mahurrum it is carefully avoided by the zealous Sheahs—the Soonies are violently opposed to the celebration of this festival. After the elephants, a band of music follows, composed of every variety of native instruments, with drums and fifes; the trumpets strike me as the greatest novelty in their band; some of them are very long and powerful in their effects."[102]

"Next in the order of procession I observe a man in deep mourning, supporting a black pole, on which two swords are suspended from a bow reversed- the swords unsheathed glittering in the sun. The person who own the banners, or his deputy, follows next on foot, attended by readers of the Musseeah (mersiya), and a large party of friends in mourning. The readers select such passages as are particularly applicable to part, Abbas Ali took in the affair at Kraabaallāh, which is chanted at intervals, the procession pausing for the purpose."[103]

"Then comes Dhull Dhull (Dul Dul or zu 'l janah)—the name of Hosein's horse at Kraabaallāh; - that selected for the present purpose is a handsome white Arab, caparisoned according to the olden style of Arabia: due care is taken to represent the probable sufferings of both animal and rider, by the bloody horsecloth—the red-stained legs—and the arrows apparently sticking in several parts of his body; on the saddle is fixed a turban in the Arabian style, with the bow and arrows;—the birdle & c. are of very rich embroidery; the stirrups and mountings of solid silver. The horse and all its attire are given after Mahurrum, in charity, to a poor Syaad (Saiyid). Footmen, with the afthaadah (Aftabgir, a sun-screen) and chowrie (Chaunri, the bushy tail of the yak, used as fly-flapper)—peculiar emblems of royalty in India – attend Dhull Dhull. The friends of the family walk near the horse; then servants of all classes, to fill up the parade, and many foot-soldiers, who occasionally fire singly, giving to the whole description a military effect."[104]

At the end, Mrs. Ali puts forward that, "I have seen many other processions on these fifth days of Mahurrum—they all partake of one style—some more splendid than others; and the very poor people parade their banners, with, perhaps, no other accompaniment than a single drum and fife, and the owner supporting his own banner."[105] According to Mrs. Ali, the shrine attendants consecrated forty or fifty thousand banners in a single day.[106]

Even today, a procession of Tāziās and 'alams takes place on the streets of Gorakhpur on 5th Muharram, led by the Sufi custodian of Imāmbārah, (constructed by Nawab Āsaf-ud Daula). This procession is famous as, "Miyan Sāhib ki Paanchvi". In this procession all the Tāziās and alams of every Mohalla are included along with music instruments. A number of horses, camels and elephants are also the part of the procession. However, Shi'as of Gorakhpur do not participate in the procession. The purpose of mentioning this procession is only to show that the date of fifth Muharram co-relates with the Lucknow-procession's date.

The next big and famous procession during Muharrum in Lucknow was maynhdi, on the seventh Muhurrum in the commemoration of the battle-field wedding of Hazrat Qāsim, the Imām Husayn's doomed nephew, to the Imām's daughter. Mrs. Ali, who was an eye witness of the procession describes it in these words: "The public display on the seventh Mahurrum is by torch-light, and called the night of Mayndhie (Menhdi), intending to represent the marriage ceremony for Cossum (Qāsim), who, it will be remembered, in the sketch of the events of Kraabaallāh, was married to his cousin Sakeena Koobraah, the favorite daughter of Hosein, on the morning of the celebrated battle.

This night presents to the public all the outward and showy parade which marks the Mayndhie procession of a real wedding ceremony, which I propose speaking further in another place. This display at Mahurrum is attended with considerable expense; consequently, the very rich only observe the outdoor formalities to be exhibited on this occasion; yet all classes, according to their means, remember the event, and celebrate it at home.

The Mayndhie procession of one great personage, in Native cities, is directed—by previous arrangement—to the Emaumbaarah of a superior. I was present, on one occasion, when the Mayndhie of the Prime Minister of Oude was sent to the King's Emaumbaarah, called Shaah Nudghiff (Shaah Najaf, built by Ghāzi-ud-deen Hayder, the king of Awadh)— from the mausoleum of Ali, of which it is an exact representation, on a small scale.

It is situated near the banks of river Goomtie (Gomati), some distance from the palace at Lucknow; the entrance to the outer court, or quadrangle, is by a handsome gateway of brickwork plastered, resembling marble. On each side of the gateway, and carried up the two sides, in a line with the building, are distinct apartments, designed for the abode of the distressed and houseless poor; the back of these apartments forms a substantial wall or enclosure. The Shaah Nudghiff faces the gateway, and appears to be a square building, on a broad base of flights of steps, with a cupola roof; the interior is paved with black and white marble tessellated, the walls and dome neatly ornamented with plaster and gold in relief, the beading, cornices, & c. of gold, to correspond on a stone-color ground. The cupola and cornices on the outside are richly ornamented with plaster designs, relieved with gold; on the summit of the dome is placed a crown of pure silver, gilt, of an immense size.

The decorations of the interior, for the season of Mahurrum, were on scale of grandeur not easily to be conveyed by description. The walls were well covered with handsome glasses and mirrors; the splendid chandeliers, one containing a hundred wax lights, in every variety, and relieved with colored lamps—amber, blue, and green, mellowing the light, and giving a fairy-like effect to the brilliant scene. In the center of the building stood the green glass Tāziā, surrounded by wax lights; on the right of which was placed an immense lion, and on the left, a fish, both formed of the same bright emerald-green glass as the Tāziā. The richness and elegance of the banners— which were numerous and well- arranged,—could be equaled only by the costliness of their several mountings.

In Asiatic buildings niches and recesses prevail in all convenient situations, and here they are appropriated for the reception of the relics of antiquity and curiosities; such as models of Mecca, the tent of Hosein, the gate of Kraabaallāh, & c., arranged with much taste, adorn the interior.

The pulpit (mimber) is of silver, and of very handsome workmanship; the whole of the fitting up and arrangements had been made under the eye of his Majesty, and to his good taste may be ascribed all the merit of the well-ordered display for these occasions. He delighted in visiting this place, which he not only designed as a tribute of his respect to the Emaums, but as the future repository for his own remains, when this world should cease to be his place of joy, or anxious care. His intention has been fulfilled—he died in 1827, aged fifty years much and justly beloved and regretted by all who knew him; his funeral obsequies were impressively grand, according to Mussulmaun custom. This good and amiable King was succeeded by his only son Naseerooddeen Hyder, who had just completed his twenty-second year when he began to reign.

On the evening of Mayndhie, the crowds of admiring people were admitted to view their Padshāh's (King's) exhibition; until the distant sounds of musketry announced the approach of the spectacle, when the multitude were desired to quit the Emaumbaarah. Hundreds still lingering, could not be prevailed to depart, except by the stripes dealt out unsparingly from the whips of the hurkaarahs (Harkara) and peons, appointed to keep order on the occasion. The place cleared, and quiet, restored, I had leisure to view the fairy-like palace of splendor, before the bustle of the procession reached the building. I could hardly persuade myself the picture before me was not a dream, instead of a reality.

I stood at the entrance to watch the approach of the minister's train, through the gateway into the illuminated quadrangle. Spacious as this court-yard is, it was nearly filled with the many people forming the Mayndhie-parade. I should imagine there could not be less than three thousand souls engaged in this service, including the match-lock soldiery. Several trays of Mayndhie are brought, with the other requisities for the usual forms of marriage gifts, such as sweetmeats, dried fruits, garlands of sweet jasmine, imitative beds of flowers, composed of uberuck: in some of the flower, fireworks were concealed, to be let off in the quadrangle. An imitative tomb on a bier is also paraded, together with the palkie and chundole of silver, which are the covered conveyances for females of the royal family, or such of the nobility as are privileged by grants from the crown; all other females used the covered palkie, mahanah, dhollee (doli), and the rutt (rath). Several bands of music follow, and torches out of number. The elephants, camels, cavalry & c. are left in the open space, outside the gateway- the gentlemen, dismounting, enter with Dhull Dhull and the trays of Mayndhie.

I trembled for the probable destruction of the brilliant ornaments in the Emaumbaarah, when I heard the noble animal was to make the circuit round the Tāziā. Dhull Dhull, being led in, went up the steps with little difficulty, and to my astonishment, the gentle creature paced the tessellated floor, in very slow time, without once slipping, or seeming concerned at the novelty of his situation; indeed, this docile animal seemed to me the only living thing present that felt no interest in the scene—rendered more attractive and conspicuous by the gentle manner of the pretty Dhull Dhull himself. The circuit being made, he was conducted back into the court-yard, without the slightest accident or confusion occurring during his visit to the Emaumbaarah.

The model of the tomb of Cossum, the chandole and palkie, the trays of Mayndhie, sweetmeats, & c. were deposited here until the tenth day, when they accompany the King's temporary Tāziā cavalcade to Kraabaallah for interment.

The ceremonies performed on this night of Mayndhie resemble, in every particular, those of the same rank of persons on the actual solemnization of a wedding, even to the distribution of money amongst the populace who crowd in multitudes on such occasions, though apparently more eager for the prize than the sight."[107]

The tenth day of Āshūrā is the climax of the mourning period. Mrs. Ali describes the tenth day of Muharrum in these words: "The most imposing spectacle in the celebration of Mahurrum, is reserved for the last day (Āshūrā); and, judging from the activity of all classes, the zealous exertions of the multitude, the deep interest marked on every face, male and female, a mere spectator might well imagine this, mourning, to be of more importance than any other in the Mussulmaun's catalogue of days.

The whole line of march is guarded in each procession by burkhandhars or Barqandaz (lightening-darter, or matchlock-men), who fire singly, at intervals on the way. Several bands of music are dispersed in the cavalcade, performing solemn dirge-like airs, peculiar to the style of composition in Hindoostaun and well- suited to the occasion—muffled drums and shrill trumpets, imitating the reiteration of 'Hasan, Hosein', when Mortem (ma'atam) is performed. I remember a fine female elephant, belonging to King Ghauzeeooddeen Hyder, which had been so well instructed, as to keep time with the soundings from her proboscis with the occasional Mortems. I cannot say that she clearly pronounced the names of the two sons of 'Ali, yet the regularity of keeping time with the music and the human voices was of itself sufficient to excite admiration—the Natives declare that she pronounces the names distinctly. Her name is Hoseinie, the feminine of Hosein."[108]

Further she writes, " There are many little observances, not of sufficient importance to make them general to all who keep Mahurrum, that need not here be detailed; but one must not be omitted, as it is a feature in the domestic observances of Mussulmauns. On the Tāziā, when about to be conveyed to Kraabaallah, I discovered small portions of corn, rice, bread, fruits, flowers, cups of water, & c.;- this is in keeping with the Mussulmaun funerals, who invariably convey food to the tomb with their dead For the same reason, at Mahurrum, camphor and rose water are always carried with the Tāziā to Kraabaallah, although there is not the same occasion for the articles.

I have seen females of rank, with their own hands, place red and green wax lights in front of the Tāziā in their halls, on the night of Mayndhie. I was told, in answer to my inquiry, What was meant by the solemn process I had witnessed?—that these ladies had some petition to make, for which they sought the Emaum's intercession at the throne of mercy. The red light was for Hosein, who died in battle; the green for Hasan, who died by poison—which these colors symbolize; and those females place great dependance on the fulfilment of their desires, who thus present to their Emaums the wax lights on the night of Mayndhie.

I have remarked that the noblemen and gentlemen generally engaged in the service of celebrating Mahurrum, walk on the tenth morning with their heads bare and their feet uncovered from their homes to the burial ground called, Kraabaallāh, whatever may be the distance,-perhaps four or five miles,— exposed to the fiery rays of the sun: some persons, who on this occasion are very scrupulous in thus humbling their nature, walk back again in the same manner, after the funeral ceremony has been duly gone through at Kraabaallāh. The magnitude of this undertaking can be only well understood by those who have experienced the state of an atmosphere in the shady rooms of a large house, when the thermometer ranges from eighty-foru toe eighty- eight, or even ninety degrees; and when, if you venture to the verandah for a few seconds, the flames of heated wind are not only insupportable to Europeans, but frequently produce severe attacks of fever. The luxurious habits of the Eastern great men may be well recollected when counting over the proofs of zeal exhibited in this undertaking, where every selfish consideration for the time is banished. The nobility (or indeed anyone who lays the slightest claim gentility) never walk from one house to another during their lives, but at this particular season; even in their gardens indulging in whatever luxury they may boast, by being conveyed round in their palkie, or thonjaun (Tamjhan)—a chair with poles, supported by bearers. On the tenth day, the good Mussulmauns rigidly fast until after the third watch; not even a drop of water, or the hookah, enters their mouths; as they believe Hosein's sufferings only concluded just before the third watch, they cautiously abstain from indulgences, until that hour has passed.

The procession having reached Kraabaallāh, the whole ceremony of a funeral is gone through. The Tāziā is committed to the grave with equal solemnity to that which is observed when their dead are deposited in the tomb: this occupies some time."[109]

The following observation of Mrs. Ali signifies the importance of Muharram on the deprived sections of society. She mentions that while, "returning to their home, the rich men are occupied in dispensing benefits among the poor. Food, money and clothes are distributed in nearly as great proportions as when they have to mourn over a recent separation by death from a beloved relative. The clothes worn during Mahurrum are never retained for the next occasion, but always distributed amongst the poor, who derive so many advantages from the annual commemoration of Mahurrum that the philanthropic heart will rather be pleased than vexed at the zeal which produce such a harvest of benefits to the necessitous."[110]

On the third day after Āshūr, as Cole writes, "men began shaving their beards again, women threw off their mourning vestments, bathed, and put on jewelry. The populace began chewing betel leaves once more. Only a few very devout persons continued to mourn for forty days."[111]

After the extension of mourning period up to forty days, the procession of Chihlum was also added. According to Saiyid Athar Abbas Rizvi, "The ta'ziya procession on the fortieth day after, 'Āshūrā, called Chihlum in Lucknow, were also impressive. From villages and small towns, the mourners visited Lucknow to pay homage to the memory of the Karbala martyrs. As on Āshūrā day, the artisans and craft-men organizing separate ta'zia processions adorning their ta'ziyas with distinctive features of their work. For example, the sweet sellers covered their bamboo frames with sweets and the humble grass-cutters covered theirs with hay or green grass."[112] According to Hollister, "The procession on the night of Chihlum is almost a repetition of the Muharram procession".[113] But Najat Husayn Khan came from Patna to Lucknow, specifically to observe the Lucknow Chihlum. He saw Shaykh Khuda Bakhsh's procession from a vantage point in the Daru'sh-Shifa mosque near Hazratganj. The procession passed through the mosque in the afternoon. He writes "It was headed by seven swift she-camels, each covered with a black cloth. Their riders were also clothed in black. Seventeen elephants covered in black, bearing tall flags and 'alams, followed. The black and red satin pennants and 'alams were embroidered with the names of Allāh and Panjatan (Muhammad, Ali, Fatima, Hasan and Husayn) in silver and gold thread Then came the officials who held gold and silver spears and clubs in their hands. They were by countless foot soldiers armed with swords and shields. This part of the procession occupied more than one mile of the road. The band, comprising sets of different instruments, played moving mourning tunes. The 'ābdār-Khānā' (A repository for drinking water including sherbet) was behind the band. It was placed on wooden benches and transported by carts. Sherbet in jugs and cups, and covered with ice, was placed on the benches and was served free to the processionists. The spectators watching from their roofs were offered cups tied to a long-poles. He further writes, that, "Behind the ābdār-Khān, the gold and silver 'alams were followed by two or three Zu'ljanahs and tabūts. Arrows pierced the tabūts. The coverings of the Zu'ljanahs were sprinkled with red color. Behind them, hundreds of poor people carried their own taziyas. At the end was Khudabakhsh's taziya. The taziyas were surrounded by countless mourners, all bare-headed and bare-footed. Tears rolled down their cheeks and constant crying had reddened their eyes. Their breasts had also become red from continued beating. Nawhas and marsiyas were recited in moving tones around the taziyas. Various ethnic and racial groups such as Ethiopeans, Mughals etc. formed separate parties of their own to perform ma'tam. The cries and beating of breasts were so moving as to make even Shimr, who had martyred Imām Husayn, cry. Some actions of the processionists were anti-shari'a, but, as their objective was to shed tears for the martyrs of Karbala, there was nothing wrong in them. Several thousand spectators watched the procession. The noblemen, viziers and dignitaries followed the procession in their conveyances."[114]

Najat Husayn also visited the Talkatora Karbala. The groups of mourners with the taziya parties, both small and large, assembled there. They performed m'atam under 'alams and buried their taziyas." In many districts Eastern Uttar Pradesh, the procession of Chihllum is brought out. The procession known as 'Amari'. Amaari of Baragaon (Shahganj, Jaunpur) is very old. It is still continuing.

In Lucknow, also another procession included on the eighth of Rabi-ul Awwal, what is known as the "Chup-ta'zia" procession, when ta'ziyas are taken to Karbala but the procession moves in complete silence. Women, as would be expected in any religious function, share deeply in the mourning of Muharram.[115]

Shi'a ulama took a critical attitude towards some of the Muharram practices. For example, Mawlana Sayyid Dildār Ali Nasirābadi, said the employ of drums were heretical innovation. An Irani scholar, Aqā Ahmad Bihbahani endeavored to convince notables in Faizabad to give up the practice of beating drums to the accompaniment of their breast -beating. According to him, 'he was successful in his mission'.[116]

The impact of political changes in Awadh could be felt on the expenses of Muharram ceremonies. The annexation of Awadh by the British completely finished the role of the Nawabs or Kings of the province. Summary settlement of 1856 also disrupted the talluqdars of Awadh and finally the revolt of 1857 finished many ta'lluqdars. The Urdu newspaper, *'Tilism'* commented, "the rites of Muharram, the annual commemorations for the martyred Imām Husayn and his family which dominated Lucknow's municipal calendar, experienced heavy depletion in tandem with the fortunes of the Nawabi elite and the realities of British policing: The doors of fortune are closed. The fire of sufferings is at its height. The Imāmbārahs (mourning halls) look deserted.'[117] Veena Oldenberg, too, writes, "The city's largest Shi'a mosque , the Āsafi-masjid, and the adjoining Āsaf-ud-Daula Imāmbārah, Lucknow's most imposing religious building, were converted into British military garrisons, their religious functions shut down: over fifty other city mosques were appropriated to uses including offices, police depots, medical dispensaries and stables for livestock."[118] According to Justin Jones, "The two decades after 1858 proved especially ruinous for Shī'īsm in north India, especially in the city of Lucknow, the former Nawabi capital."[119] He further writes that, "New land-settlement policies, rewritten in 1858 around principles of perceived 'loyalty' to the British Raj, shut off got the stipends of inherited land revenue on which many noble Shi'a families and religious scholars had depended. Meanwhile, with the kings of Awadh no longer representing a solid source of patronage for Shi'a scholars and preachers, the transnational clerical traffic between Iraq, Persia and India largely evaporated."[120] The two or three decades after 1857 was an era of religious weakness and disorder (mazahabi kamzori, fitna-parwazi). According to Ahmad Ali, one of the Lucknow's leading scholars, 'the Shi'as had no sense of common brotherhood with one another.[121] But, despite all these odds, the remaining Muslim landowning class, the zamindars, the Muslim dignitaries of the Hindu talluqadars and the beneficiaries from the bequests of the Awadh Nawabs and Begums, known as wasiqadars, and common people followed their ancestral traditions in commemorating the mourning ceremonies of Muharram. The 'Fasānā-i-Āzād' by Ratan Nath Sarshār (d.1902) gives an impressive account of the processions, ta'zias, marsia- reciters and the crowds that headed towards Talkatora. The enormous gathering of mourners within the Karbala four walls in Talkatora had made movement from one corner to the other impossible.[122]

Hollister, whose book was published in 1953, writes, "The connecting strand which runs through, and gives unity to the programme during the ten days, or more, of mourning, is in the Majālis, mourning assemblies, where step by step, the day- to-day events are remembered, from the time that Husayn received the invitation from the Kūfans to the time of his martyrdom. Details in the programme vary from place to place. My friend, Sayyid Akhlaq Husayn, has given me this order of observance in and near Lucknow. On the first and second days there is much visiting among relatives and the story of Husayn's setting forth against the earnest entreaties of his family, his travel and his arrival at Karbala recounted. Owing to a rumor that Yazīd proposed to kill him he had not gone that year on pilgrimage, and so started for Kūfā via Mecca. In this journey he met the troops of Hur. On third day, they recall the encampment at Karbala, Husayn's moving back from the river, and arrangement with the Bani- Asad for the burial of those who might be killed. On the fourth and fifth days, the difficulties of Husayn and his party are recited; on the sixth, the valor and death of 'Ali Akbar, Husayn's son. On the seventh, the heroism of Qāsim, a son of Imām Hasan and an account of his betrothal to Husayn's daughter is recalled. The eighth and ninth days are given to a recounting of the part that Hadrat' Abbas and others of seventy-two martyrs had, while on the tenth the poignant circumstances in which Husayn himself was killed in the center of thought for all."[123]

We find same changes in the programme of Muharram in the twentieth century. But Hollister took no notice of them. For example. Abdul Halim 'Sharar' writes, "In Lucknow, the Majālis held on the nineth day of Muharram in the Ghufran Ma'ab Imāmbārah is very impressive and people come from great distances to attend it. On this occasion, after the orations, camels are brought before the audience to represent the ruined caravan of Husayn's family. Their saddles and panniers are draped with the black cloth of mourning. This sorrowful spectacle affects some people so much that they faint."[124] Now a days the procession of the camel is prohibited.

In the same way, Hoollister does not mention, the famous majlis of *Shaam-i-Ghareeban*. Earlier, no majlis was held in the evening of tenth Muharram. But on 21st July 1926 AD/1045 Hijri a majlis was organized in the Imāmbārah of Ghufran Ma'ab in special circumstances. Syeed Swaleh, a *Visitor* and the guest from Arab, who was staying in the premises of Imāmbārah, expressed his desire for a majlis after ' Fāqā-Shiknī'. The arrangement for 'Fāqā- shikni' was made at Imāmbārah. Mawlana Kalbe Husayn Sahib (father of Late Mawlana Kalbe Abid Sahib and grand- father of Mawlana Kalbe Jawwā Sahib of Ghufran Ma'ab Imāmbārah) and others, presented there, accepted his proposal. Announcements were made immediately in the near by located muhallas and within a short-time seventy to eighty persons gathered in the Imāmbārah, Sayyid Sibte Muhammad *Hādī* urf Kallan Sahib addressed the majlis. He narrated those events which occurred after the martyrdom of Imam Husayn and drew a scene of that time in such a pathetic way that many of the mourners fainted. He told the mourners that yazid's army attacked on the camp of *Ahl-i-bayt*, where only children and widows were left. They were suffering from hunger and thirst since last three days. In the name of gents, only Imām Zaynul, Ābideen (a.s) was there, who was ill and unconscious at that time. The army looted and burned the camps. But Bibi Zainab saved her nephew and brought him out of the burning camp. There was no limit of atrocities. All the children and women were frightened and unsafe. They were sitting under open sky. The darkness of the night was growing. Before making them captive, the commander of yazid's army, thought to provide some water and food to them. But no one was ready to do this work because they had no courage to face the women and children of Prophet's family. At last, the commander requested to Hurr's wife. Hurr was also a commander of yazeed's army and had brought the Imām Husayn to Karbala. But he felt that he was on wrong side. So, he changed his party on 10th Muharram, fought for Husayn and was killed in the battle of Karbala. His wife was also aggrieved. But she had the courage to face them due to her husband's sacrifice for Imām Husayn. She came along with some women to serve food and water. The conversation between both parties was heart-breaking. Mawlana Kallan Sahib set the pattern of majlis for future. We still hear those events in the majlis of "Shaam-i-Ghareebān". I have attended many times the majlis of Shaam-i-Ghareeban at the Imāmbārah of Ghufran Ma'ab, Lucknow, addressed by Late Mawlana Kalbe Abid Sahib and Mawlana Kalbe Jawwad Sahib: Noor Nabi Abaasi, the Hindi-translator of Sharar's *Ghuzishta i Lucknow*, also mentions the majlis i-Shaam-Ghareeban' in his note.

The majlis was so impressive that it was decided that the similar type of majlis will be organised every year on the same date of Muharram and at the same time in the Imāmbārah. In 1928 AD Munne Aghā Sahib, one of the senior most members, named this majlis as, "Zikr-i-Aseerān-Ahl-i-Bayt", or "Sham-i-Ghareeban." The majlis is continuing since then and it became famous in the subcontinent. One of the main feature of this majlis is that nothing is laid on the floor of Imāmbārah nor lights are switched on during the majlis. Later on, a new feature was also added in the majlis. When Zakir narrates about Hurr's wife, then two or three men, wearing naqāb or veil, appear in the midst of the mourners. They have trays in their hands, in which there are burning candles, jug of water and plates covered with cloths. This reminds the mourners about the post-martyrdom incidents of Imam Husayn at Karbala." Later Jhannu Lal Dilgir's pathetic poem *Ghabra yegi Zainab*, was also included in the majlis. Every year some one recites this poem after Zakir's address.

The above mentioned programme along with new additions, more or less, are in practice in the districts of Eastern Uttar Pradesh. Gorakhpur is no exception to it. But no procession of Mayndhie is bring out on the day of seventh. They mourn this day in their families and only majlises are held. One special feature of the day, is that the most of the children and even some adults also, wearing the green Kurta or shirt, beg money as a faqīr, in the name of Hazrat Qāsim. The collection is used for a majlis on any other day or for the 'nazr' of Hazrat Qāsim. Generally, they become faqīr for three to five years on this specific day or as the parents' oath (mannat) for their children. Generally, the children below ten years, become faqīr. On this day only 'Sherbat' is distributed in place of taburruq in majlises.

The number and days of processions vary in the different districts. For example, in Jaunpur the Shi'a of one muhalla started to take out the Mayndhie procession to mark Sakina Kubrā's wedding on 7th Muharram, primarily a large Lucknawi custom, for the first time around 1899 AD.[125] My mother (1919-1999), who was from Jaunpur, used to tell us that before the partition, her younger brother was member of a ma'tami -anjuman, and used to participate in the different processions of Muharram in the city including Maynhdi Jaloos. More or less in every district of Eastern Uttar Pradesh, a procession, in the night of eighth Muharram, is taken out in the memory of Hazrat 'Abbas. An 'alam and also in some places, Duldul, is its main feature. In Gorakhpur in the second half of the twentieth century or earlier two processions were brought out. One, on the night of sixth Muharram and the second on eighth Muharram's night. The first procession includes an a'lam attached with a small mashk, a mynhdi (in the shape of a boat) and a Duldul. As for as, I remember, Late, Syed Wasi Haider, an Urdu Journalist, who also published a weekly Urdu paper, was the originator of this procession in Gorakhpur. According to oral sources, he came from Saharanpur to Gorakhpur, in the first half of twentieth century and settled there. Second procession, includes an a'lam and a Duldul. This is the 'Qadimi- Juloos' (old procession) and is generally famous as, 'Āghā Saahiban ka Julus' or 'Aathvi ka Juloos'. Now, Hallaur association of Gorakhpur also brings out a procession on Fifth Muharram, since the last decade of twentieth century. At the end of Juloos, the Association occasionally organizes the ma'tam on fire (Aag ka ma'tam) in the premises of Qadimi-Imāmbārah. Late Mohd. Mehdi Advocate, with the permission of Government, in 1978 AD, started a new procession on the fourth Muharram in the day hours, from his house, situated in Mohalla Basantpur-Mutnaza. Besides, these processions, an a'lam on the eve of 1st Muharram and on twentieth Safar (40th day of martydom), a tābūt with alam are also brought out from the residence of Late, Syed Haidar Raza which is situated in Mohalla Miyan Bazaar. All the above mentioned processions are still continuing.

The main feature of the above mentioned processions is flagellation (ma'tam), which attracts the other communities.

Generally, a big crowd of Sunnī- Muslims and Hindus come to see the ma'tam. All through the way of procession, 'chest-beating' and *zanzir ka ma'tam* (iron chains attached with sharp blades) are being done by the mourners. Children, youths and even old people actively participate in the ma'tam. Sometimes one or two youths do the ma'tam of Qamā (the use of swords and knives to cut the forehead or tatbir). But the elders discourage them. I saw the ma'tam on fire, for the first time, approximately around 1960 at the age of ten years. It was arranged in the open ground adjacent to Khādim Qadā. An anjuman was, especially invited from Faizabad, for the same. But, during the last sixty years, as I recall, only five to ten times, the 'ma'tam on fire' was organised in Gorakhpur. Other communities respect the Shi'as due to their ma'tam.

Earlier, for the Shi'a-women, a partition of curtain was arranged because they had no separate Imāmbārah. Still there is no separate Imāmbārah for them. But during the days of ayyām-e-Azā, they convert a part of their houses into Imāmbārah and organize Majlises there. Their number is increasing day by day. Sometimes, due to non-availability of Zakira and short of time, only nauha, ma'tam and ziyārat, complete their majlises.

There is an old Imāmbārah, constructed by Begum Ashraf-un-Nishā Khanum. This lady belonged to the Mirzā family of Captainganj. The family had played an active role against the British in the revolt of 1857. This was the richest family of Gorakhpur before the revolt. After the revolt, some or half of the property came in the hand of Mirzā Nawāzis Ali, who was loyal to the government.[126] Begum Ashraf-un-Nishā, Khanum, wife of Mirzā Bande Ali, was his daughter in-law. She is also known as, 'Rani-Sahiba'. She died issueless and the management of property went in to the hands of Āgha Family. During my childhood, the Imāmbārah, was known as, "Āghā Rabbi ka Imāmbārah", but now as, "Āghā Saahibān ka Imāmbārah." Previously it was badly damaged. However, Late Āghā Muzaffar Husayn Sahib of this family, after his retirement, reconstructed its roof and also did some other repairing works which he financed from his provident fund received from Railway. But still the repair work is not complete. At present, his son, Āghā Ali Mohammad Advocate, is the caretaker of the Imāmbārah. Recently nearly a decade ago, another Shi'a Imāmbārah was built by (Late) Mohd. Mehdi Advocate, on the first floor of his old, but newly constructed house at Askarganj, Reti-Road, Gorakhpur.

During the ten days of Muharram, three to four Majlises in the morning and the same number in the evening, are held. The first majlis in the morning is held at the old residence of Mohd. Mehdi Advocate and since last many years, the *baani-e-majlis* arrange the varieties of rich breakfast for mourners. An attractive tabarruq was also distributed there. Mohd. Mehdi Advocate died in May 2021.The second majlis of the morning is held at old Imāmbārah of Shaykhpur, where Āghā Ali Mohammad Advocate receives the mourners. In my early days the second majlis was held at the residence of Late Master Sibtain Sahib, a teacher of D.A.V. College. He lived in Chaurahiya-Gola (a famous grain market of the city). The plea behind the timing was that he had to go to college at nine O'clock in moring. After his death, the order of majlis changed. Now, the second majlis is held in the Imāmbārah of Āgha Sahiban. The third and fourth Majlis are held at the residences of (Late) Kallana Shib (1977) and Mr. Sabir. Both the houses are in Mohalla Jafra- Bazaar. Mr. Sabir's father had come Gorakhpur in connection of his service. He was a postman. Mr. Sabir also served in the postal department as a postman.

The first Majlis in the evening, is held at Khādim Qadā, a known center of Shi'as' religious activities. (Late) Mirzā Khādim Husayn and his sons were the baani-e-majlis. (Late) Mirzā Ishrat Hussain, Naurozi Sahib and Dostdar Hussain of this family were famous for marsiya and nauha-khwani. Now the third generation of the family is maintaining the old tradition of holding the Majlis and other rituals. One of them is,'Haziri' of Hazrat Abbas on 8th Muharram and another, is 'Faaqa-shikni' on 10th of Muharram.

The second majlis is held at 'Late Mirzā Nabban's Imāmbārah, (an old house, a part of it is reserved for the observance of Muharram). I have not seen Late Mirzā Nabban. But it is well known that he was owner of a cycle-store. He did not had any off spring. So, he made his house waqf. The upper story was given on rent and the entire rent collected through the year was used for meeting the expenses of organizeing the majileses. A very interesting point is to note here in regard of his registered 'waqf-deed' is that in the five members committee, he had included two of his Hindu friends. This shows the post partiton Shī'īs'- Hindu, relationship. During the life of Mrs. Nabban, my mother used to stay with her since the sixth Muharram up to eleventh Muharram, because our house was out of the city. Mrs. Nabban was a very pious lady. She paid much respect to my mother due to her Saiyyid-origin. I was fortunate to see her in my childhood. After her demise, Late Haider Raza Sahib used to manage the affair but the maid-servant of Mirzā- family, Niyājan Buā, though a Sunnī by faith, was the custodian of majlis till her death. She used to wait the mourners on the door of the house, whenever, they reached late. A burning lamp (Laltern) of kerosene oil, was always in her hand to show the path, because the house is in a lane. (Late) HaiderRaza Sahib was custodian till his death. Now his son Syed Wasi Raza is the caretaker of the Imāmbārah of Mirzā Nabban.

The third majlis is organized at the residence of (Late) Iqbal Sahib since last fifty years. His sons, Syed Alamdar Husayn Rizvi or Intizar Bhai and Ajaz Husayn Rizvi urf Babu Bhai are making all the arrangements for holding the majlis. Intizar Bhai's son,Taqī is at present, the elected treasurer of Babul Ilm, Shia Committee of Okhla Vihar, Jamia Nagar, New Delhi, which indicates the religious activities of this family. The fourth and last majlis at the residence of (Late) Nisar Sahib.

Now, these Majlises are counted in the list of Qadīmī (old) Majlises. These are held regularly. But every year, on holy days, the number of Majlises increases so much that no one can return home in the day hours. Every Shi'a family tries to hold a majlis, during the period of Ashra (the first ten days of Muharram).

In Gorakhpur, there is no Shi'a Karbala and therefore the Tāziās are immersed in the river Rapti at Rajghaut. For the immersion of ta'zias on 10th Muharram, all the mourners join the procession from Imāmbārah to the ghaut of the river with bare-head and bare-foot. Many mourners have chaff on their heads which is an old ritual. As early as 1000 AD, the people of Baghdad used to throw dust and ashes about the streets, and dress in black sackcloth on the death anniversary of Imām Husayn.[127] The procession moves from Imāmbārah-Āghā Sahiban in the style of Lucknow procession and after covering some distance (forty steps) the mourners begin to read nauha and do the m'atam throughout the way, until they reach the Ghaut of the river.[128] One peculiar tradition of Shi'as in Gorakhpur is that they complete their procession after immersing them into water before 11 A.M. After returning from Ghaut, they do the aamaal in open ground or on the roof of Imāmbārah or mosque before noon prayer. In the afternoon, most of the Shi'as assemble at Khādim-Qada between around four to five p.m. They read special ziyārut of the day and break the Fāqā (fast) by taking the *chuni-roti* (bread made of jau or barley flour) with spinach or *chaulai ka saag*, bhuna chana (dry roasted chana or gram) and roasted rice along with tea. Within few minutes, all the members take rice, *masoor ki daal* and paarcha (grave based non-veg.). We find a separate arrangement for the women also. The family members of Khādim Qadā arrange all these very nicely. It is well known that on this day every member of the community keeps Fāqā since morning Azā'n. It is not called a fast because two or three grains of salt put on the tongue in the morning to prevent its being a fast. Nobody burn his or her stove or gas chulha in the kichen on this day. Even the mothers do not feed their six month old or above, till the noon (sawaa pahar tak).[128A] They remember Janāb Asghar, the six months old son of Imām Husayn, who was killed by the army of enemies, at Karbala. When Imām Husayn brought him in the battlefield and put him on the burning ground before the enemies with a request to give him water to quench thirst. It was the time between one and two P.M.. But, instead of supplying water they killed him. One can easly assess the sorrows of Shi'as on this day.

Then the majlis known as, *Shaam-i-Ghareebān*, follows in the Imāmbārah (A part of the house reserved as a Imāmbārah). In this majles the tradition of Lucknow is followed. Two or three persons appear in veil along with burning lamp or candles and a jug in the tray in the mid of the majlis.

Here it is noteworthy that even today there are no more than fifty houses of the Shi'as in the district of Gorakhpur and many among them live on rent. But in the observance of Muharram, Shi'as get all kind of support from Sunnī -Muslims and Hindus. I have never seen any communal tension in my life for the observance of Muharram in Gorakhpur. Now one can observe a change in the attitude of the society. Earlier, a large number of Hindu-youths participated in the night of 9th. Muharram as a paik (payak), but now day by day their numbers are decreasing.[129]

Sometimes the Shia Zākirs are criticized by their Sunnī counterparts and the other Muslims, for the exaggeration of the events of martyrdom of Karbala. The suggestion of Ayoub, Mahmūd, is mentionable here, "That for scholars of religion, the focus needs to be less on the history of the actual event than the history of the way a community imagines, interiorizes and lives it."[130] But it is wrong to say that historical accuracy is not an issue among Shias themselves. Murtadā Mutaharri's scathing comments about the popular rendition of the martyrdom of Husayn, is an answer for the critics.[131]

The description of Muharram, mentioned above, shows some symbols also. The Muharram symbols are designed to arouse memories of the tragedy at Karbala and to promote devotion towards the family of *Prophet*. The earliest known Muharram symbol in India is the 'a'lam (a standard or an ensign). It is intended to remind the mourners of the 'alam which, on 10th Muharram, Imām Husayn assigned to his half- brother 'Abbas, an invincible warrior and a redoubtable personality. Often 'Abbas had wished to march deep into the enemy ranks and destroy them but Imām Husayn did not approve of annihilation even for the nominal followers of his grand-father. Ultimately, 'Abbas was urged to fetch water for the children who lay prostrate for three days without a drop of water. 'Abbas fought gallantly, broke the enemies' ranks and reached the Euphrates. He filled the leather bag (*mashk*) with water that was given by Husayn's little daughter Sakina and moved toward the camp without himself drinking a single drop of water. The enemies had closed the ranks and martyred 'Abbas. The 'alam, instantly reminds mourners of the children's thirst and 'Abbas' self -sacrifice filling them with an ecstasy of grief.[132]

The metal crests of the 'alams are cast in different patterns. They are generally in the shape of the palm of a hand, whose five fingers represent Prophet Muhammad, 'Ali, Fatima, Hasan and Husayn. In more ornamented crests, the palms are artistically designed and leaves and sword blades, representing fingers are added. Arabesques floral designs and inscriptions, comprising the names of the Prophet, his daughter and the Imāms are carved on the surfaces of the crest. Much of the elaborately decorated crests are inlaid with precious stones. Pierced works on metal sheets are frequently used for 'alam crests.[133] *Jhoola* is also a symbol of Janāb Asghar, the six months' old son of Imām Husayn.

The Majlises and processions of Muharram were organized in all the districts of eastern Uttar Pradesh, in large scale specially where Shī'īs' population existed. The centers of Shi'a population as revealed by the 1881 census, were Jaunpur and Azamgarh. Hollister writes, "Owing to the long continuance of the Shiite court at Jaunpur, there is a large proportion of Shi'as now resident there than in any other district of the United Provinces except Lucknow."[134] Justin Jones mentions Kajgaon, Baragaon and Machhli shehr as rural outposts of Jaunpur, where the Shi'as were in large numbers.[135] In present times their numbers is no less. Therefore, the Shi'as of these districts are following the tradition of Lucknow and subsequently arranging the Majlises and processions. Previous evidences show that sometimes, they openly recited 'tabarra' and organized the munāzarā type Majlises. For example, in 1904 AD they invited Hāji Maqbool Ahmad, a famous maulvi for reciting overt tabarra type majlises. Benares and Ghazipur also consist a good number of Shi'as in its Muslim-population, though lesser in number than Jaunpur. Shias of these districts actively participate in Muharram. Shaykh Ali Hazīn, an Usūlī mujtahid of Iran, sowed the seeds of Shī-īsm in the district of Benares. He constructed a 'rauza' of Bibi Fatima, which later became a Shi'a center of Benares. Hazīn wrote a voluminous book, namely *Fath-ul Sabīl*. It contains a detailed account of Shia beliefs.[136] He also taught many students of neighboring districts who are famous as a Shi'a ālim. In Ghazipur, we find the evidence of the Imāmbārah of Fazal 'Ali Khan of Ghazipur. He was an Ijaradar (Revenue-farmer) during the period of Shujā-ud Daula.[137] Though we do not get any detail of the observance of Muharram, but the existence of an Imāmbārah is itself a proof for the commemoration of Muharram. We again find a rich scholarship there. Ziya'u'llah bin Sayyid Muhammad Fakhir Husayn of Zangipur (Ghazipur) studied Hadīs, fiqh and Hikma under Shī'ī ulama in Dacca. After completing his education, he returned Ghazipur and fearlessly disseminated Shī'īsm. He died on 21 October 1754 AD. His piety and religious zeal made Shī'īsm popular in Ghazipur and the neighboring districts of Eastern India. His most prominent disciple was Mawlana Sayyid Atā Husayn bin Ghulām Murtazā Zangipuri. He died in 1797AD. Other centers of Shī'ī education were based in Nawnahra, Pārā and Ghazipur. The leading Shī'ī ulama and authors in19th century Ghazipur were Najaf Ali Nawnahrawi (d.1845), Karam Husayn Zangipuri (d.1846), Mansab Ali Ghazipuri (d. 1850), Safdar Ali Zangipuri (d.1852), Asghar Husayn, Zangipuri,(d. after,1853), Husayn bin Ramzan Ali (d. 1854) and Ramzan Ali Nawnahrawi (d.1857). But Abdul Ali of Deva-Khatta (Ghazipur1749-1827) was the most famous Shi'a scholar. Among Mawlana's disciples were a number of students from Ghazipur, Azamgarh and Jaunpur. The most prominent among them was Mawlana Sayyid Ahmad Ali bin Ināyat Haider of Muhammadabad in Azamgarh.[138] Even today, the deep-rooted impact of the abovementioned scholars and other community members may be felt in the commemoration of Muharram in these districts of Eastern Uttar Pradesh.

J. Thomson, the collector of Azamgarh, mentions in his report of 1835 AD, published in 1837 AD, about the tension of Shi'a–Sunnī. He states that, The weavers of the district were under the influence of Saiyyid Ahmad Shahid of Rai Bareli and were opposing the Shi'a rituals in Muharram.[139] The report of J. R. Reid, published in 1877, mentions the presence of Shi'a zamindars in the district. For example, the Saiyids of Sarai Mīr, the Saiyids of Kusawe, the Huseini-Saiyids of Patār and other villages, the Saiyids of Baraganw (Baragaon) in Pargana Ghosi, were Shi'a zamindars.[140] These places are still famous as the Shia centers, where the observance of Muharram is continuing, though the zamindari was abolished in 1952 by the Uttar Pradesh Government. Dr. Alauddin Khan of Shibli P.G. College, Azamgarh, has given the details of Shi'a Azādārī in Azamgarh district along with its history.[141] In mauza Koth of pargana Sikandarpur of district Ballia, where Ghardezi-Saiyids settled during the Sultanate period, observe the Shia rituals. Here also, the Majlises are held during the Muharram and a procession of 'alam is taken out on the eighth Muharram.[142]

Thus, the annexation of Oudh by British, their economic policies, the partition of the nation and the abolition of zamindari in Uttar Pradesh did not effect the observance of Muharram. Now every Shia contributes his share according to his status and participates in the rituals of Muharram. Today the observance of Muharram is spreading not only in Uttar Pradesh or India but all-over world, despite the opposition of the communal forces.

NOTES AND REFERENCES

1. Umar, Muhammad, *Islam in Northern India During the Eighteenth Century*, pp.176-77, Also, reference nos.103 to 105 on p. 234, New Delhi, 1993. (Hereafter, mentioned as Umar, Muhammad); According to Yann Richard, "India, which today is the second largest Muslim country in the world, contains about 80 million Muslims (12 per cent of the total population). Out of the community it is estimated that between 15 and 20 per cent are Shī'ītes, both Imāmis and Ismailies." See, *SHI'ITE ISLĀM*, (Translated by Antonia Nevill in English), pp. 3-4. The original book in French was published in 1988 and English translation in 1995, Blackwell Publishers, Cambridge, Massachusetts, o2142, U.S.A. 1995. (Hereafter mentioned as, Richard, Yann.); J. R. I. Cole writes that, "The north Indian Shī'ī population in the eighteenth century can only be guessed at, and not until after the fall of the Awadh kingdom, do population statistics become available for the area. Tables, as of 1881, give Sunnī and Shī'ī population figures in each district of combined British administrative unit of the North-Western Provinces and Oudh (an area nearly equivalent to the Greater Awadh ruled by Shujā' ud- Daula in the eighteenth century). But census takers did not divide Muslims by sect when they recorded their occupations." See, *Roots of North Indian Shī'īsm in Iran and Iraq*, pp. 69-71, OUP, Delhi, 1989. (Hereafter referred as, Cole.); Nevil, H. R., *District Gazetteers of the United Provinces of Agra and Oudh*, volume-XXXVII: Lucknow (Allāhabad, 1904), p. 65.; John Norman Hollister only writes that, "Shi'as are scattered throughout India. According to the 1921 census———Similarly, many of the taalluqdars in Oudh are Shi'as. Fyzabad, as an old capital, has a large and influential Shiite community in the district." A considerable community of Shias at Amroha in Uited Provinces may be traced. See, Hollister, John Norman *'The Shi'a of India'*, pp. 181-82, second edition, 1979, New Delhi. (Hereafter referred as, Hollister.)
2. Hasnain, Nadeem and Abrar Husayn, *Shias and Shia Islam in India*, p. 5, New Delhi, 1988.
3. Momen, Moojan, *Shī'ī Islam, A Beginner's Guide*, pp. 259-61, London,

2016. (Hereafter referred as Momen, Moojan)

4. Donaldson, D.M., *The Shī'īte Religion*, p. 277. cf. Hollister, op. cit., p. 164.
5. Jones, Justin, *'Shi'a Islam in Colonial India'*, pp. 91-92. Cambridge, 2012.
6. Mrs. Meer Hassan Ali, *Observations* on *The Mussulmauns of India, Descriptive of Their Manners, Customs, Habits And Religious Opinions, made during a Twelve Years' Residence in Their Immediate Society*, p. 7, Second Edition, edited with notes and an Introduction by W. Crooke, Deep Publication reprint, New Delhi, 1975. (Hereafter mentioned as, Mrs. Ali.)
7. Mrs. Ali, ibid., p. 7.
8. Ibid., pp. 7-11. Mrs. Ali has wrongly mentioned "Shaam". It was the Kūfā, the capital of Late Hazrat Ali. Therefore I have corrected it. For details, also see, Shaykh al-Mufīd, *Kitāb Al-Irshād*, (English translation by I.K.A. Howard), pp. 303-26, 332-33.
9. Mrs. Ali writes, "The ancient writings of Arabia say, Mahumud had predicted the death of Hosein, by the hands of men professing to be of 'the true faith', at this very place Kraabaalah or Hurth Maree." see, ibid., pp. 11-12.; According to both Shī'ī and Sunnī authorities, the Prophet Muhammad foretold the tragedy of Karbala. Among the transmitters were the Prophet's wives, Umm-e Salama and Aishā. Umme Salma recounts that one day in her house, when Imām Husayn was playing on the Prophet's chest, she was surprised to see soil in the Prophet's hand and tears rolling down his cheeks. When Imām Husayn had left, Umme Salama asked the reason for the Prophet's anguish and the handful of soil. The Prophet replied that he had been happily watching Husayn play when Gabriel appeared. The angel gave him some soil and told him that it came from the place where Husayn would be martyred. This terrible news had made the Prophet burst into tears. See, Saiyid Athar Abbas Rizvi, *A Socio-Intellectual History of the Isnā 'Ashari Shī'īs in India*, vol.-II, pp. 284-85, Delhi, 1986. (Hereafter referred as Rizvi, vol. II.); Also see, Shaykh al-Mufīd, *Kitab Al-Irshād* (English translation by Howard, I.K.A.) pp. 375-76; Ansariyan Publications, Qum (Iran).
10. Mrs. Ali, p.12.

11. Ibid.
12. Ibid.
13. Ibid., pp. 12-13.
14. Ibid., pp. 13-14.
15. Ibid., p. 14.
16. Richard, Yann, op. cit., pp. 28-29.; Also, see, Momen, Moojan, op. cit., pp. 37-40.
17. Richard, Yann, Ibid., p. 29.
18. Rizvi, vol. II, op. cit., p. 286.
19. Ibid.
20. Ibid., Richard, Yann, op. cit., pp. 38-39.; Allamā Sayyid Muhammad Husayn Tabātabāī, *SH'IA* (English translation by Sayyid Husayn Nasr), pp. 59-63, Qum, Iran, Feb.1989. (Hereafter referred as *SHI'A*); Rizvi, vol. I, op. cit., pp. 59-68.; Momen, Moojan, op. cit., pp. 42-43, 45-47 & 61.
21. Hollister, op. cit., p. 164; Rizvi, vol. II, op. cit., p. 288.
22. Ibid.
23. Hollister, Ibid., p. 164.
24. Momen, Moojan, op. cit., pp. 79-80; Cole, op. cit., pp. 22-24.; Umar, Muhammad, op. cit., p. 196; Rizvi, vol. II, pp. 335-46, 346-47; Richard, Yann, op. cit., p. 143.
25. Momen, Moorjan, op.cit., p. 80; Hollister, op. cit., p.148; Cole, op. cit., p. 25; Umar, Muhammad, op. cit., pp. 190-92.
26. Umar, Muhammad, op. cit., p. 192.
27. Ibid., p. 193-94.
28. Ibid., p. 194
29. Ibid. pp. 194-95.
30. Abū Talib, *Tafzīhu'l Ghafilīn*; translated by W. Hoey, *A History of Āsaf ud Daula*, pp. 93-94; cf.: Hollister, op. cit., p. 157.
31. Rizvi, vol. II, p. 309-16.; In Faizabad, Bahu-Begum used to visit her nephew's ta'ziakhana at his house every year, see, *Memoirs of Faizabad* (English transltion by William Hoey), pp. 293, Govt. Press of NWP and Oudh, 1889.
32. Cole, op. cit., p. 102.
33. For details, see, Cole, op. cit., pp. 98-101; Hollister op. cit., p. 159.
34. Nasreen, Farhat (translator), *Kashful-Baghāvat*, Gorakhpur,

Introduction, p. xvi-xvii; Jones, Justin, op. cit., pp.131-32; Sufi, Waheedul Hasan, '*Mashayikh Gorakhpur*', (Urdu) pp. 96-97. Bangar Mau, Unnao, U.P. 1993. According to Montgomery Martin the Imāmbārah was built by the Shujā ud Daula see, *the History, Antiquities, Topography and Statistics of Eastern India* Vol. II, p. 347, Reprint, Cosmo Publications, Delhi, 1976. But his statement is wrong. He also writes that, "The Keeper of the Imāmbārah, Shāh Raushunali, has large endowments. He is a native Persian, now very old and exceedingly reserved towards infidels, He seldom resides in Imāmbārah, but usually supports there from 15 to 20 Fukirs, all unmarried, as he himself is. During the ten days of the Muhurrum they distribute daily from 25 to 30 mans (each 113, 9/10 lb.) of boiled rice and pulse (khichri) seasoned with butter, salt and spices and from 4 to 5 mans of sugar and molasses in sherbat.". see, ibid., p. 349.

35. Rizvi, vol. II, pp. 79, 316; Cole, op. cit., p. 102; Hollister, op. cit., pp. 158-59.
36. Abdul Halim 'Sharār', *Guzishtā Lucknow*, pp. 52-54., cf., Umar, Muhammad, op. cit., p.199, and footnote no. 362 on p. 248; Rizvi, vol. II, p. 80-81, 316; Hollister, op. cit., p. 159.
37. Rizvi, vol. II, p. 316.; Also see, Umar, Muhammad, op. cit., p. 199, and Footnote nos, 358-60. on p. 248.
38. Knighton, William, *The Private Life Of An Eastern King*, Oxford, 1921, pp. 176-191.; cf: Rizvi, vol. II, op. cit., p. 317.
39. Umar, Muhammad, op. cit., p.199 and Footnote no. 364 on p. 248.; Hollister, op. cit., p.160.
40. Hollister, op. cit., p. 160; Rizvi, vol. II, p. 330. According to Rizvi, "He also founded the zarih procession of the first Muharram. The wax zarih was installed in the Āsafi Imāmbārah and, from there, was taken in procession through Chawk to his newly built Imāmbārah. The zarih was followed by an impressive band dressed in mourning mahi-marātib (royal emblems), camels and elephants. Sherbat was freely distributed and a large crowd followed the procession. "See, ibid. .
41. Hollister, op. cit., p.160; Jones, Justin, op. cit., p. 125.
42. *Guzishtā Lucknow*, (Hindi), p. 4;"His Imambarah, Sibtainabad,——

—, is situated at the side of the road in the western part of Hazrat Gunj. It was built after his death by Wajid Ali Shah at the cost of ten lakhs of rupees. This Imambarah is bad imitation of Husaynabad——." See, the English translation by Harcourt, E.S. and Fakhir Hussain, p. 61.

43. Manzar Hussain Rizvi, *Tarikh-e-Sultan-e-Awadh*, p. 361.; Hollister op. cit., p. 162.
44. Memoirs of Faizabad, Vol. II, P. 250. Rizvi, vol. II, pp. 308-09, 331; Hollister, op. cit., p. 155.
45. Muhammad Faiz Bakhsh Kakoravi, *Tarikh-Farāh Bakhsh*, ff.231a, 253b, 306b; *Memoirs of Delhi and Faizabad*, Vol. II, p. 266., Umar, Muhammad, op. cit., p. 195; *Memories of Faizabad* (English translation by William Hoey), p. 60, The Govt. Press of N.W.P. and Oudh, Allahabad, 1889.
46. Umar, Muhammad, op. cit., p. 195; *Memories of Faizabad*, op. cit., pp. 60, 266.
47. Umar Muhamma, Ibid.
48. Ibid.
49. Ibid.
50. According to Cole, in the early 1800s some 2000 large Imāmbārahs and 6000 smaller tāziā-khanas embellished Lucknow. He also mentions some large Imāmbārahs. See, Cole, op. cit., p. 96.
51. Mrs. Ali, op. cit., p. 19 and footnote no.1 on p. 18 by W. Crooke.
52. Ibid.
53. Ibid.
54. Ibid.
55. Mrs. Ali, ibid., p. 30.
56. Ibid., p. 18.
57. Ibid., Knighton, William, *The Private life of an Eastern Queen*, p. 93.
58. Even today in Gorakhpur the Shi'as immerse their tāziās in the water of the river.
59. W. Crooke's, Footnote no. 2 on Mrs. Ali's Observations...p. 18.; According to S. A. A. Rizvi, "Timur's respect for Fatima's relic suggests that he attended mourning assemblies in Muharram, particularly after his conquest of Iraq in 795AH/1393 AD." See, S.A.A. Rizvi, vol. II. p. 296.
60. Mrs. Ali, op. cit., p. 20.; Almost seventy years later, Abdul Halim

Sharar also writes, "Majlises are addressed from a wooden pulpit with seven or eight steps that is placed on one side of a hall or room, with the audience sitting all around on an immaculate farsh. If there is a large attendance, all the space filled. When sufficient people have arrived, the orator mounts the pulpit, raises his hand and says, 'Fatiha', upon which everyone raise his hand and quietly repeats a part of the opening verse of the Qur'ān. After that the orator, if he is a hadis khwan or a vaqiakhwan, opens his book and begins to speak. If he is reciter of marsiyas he begins with the pages of his composition."See, Lucknow, *The Last Phase of an Orintal Culture*, op. cit., p. 216; Sharar, Mawlana Abdul Halim, *Guzishtā Lucknow*, (Urdu), Hindi transliteration by Mrs. Humaira Siddiqi, pp. 290-91., Lucknow, Bhuwan Vani Trust, Third Edition, 1999. (Hereafter mentioned as Humaira, Siddiqi.)

61. *Lucknow, The Last Phase of an Oriental Culture*, op. cit., p. 216; Humaira Siddiqi, op. cit., pp. 290-91.
62. Mrs. Ali., op. cit., p. 20.
63. Ibid., pp. 20-21.
64. Ibid., footnote no. 1.
65. Ibid., p. 21.
66. Ibid.
67. Ibid., p. 21-22.
68. Ibid., p. 22.
69. Ibid.
70. Ibid.
71. Cole, op. cit., p.107.
72. Ibid., p.107.; Mrs. Ali, op. cit., p. 23.
73. Ibid., Mrs. Ali, ibid.
74. Cole, op. cit., p. 107.
75. Ibid., For details, see, Sharar, Abdul Halim, *Guzishtā Lucknow* (English translation as, *Lucknow, The Last Phase of an Oriental Culture*, by Harcourt, E.S. and Hussain Fakhir) pp. 147-150.
76. Mrs. Ali, op. cit., p. 23; But according to S. A. A. Rizvi, "the public recital of *tabarrā* was not a part of Muharram rituals. Only the extremist Shi'as insisted on it." See. Rizvi, vol. II, pp. 307, 331-32.
77. Mrs. Ali, op.cit., p. 22.

78. Mrs. Ali., ibid. pp. 22-23.
79. Cole, op. cit., p. 105.
80. Mrs. Ali, op. cit., p. 30; Cole, op. cit., p. 108.
81. Cf: Umar, Muhammad, op. cit., p. 218.
82. Ibid, pp. 218-19.
83. Sweetman, J. W., Some Additional Notes on Muharram, News and Notes June 1935, p.46. cf. Hollister, op. cit., p.170
84. Mrs. Ali also writes that, "Everyone is expected, on entering the outward verandah, to leave their shoes at the threshold of the sanctuary; none but Europeans have any occasion to be reminded of this, as it is a well-known and general observance with all degrees of natives of Asia. The servants, in charge of the Imāmbārah, are responsible for the due observance of respect to the place, and when any foreigners are advancing, they are politely requested to leave their shoes outside; which must be complied with, or they cannot possibly be admitted."Mrs. Ali, op. cit., p. 27.
85. Ibid., p. 27-28.
86. Ibid., p. 24.
87. Ibid., p.24-25.
88. Ibid., p.25.
89. Ibid.
90. Ibid.
91. Ibid., p. 25-27. Also see the Elihu Jan's story. She was the maid servant of Khas Mahal (The Chief Wife of Amjad Ali Shah and mother of Wajid Ali Shah). According to her, "During this fast or festival of woe (Muharram) no tobacco or pawn (betel-nut chewed with spices and lime) is used and men and women are not to indulage in any sensual pleasures, but all ought mourn and lament with soul and body. The queen kept the Mohurrim so strictly, that she would not change her clothes those forty days, used no oil or sweet scents, pun no misee (tooth-powder) to her teeth, nor mayndee (Colouring matter like rouge) to her hands or feet and let off all her ornaments. No marriages ought to be celebrated, or contracted during the Mohurrim and in properly conducted households the men and women live separately at that time". Knighton, William, *The Private life of an Eastern Queen*, pp. 84-85,

London, 1865.

92. Ibid, p. 27.
93. Ibid., p. 29.
94. Ibid., Cole, op. cit., p. 110.
95. Cole. op. cit., p. 110.
96. Cf: Hollister, op. cit., p.174.
97. Mrs. Ali. op. cit., pp. 17-18.
98. Cole, op. cit., p. 111.
99. Mrs. Ali, op. cit., pp.17-18; Cole, ibid., p. 111.
100. Mrs. Ali., ibid., p. 32.
101. Ibid., p. 36.
102. Ibid., pp. 36-37.
103. Ibid., p. 37.
104. Ibid., pp. 37-38.
105. Ibid., p.38.
106. Ibid., p. 36.
107. Ibid., pp. 42-46.
108. Ibid., pp. 46-50.
109. Ibid., pp.51-52.
110. Ibid., p. 53.
111. Cole, op. cit., p. 113.
112. Rizvi, vol. II. p. 330.
113. Hollister op. cit., p. 177.
114. Rizvi, vol.-II. p. 330-31.
115. Hollister, op. cit., p. 174.; After 1880, perhaps in 1894 AD, Akbar Ali Khan, a former Nawabi official, brought out a new procession on 8 Rabi'-ul-awwal on the death anniversary of Imām Hasan al-'Askari' (a.s.) the eleventh Imām. The Government's condition was that the procession would be conducted in silence to avoid excessive public disturbances. It became known as the *Chup* (silent) tāzia procession. See, Jones, Justin, op. cit., p.97.
116. Cole, op. cit., pp. 113-14; In 1870s-80s, a number of ulama in Lucknow were also issuing edicts against the undue dramatization of m'atam, the parading of the 'alams of Abbas', and the belief in hāzari, the spiritual presence of the Imāms within ta'ziyas. But in 1910 AD Sharar writes that, while 'mujtahid and Shia prelates do not approve

of such innovations but popular interest in them is increasing day by day.' See, Harcourt E.S. and Fakhir Hussain, *Lucknow, The Last Phase of an Oriental Culture*, p. 217; Jones, Justin, op. cit., p. 108.

117. Faruqui Anjum Tabān, 'The coming of the revolt in Awadh: the evidence of Urdu newspapers', *Social Scientist*-26 (1998), pp. 19-20, cf.: Jones, Justin, op. cit., p. 2.
118. Veena Oldenburg, *The Making of Colonial Lucknow: 1856-1877* (Princeton, 1984) pp. 35-37. cf. Jones, Justin, op. cit., p. 2.
119. Jones, Justin, op. cit., pp. 2-3.
120. Ibid., p. 3.
121. Ibid.
122. Cf. Rizvi, vol. II., p. 331.
123. Hollister. op. cit., p.165.
124. *Lucknow, The Last Phase of an Oriental Culture* (English translation of *Guzishtā Lucknow*) op. cit., p. 216.
125. Jones, Justin, op. cit., p. 98.
126. For details of the family, see, Rizvi, Syed Najmul Raza, *The Rebel World of 1857: Eastern Uttar Pradesh*, pp. 162-64.
127. Mrs. Ali, op. cit., p. 48, Foot-note no. 3 by W. Crooke, cited from, *Ockley, History of the Saracens*, p. 418; This tradition was also followed by Royal family of Awadh during the reign of Amjad Ali Shah. For the further datails, See, Kinghton, William. *The Privali life of an Eastern Queen*, p. 94
128. Finally, after reaching the ghaut of the river, all the mourners, perform the m'atam and recite the lines of a nawha (dirge), "Albida, Aai Husayn! Albida. Zinda rahe gar to, agle Saal bhi ma'tam karenge Ham. Aai, Husayn! Albida.... ." Then, after recitation of ziyārat, tāziās are taken on the boats and are immersed in the middle of the river. Thereafter, most of the mourners return to Imāmbārah and do the 'aamaal' of 10th Muharram, under the leadership of an ālim or pesh-namāz.

128A. During the reign of Amjad Ali Shah, this tradition was existing. For details, See, Knighton, William, *The Private Life of an Eastern Queen*, p. 96.

129. In Bihar also, the Hindus serve as payak during the Muharram for a period of years, usually three to five, but sometimes for a lifetime.

These refrain salt, animal food and all the luxuries during this period. They wear small bells as girdle around the waist, have a small cone-shaped turban and carry a yak's tail (or peacock's tail or morepankhi) in their hands While they run as a sewak (servant of Imām Husayn) from one chawk to another fanning the Tāzias, whole night of the 9th Muharram. Gorakhpur is the neighboring district of Bihar. So, it may be the impact of Gorakhpur on Bihar or Bihar on Gorakhpur, I am not sure. But during the period of 1965 to 1985, I have seen hundreds of payaks in the Imāmbārahs and Imām-Chawks of Gorakhpur city. For Bihar, see, Hollister, op. cit., p. 178.

130. Ayoub, Mahmud, *Redemptive Suffering in Islam: A Study of the Devotional Aspects of 'Āshūrā' in Twelver Shī'īsm,* The Hague, Netherland, cf: D'souza, Diane, *Shia Women, Muslim Faith and Practice*, p. 2, Zubaan, an Association of Kali for Women Publications, 2012.
131. Mutahharī, Murtadā, *Āshūrā': History and Popular Legend*, A.A. Q.Q., trans. Al- Tawhid, 8, 3: 41-74.
132. Rizvi, vol. II, p. 347.
133. Ibid.
134. Hollister, op. cit., p. 183.
135. Jones, Justin, op. cit., p. 10.
136. Cole, op. cit., pp. 51-52.; Rizvi, vol. II, pp. 116-17.; Umar, Muhammad, op. cit., p. 219.
137. Rizvi, S. N. R., *Zamindars and Revenue Farmers of Eastern Uttar Pradesh*, p.138-39. New Delhi, 2004.
138. Rizvi, vol. II, pp. 127-28.
139. Thomson, J., *Report of the Collector of Azim Gurh on the Settlement of the Ceded Portion of the district, commonly called Chakla Azimgurh*, para, Agra, 12, page. 5, 16 Dec. 1837.
140. Reid, J. R., *Report on the District of Azamgarh*, compiled in connection with the completion of the Sixth Settlement, pp. 68-69, 70, 79, Allāhabad, 1877.
141. Khan, Dr. Alauddin, "Zila Azamgarh Mein Azādāri ki Rawayat" in *Raah-e Islam*, pp. 49-66, Issue no. 203-204, January to June 2007, Chief Editor: Muhammad Husayn Muzaffari, Khana Farhang Jamhoori

Islami, Iran,18, Tilak Marg, New Delhi

142. Vaughan, J., *Report on the Settlement Operations in Parganas, Sikandarpur and Bhadaon, District Azamgarh for 1875-1879*, pp. 7-8, Para 35-f. Allāhabad, 1880. My personal experience of village Koth during the Muharram. This village is situated to the south-west, near about three miles away from Sikandarpur.

Conclusion

After the death of Prophet Muhammad, the Muslim community divided into two groups on the issue of the successor or Caliph. In the meeting at Saqifā, after some deliberation, Abū Bakr was unanimously declared as the Caliph of the Muslims. But Hazrat Ali and his close associates were not present there. They were occupied with the funeral of Prophet Muhammad Later, they disagreed with the decision. Their belief was that Hazrat Ali is the successor of Prophet Muhammad because he is selected and nominated by God. Prophet Muhammad had already declared him as his successor during his last pilgrimage (Haj) at the place of Ghadir-i-Khum. Therefore, the decision taken at Saqifā had no value. When Hazrat Umar was declared the Caliph, the numbers of dissenters increased and during the Caliphate of Uthman, a confrontation started between both the groups. After the murder of Uthman, no one challenged Hazrat Ali and he was accepted by the Muslim community as the Caliph. Later, Muawiyya challenged his caliphate, fought against him and after his murder through a conspiracy, he forced Imām Hasan, the son and successor of Hazrat Ali, to abdicate the post of Caliph or Imām through a treaty. Muawiyya's son Yazīd wanted to finish the challenge forever from Prophet's household. Therefore, on his order, Imām Husayn, and his family along with some supporters were massacred in Karbala. Only one son of Imām Husayn, who was seriously ill at that time, was not killed by the soldiers at the request of Bibi Zainab, the sister of Imām Husayn. But the enemies took him captive and he was taken away to Shaam (Seriya), to the court of Yazīd along with other captives. He suffered a lot of torture at every stage. But the Imāmate continued through his progeny. The incident of Karbala divided the Muslim community forever. The winning group called themselves as Sunnī Musalman and they were in majority. Those others who protested against this tyranny, were called Shī'ī. Thus, Shī'īsm rose as a dissenting group in opposition to the Muslim majority.

Most of the Sufi orders trace their origin from Hazrat Ali except one or two. They call themselves as Sufis. There are many similarities among the Shi'as and Sufis. But also their many behaviors are against the Islam. Therefore, Shi'as and puritan Sunnīs oppose them. However, Sufism is deeply rooted in Sunnīsm. By showing respect to the martyrs of Karbala, they tried to win over the Shi'as to their side and tried to check the expansion of Shī'īsm in India. Though the situation was opposite in Iran during the Safavid period but in India they enjoyed the protection and support of Sunnī rulers. They received cash and land-grants for their Khanqah and for the expenditure of Langar to feed the poor. Sufis gave the moral support to the rulers and used their influence for the conversion and to check the Shī'īsm.[1] Some Shi'as were also benefited by adopting the Sufism. They applied the rule of taqqaiya on themselves and in the garb of Sufism they tried to spread Shī'īsm.

After the disintegration of Mughal empire, the Shī'ī rule established in Awadh and the circumstances changed. The Usūli ulama openly attacked Sufism. Therefore, the influence of Sufis decreased on Shi'a society. With the open support of the rulers of Awadh, the Usūlī ulama successfully established the Shī'īsm as a religion and provided it an identity in Awadh.

The two Shi'a scholars played an important role in the propagation of Usūlī-fiqh in the region of Awadh and Benares during the second half of the eighteenth century and in the first half of the nineteenth century. A famous Persian poet of Sabk-hindi and mujtahid, who fled from Iran due to the rise of Sunnī ruler Nādir Shāh and took refuge in India, was Shaykh Ali Hazīn. He preferred Benares for his abode, a Hindu sacred place, dominated by the Hindu population. He lived a respectful life there, promoted Persian language and literature. Many students of the region progressed in religious education under his guidance. He produced enormous religious literature and developed the Usūlī faith in the region. He also built a rauza of Bibi Fatima for his personal prayer and put the foundation of remembering the family of *Ahl-i-bayt*. He did all the above-mentioned deeds without annoying the Hindu or Sunnī-majority. In practice he followed the theory of co-existence, in practice.

The second scholar and the first Shi'a mujtahid of Awadh, was Sayyid Dildār Ali Ghufran Ma'ab. He took confrontation with Akhbārīs and with the support of Nawab Āsaf-ud Daulah and his Deputy, Nawab Hasan Riza Khan established the congregational Friday prayers in Lucknow, the capital of Awadh. He eroded the Akhbārīs and attacked on Sufism and declared them najis. His followers used to abuse the Sufis in public. He destroyed the influence of Sufis on Shī'īs to a large extent. His tirade against Sufis continued after his death. He set a pattern for commemorating the Muharram and brought many changes in the prevailing customs of nikah, talaq and burial according to Shī'ī laws. Mawlana also responded to Shāh Abdul Aziz Dehlawi by writing rebuttal of many chapters of *Tuhfa-i-Isnā-Ashariya*. He did great services to the Shi'a community, not only of Awadh but also all-over India.

Stress on 'Ilm' in Shī'īsm is much higher in comparison to others. The Shi'as were guided by their Imāms before the occultation. The authority of Imām was measured by the 'Ilm' (divinely bestowed knowledge) that the Imām had reportedly inherited from the Prophet. The Shi'a also maintain that the 'Ilm' of an Imām is transmitted in a linked chain to all subsequent Imāms. After occultation, this direct chain of knowledge broke down but the naibs of the Imām guided their followers and one of them, Shaykh at-Taifa established 'Hawzā al-ilmiyya', a Shī'ī madrasa in Baghdad This development shows that how much the leader of the age was cautious about the education of the community. Development of Usūlī fiqh on the theory of syllogism also shows that the education should be based on reasoning and not on the traditional knowledge. In the state of Shi'a Awadh, the rulers did not pay the attention towards the religious education. The only Shī'ī madrasa was established by King Amjad Ali Shāh in 1843 AD which was closed during the rebellion of 1857. But there was need of Shi'a madrasās for the society. Shi'a scholars felt this need and tried to establish the madrasa. Abbū Sahib was the first, who established the *madrasa i- imāniyya* in 1872. But this madrasa was closed very soon and he was so much disappointed that he thought to settle in Najaf or some other place of Iraq. However, after sometime, he changed his mind and again founded another madrasa named, the *Madrasa-i-nāzimiyya*, and then, with the help of other Shī'ī ulama, 'Sultan al madāris' in Lucknow was establshed. After sometime, with the help of Raja Mahmūdabad and his brother, the madrasa waizin was also established. These madrasas are still, the famous Shi'a centers of Islamic education and are disseminating the knowledge. Many other organizations, like *Tanzim ul makatib*, are also active in the field of religious education.

The members of Shi'a community have attached themselves with the Prophet Muhammad and his *Ahl-i-Bayt* that they enjoy or express sorrow according to the incidents related to them. They celebrate Id-i Zehrā, Id-i Ghadīr besides the Id ul Fitr and Id uz Zuha. They celebrate birthday of Imāms, Bibi Fatima and Sāni-e Zehra. The festival of Nauroz is celebrated by them due to those incidents which are described in *Tohfat ul Imām*. They express their sorrow on the death anniversary of Imāms by organizing majlis. But Karbala episode is the most important for them. The period of ten days of commemoration of Muharram, which later extended upto forty days, is together known as ayyam-i- Azā, and has really become the synonym of Shī'īsm. It gives a message to the world to fight against the injustice and atrocities but through pious path.

Thus, the Shi'a scholarship, their educational system and the culture, that have been largely neglected, do hold a specific place in history.

Reference

1. Rizvi, Saiyid Athar Abbas, *A History of Sufism in India*, Vol. II, pp. 98, 427, New Delhi, 2002.

Select Glossary of Terms

ahal e bait	Literally, the people of the house i.e., the immediate family of Muhammad which includes besides the Prophet, Ali, Fatima, Hasan and Husayn.
akhbar	A term often used for Hadīth by Shi'as.
'alam	The standard, or crest of the standard, carried in Muharram processions.
'ālim	A scholar of Islamic knowledge.
'ashra	the first ten days of Muharram.
'āshurā	The tenth day of Muharram, upon which the death of Husayn is commemorated.
azādāri	The practice of mourning for Imām Husayn observed during Muharram.
azāāan	the call to daily prayer.
begam	A married Muslim lady of high rank
bilafasl	Without interruption, a phrase used periodically by the Shi'as to describe Ali's succession of MuhammAD
caliph (Khalifa)	The personage charged with rightful succession of the Prophet according to Sunnī Islam.
dargah	Shrine, tomb of a saint.
dars-i-Khārij	The course of a study to become a mujtahid.
duldul	Effigy of the steed upon which Imām Husayn was mounted at Karbala.

fazil	Distinction, often denoting the degree gained from education within a Madrasa.
fiqh	The science of Islamic jurisprudence.
firqa	Faction, sect.
hadīs	An oral report transmitted by generations of Muslim scholars going back to the Prophet or the Imāms; compliments the Qur'ān as a source of Islamic law.
hajj	Pilgrimage, as prescribed in Islam.
hauza	Circle of scholars, denoting a place of learning.
hazrat	Muslim notables.
hujjat	Proof, a high position in the hierarchy of mujtahids.
ijāzā	Certificate, authorizing its recipient to exercise ijtihād.
ijtihād	The application of reasoned effort to the derivation of a ruling from the scriptural text, sometimes involving a limited sort of syllogism or analogy. A jurisprudential method, accepted by Usūlīs from the fourteenth century.
imām	One of the descendants and legitimate successor of the Prophet, beginning with Ali and ending with the twelfth Imām, the personages at the doctrinal and devotional heart of Shī'īsm.
imāmbārah	A place set apart for the holding of Majlis for remembering the imāms.
isnā 'ashari	Literally "twelver", those Shi'as who recognize only twelve Imāms, the last of whom is in great occultation.
jihad	War for the shake of God and Islam. In Shī'īsm such a war was classically believed to be, legitimately led only by an Imām, and after the last Imām disappeared the duty to wage it, lapsed, except in self defence.

jum'ah	Friday congregational prayers.
kalam	Dialectical theology.
karbala	A piece of ground symbolic of the land in Iraq upon which Imām Husayn was martyred, where ta'ziyas are buried during Muharram.
kashf	Mystical inspiration from God.
khanqah	A building where Sufis gathered for chanting and meditation sessions.
khirqah	The patched cloak bestowed upon a Sufi adapt by his master upon his initiation into a Sufi order.
khums	A Muslim religious tax of 20% on certain kinds of income, which among Shī'īs, is distributed to poor Sayyids. Usūlīs held that half of the income from this tax should go to religious jurisprudents.
khutba	The sermon delivered together with Friday prayers and on other occasions.
madad-i ma'sh	Land grants to Muslim religious functionaries, scholars and mystics for their support.
madrasah	Seminary or Muslim institution for higher studies.
majlis	A mourning assembly held during Muharram or in commemoration of the Imāms.
mantiq	The discipline of logic.
marja'-i-taqlid	A jurisprudent or mujtahid.
marsiya	Shī'ī elegiac poetry, used in Muharram majlis.
mashk	A leather bag for carrying water, a replica of the empty and dry water bag of Husayn's daughter Sakeena at Karbala.
masjid	Mosque.
ma'sum	Sinless, an attribute in Shī'īsm of Prophet and the Imāms.
ma'tam	Self-flagellation in mourning for the Imāms.

mawlana	Designation of religious distinction and authority.
maulvi	Religious speaker or preacher, learned man.
mehdi or Mahdi	In Shī'īsm, the twelfth or last Imām who is in great occultation.
menhdi	The procession during Muharram commemorating the death of Qasim, the son of Imām Hasan.
mimber	A stairway-like pulpit from which preachers speak in the mosque or Imāmbārah.
mominin	Followers, often used in juxtaposition with the leading sadat of Shī'īsm.
mu'afidar	A landholder of revenue-free grant.
muharram	The first month of the Muslim calender, during which the martyrdom of Imām Husayn and other personages is commemorated.
mujtahid	A jurisprudent who practices ijtihād or legal reasoning.
mutwalli	The trustee of a waqf or religious institution.
najis	In Shī'ī law, something ritually impure or polluted.
qasba	A small town or large village.
qiyas	Analogy or deduction by analogy.
risālā	Treatise or tract.
roza	fast.
sadat	See, Sayyid.
sanad	A certificate or document.
sayyid	A descendant of Prophet Muhammad
soz	Lyrical dirge for Imām Husayn.
sufism	A mystical side of Islam whose followers are called Sufis.
sunna	The established practice of the Prophet and his immediate successors, which has the force of law in Islam.
sunnī Islam	The majority branch who recognizes four pious

	successors or caliphs of Prophet Muhammad
ta'aluqdar	A large rural landholder in Awadh.
tabarra	Comminations or curses against the first three caliphswhom Shi'as consider as usurpers of Hazrat Ali's rights.
tafsir	A commentary.
taqiyyā	Dissimulation or the concealing the religious beliefs.
tasawwuf	Islamic mysticism or the principles of Sufism
tauhid	The oneness of God.
tawa'if	Prostitute.
tawalla	Praying and blessing of the Prophet and the Twelve Imāms whom Shī'īs believe to be his legitimate successors.
tazia	Miniatures of the tombs of Husayn carried in processions or placed in Imāmbārah or chawk.
ulama	Muslim religious scholars.
usūlī	Who believe in ijtihād or reasoning in jurisprudence.
wahabi	A reformist, who opposes all those customs which undermine the oneness of God.
wahdat al-wujud	The doctrine adhered by Muslim mystics or Sufis, that existence is ultimately monistic in nature rather than plural. Opponents of the doctrine branded it pantheistic.
waiz	Preacher.
wujub-i 'ayni'	A religious duty incumbent on each believer.
wujub -i takhiyri	An obligation of preference.
wajd	A state of mystical ecstacy.
waqf	A religious endowment.
wazir	The Prime Minister.
zakat	A Muslim religious tax for the poors.
zakir	A preacher who renders the significances of the Imām in majlises during the Muharram or any

	time.
zamindar	Landlord or owner of the land during British period.
zann	In jurisprudence, a considered opinion: differentiated from certain knowledge based on conclusive evidence.
zarih	An imitation of the grave of an Imām.
ziyarat	Religious visitation or pilgrimage.
zuhr	Noon prayer

Select Bibliography

I. Unpublished Sources

A. National Archives, New Delhi.

1. archive.org>internet.dli-201580932

B. Arabic

1. Ali Akhbārī, Sayyid Fidā: *Risālah fī radd hujjat al-ijma,* Lucknow Nasiriyyah Library, Usul al Fiqh Shi'ah, MS. 31.
2. Astarābādī, Muhammad Amīn: *Al-fawāid al-Madanniyyah,* Lucknow. Nasiriyyah Library, Usul al-Fiqh Shi'ah, MS. 49.
3. Nasīrābadī, Sayyid Dildār Ali: *Imād al-Islam fī 'ilm al- kalām,* 5 volumes, Lucknow, Nasiriyyah Library, MSS 163-167 —: *Ithārat al-ahzān,* Patna. Khudabakhsh Oriental Public Library, MS H.L. 2292. —: *Risālah fī ahkām al-aradīn,* Rampur Raza Library, Fiqh, MS. 2842. ———: *Ash-shihāb ath-thāqib,* (I.O.L.), MS. 2182.
4. Shushtari, Nurullah: *Al-lum'ah fī tahqīq salāt al-jum'ah,* Lucknow. Nasiriyyah Library, Fiqh Shi'ah, MS.187.

C. Persian

1. *Ā'inah-i haqq-namā,* Lucknow, Nasiriyyah Library, Rijal Shi'ah, MS. No. 1.
2. Bihbahani, Aqā Ahmad: *Mir'at al-ahvāl-i Jahān-numā,*

Khudabakhsh Oriental Public Library, Bankipur (Patna). Buhar Collection, MS. No. 96 ———: *Tanbīh al – ghāfilīn*, Lucknow, Nasiriyyah Library, Usul al-Fiqh Shi'ah, MS. No. 10.

3. Illahabadi, Khayru'd-Din Muhammad: *Tuhfāh-i Tazāh*, Khudabakhsh Oriental Public Library, Bankipur (Patna), MS. No. 160 ———: *Tadhkirt al -Ulama*, Calcutta, Asiatic Society Library, MS. No. 203.
4. Khan, Ghulam Husayn: *Tārikh- i- Benaras*, Khudabakhsh Oriental Public Library Bankipur (Patna), MS. No. 159.
5. Khan, Subhān Ali (Editor): *Balwand-nāmāh*, National Archives, New Delhi, MS. No. 2210.
6. Nasīrābadī, Sayyid Dildār Ali: *Ris alah dar radd-i mazhab-I sufiyyah*, Lucknow, Nasiriyyah Library, Kalam Shi'ah, MS. No.111. ———: *Najat as-sa'ilin*, MS. No. 256, Fiqh Shi'ah, Nasiriyyah Library, Lucknow ——: *Sharh-i Hadiqat al-muttaqin, bab-i swam*, MS..No-40, Tagore Library, Lucknow University, Lucknow.
7. Zaidi, Mawlvi Noor ud-din: *Tazallī-i-Noor*. (Rampur, MS.)

II. **Published Sources**.

A. Digital Library India (Jai Gyan)

B. Arabic

1. *Qur'ān*
2. Nasīrābadī, Sayyid Dildār Ali:

   –*Asās al-usūl*, Lucknow: Matba'ah-i' Muhammadi, 1264 Hijri/ 1848 AD

   –*Mir'at al-uqūl fī 'ilm al-usūl*, 3 volumes. Lucknow: Matba' 'Imād al Islam, 1320 Hijri/1902 AD

   – *Muntahā al afkār*, Lucknow, Matba' Taswir al-Alam, 1330 Hijri/1912 AD

C. Persian

1. Anonymous: *Tārīkh -i- Farrukhsiyar*, edited by Syed Hasan Askari, Patna, 1980.
2. Bilgrami, Ghulam Ali Azad:
   – *Khizānāh-i 'amīrah*, Naval Kishor Press, Kanpur, 1871.
   – *Ma'āthir al-Kirām*, volume. I, Agra, 1910.
   – *Ma'āthir al-Kirām*, volume. II., Lahore, 1913.
3. Bilgrami, Murtaza Husayn: *Hadīqat al-Aqālim*, MS, Regional Archives, Allahabad.
4. Dihlavi, Shah 'Abdu'l 'Aziz [Ghulam Halim]: *'Tuhfah-'i isna Ashariyyah*, Calcutta, 1824 AD.
5. Isfahani, Abū Talib Khan: *Tafdīh al-Ghāfilīn*, edited by Abid Raza, Bedar, Rampur, 1965.
6. Kashmiri, Muhammad Ali: *Nujūm as-samā* fī tarajim al-'ulama', Lucknow, 1884-85.
7. Kashmiri, Muhammad Mīhdī Lakhnawi: *Nujūm as-Samā*: takmilah, Qum,1977.
8. Khan, Ghulam Husayn: *Tārīkh- i Banāras'*, Khudabakhsh Qriental Public Library, Bankipur, Patna, MS. No.159.
9. Naqvi, Ghulam 'Ali: *Imād as-Sa'ādat'*, Naval Kishor Press, Lucknow,1897.
10. Nasīrābadī, Sayyid Dildār Ali:
    – *Dhu'l -Fiqār*, Ludhiana, 1864-65.
    – *Savārim-i Ilāhiyy āt va tvaHusām al-Islam*, Calcutta, 1803.
    – *Nasīrābadī, Sayyid Muhammad: Risālah-i taqiyyah*, Lucknow, no date.
11. Prasad, Kunwar Durga: *Bustān-i Awadh*, Lucknow, 1891.
12. Safavi, Shah Husayn: *Tazkīrāt al-Muhaqqīqīn*, Lucknow.
13. Shah, Syed Taqui Wāhidī Saleh Ali: *'Az Kue Sufiyān Ta Hūzūr-e Ārifān'*, Qum. (Iran).
14. Shirvani, *Zaynu'l 'Ābidīn: Bustān as-Siyāhāh*, Tehran, 1897.
15. Shushtari, Nurullah: *'Majlis al- mu'minīn'*, 2 volumes., Tehran, 1897.

16. Tabātabāī, Ghulam Husayn Khan: 'Siyar al- Mutakhkhīrīn', Two volumes, Calcutta, 1832-33.

D. Urdu

1. Ali, Sarvat (Dr.), *Tārīkh -e Āsifī* (translation of Tafzīh ul Ghāfilīn of Abū Talib Londoni), Delhi,1968.
2. Azad, Muhammad, *'Ali: Aab -i-Hayāt'*, Allahabad, Ram Narainlal, Beni Madho. 1980.
   –*Nigāristāni-Fāras*, Lahore, matba Kareemia Press,1922.
3. Aziz, Shah Abdul: *Risāla Ta'ziādarī*, Aligarh.
4. Banarasi, Munsi Ghulam Husayn Khan 'Āfāq', *'Risālā-i Tazkirāh-i- Hāzīn'*, Lucknow, 1917.
5. Chakbast, Brij Narain: *Subah-e Watan*, Second Edition, Allahabad, 1927.
6. Farrukhabadi, Munshi Jawala Prasad "Akhtar", *Anwār ul Sa'ādat*, 1296 Hijri/1878 AD.
7. Hanswi, Sayyid Sibt ul-Hasan, *Azādārī ki Tārīkh*, Lucknow, 1941.
8. Hasan, Mawlana Saiyyid Jafar: *Aqāid-ul-Shi'a.*
9. Hasan, Sayyid Mazahar: *Tārīkh -i-Banāras.* vol. I, 1916 and vol. II., 1926.
10. Hasan, Sufi Waheed al, *Mashā'ikh -i Gorakhpur*, Bangarmau, Unnao,1993.
11. Husayn, Azizuddin S. M., *Qāzī Saiyid Nūrūllah Shustrī,* (1542-1610), New Delhi, 2001.
12. Husayn, Sayyid Murtazā, *'Matlā '-i- Anwār, Karachi,* Khurasan Islamic Research Centre,1981.
13. Husayn, Safdar (Dr.), *Lakhna'u ki Tahzībī Mirās*, Lahore, Bargah- i Adab, 1975.
14. Jaisi, Mustafa Husayn Asif [Editor]:
   – *Khāndān-i-ijtihād number* (Lucknow, 2005). Jaisi, Mawlana Mustafa Husayn Naqvī [Editor]: *Hindustan mein Shi'at ki Tarikh*, 2. vols., Wīlayat Publication, New Delhi, 2018.
   – *Khāndan Ijtāhād*, Vol. I, 2018; vol. II, 2018; vol. III 2019 and

vol. IV, 2019. Wilayat Publication, New Delhi.

– *Majaddid Shariat*, Ghufra'n Ma'ab aur Unke Paanch Mujtahīd Farzand. Feb. 2018. [Note: Above mentioned Jaisi's volumes arrived after this book was completed for Press.

15. Jan, Mirzā, *Hadīqah-i Shuhadā*, 1855.
16. Lakhna'ui, Sayyid Baqar Shams, *Hindustān mein Shi'at kā Tārikh aur Shī'ī Aqāid kā Tafsīl.*
17. Mashhadi, Kamalu'd-Din Haydar Husayni:
    – *Qaiser at-tawārīkh*, Nawal Kishor, Lucknow, 1896.
    – *Sawānihāt-i salātin-i Awadh*, Nawal Kishor, Lucknow, 1896.
18. Nadvi, Saiyyid Muhammad Ibrahim (translator): *Tārīkh-Tabrī'*, Devband, U.P., 1983.
19. Najmul Ghani, *Tarikh - i- Awadh*, 5-volumes., Lucknow, 1919.
20. Naqvī, Mawlana Syed Manzoor Hussain, *Tohfā -Tul -Awām* (Jadeed).
21. Naqvi, Sayyid Zafar, (Translator), *Usūl-i-Kāfi* of Shaykh Abu Jafar Muhammad Kulayni, as *'ASHAFI'*, Nazimabad, Karachi-2.
22. Naqvi, Sibte Muhammad, *Amjad 'Ali Shāh*, Naadan Mahal, Lucknow, 1976.
23. Qatil, Mirzā Muhammad Hasan [Dr. Muhammad Umar, translator in Urdu], *Haft Tamāshā*, Maktaba Burhan, Urdu Baazār, Delhi, 1968.
24. Rizvi, Sayyid Manzar Husayn, *Tārīkh -i-Sultān-i-Awadh.*
25. Rizvi, Sayyid Muhammad Raza, *Farishtgān-i Jahān*, {Lakhna'u; Baqar- ulum Foundation. 2003}
26. Rizvi, Sayyid Saee Akhtar, *Khurshīd Khāwar*, 2nd Edition, Gopalpur (Bihar), 2002, Maruf Publication.
27. Sarshar, Pandit Ratan Nath, *Fasānā -i- Āzād*, vol. I, Lucknow, 1949.
28. Sharar, Abdul Halim, *Guzishta Lucknow* or *Mashrīq Ke Tamaddun Ka Akhiri Namūnā*, Lucknow, 1974, Nasim Book Depot.
29. Shāyān, Tota Ram, *Tawārīkh-i Nādir al-asr*, Nawal Kishor,

Lucknow, 1863.

30. Tamanna, Munshi Ram Sahay:
 –*Afzal at-Tawārīkh*, Lucknow, 1879.
 –*Ahsan at-Tawārīkh*, Lucknow, 1876.
31. Tasadduk Husayn, Shaykh: *Begumat e-Awadh'*, Kitab Nagar, Deen Dayal Road, Lucknow,1964.

E. English Translations from Asian Languages Sources

1. Abu'l Fazal Allami, *The Āin-i-Akbarī*, [Trans. Blochmann, vol. I, Reprint, 1989, New Delhi.]
2. Bada'uni, Abdul Qadir, *Muntakhab-ut-Tawārikh*, [Trans. Ranking, vol. I, Lowe, W.H., vol-II, Haig, W., vol-III.]
3. Barani, Ziaud din:
 –*Tarikh -i- Firuzshāhī*. (Urdu translation is available)
 – *Fatawā-i-Firuz Shāhī*. [Trans. Mohd. Habib & Dr. Mrs. Afsar Umar Salim Khan, Allahabad]
4. Behbahānī, Ahmad, *Mir'at ul-Ahwāl-i-Jahān 'Numā'*. [Trans., Prof. A.F. Haider, Patna, 1996.].
5. Fayzbakhsh, Muhammad, *Tarikh Farāhbakhsh*, 2 volumes. [Trans. Hoey, W. Allahabad,1888-89] translated as *Memoirs of Delhi Faizabad.*
6. Ferishta, Abul Qasim Hindu Shah, *Tarikh - i- Ferishtā* [Trans. John Briggs, 4 volumes, Calcutta,1909-10], translated as, *History of the Rise of Muhammadan Power in India.*
7. Firdausi, *The Shāh-Nāmā of Firdausi* [Trans. Alexander Rogers, New Delhi, 1989.]
8. Hazīn Gilani, Shaykh Muhammad Ali, *The Life of Shaykh Mohammed Ali Hazīn written by Himself*; Translated from two Persian Manuscripts. [Trans. Belfour, F.C. London,1830.]
9. Ilahabadi, Khayrud-din Muhammad:
 – *Tazkirāt-ul- Ulama.* [Ed. & Trans. Muhammad Sanaullah, Calcutta,1934.] translated as, *A Memoir of the Learned Men of Jaunpur.*

–*Tuhfā-i- Tāzāh* [Trans. Curven, F. Allahabad,1875].

10. Isfahani, Abū Talib, *Tafzihu lGhāfilin* [Trans. Hoey, W., Reprint, Lucknow, 1971], translated as, *History of Asafu'd Dawlah Nawab vizier of Oudh.*
11. Ali, Ebrahimi (Trans.) *History of Caliphs (From the death of the Messenger(s) to the decline of the Umayyad Dynasty*, vol. II, Qum, 2003]
12. Jahangir, *Tuzuk-i-Jahāngīrī* [Trans. Rogers and Bevridge, New Delhi,1978].
13. Khafi Khan, Muhammad Hashim, *Muntakhab al Lubāb* [Trans. S. Moinul Haq, Karachi,1975].
14. Lakhnawi, Shiv Das, *Shāhnāmā Munawwar Kalām* [Trans. Syed Hasan Askari, Patna, 1980.]
15. Minhaj us Siraj, *Tabqāt-i-Nāsīrī.* [Trans. Raverty H. G., Reprint, New Delhi, 1970].
16. Mufid, Shaykh al, *Kitāb al- Irsh ad* [Trans. Howard, I.K.A., Qum]
17. Rabit Ametavi, Abdul Ahad, *Vaqāi-i-Dilpazir* [Trans. Ahmad, Muhammad Taqī, Allahabad, 1938], translated as, *Bādshāh-Begam.*
18. Tabātabāī, Sayyid Ghulam Husayn, *Siyar al-Mutākhkhīrīn*, [Trans. M. Hajji Mustapha, Raymond, 4 volumes, Calcutta, 1902.]
19. Yusuf Ali Khan bin Ghulam Ali Khan, *Tarikh-i-Bangālā-Mahābat Jangi* [Trans.Sir Jadunath Sarkar, Calcutta, 1952]

F. Hindi

1. Abbasi, Noor Nabi (translator), Abdul Halim Sharar, *Purana Lucknow*, New Delhi,1971, National Book Trust.
2. Ahmad, Sayyid Iqbal, *Sharqi Rajya Jaunpur ka Itihas*, Jaunpur, 1968.
3. Chandra, Moti, *Kashi ka Itihas*, 3rd Edition, Varanasi, 2003.
4. Lakhnawi, Ali Imām Zaidi 'Gauhar' (Transator): *Shahaan -e Awadh aur Shi'at of Allama Farogh Kazmi*, Delhi,1999.

5. Naqvī, Mujtahid Mawlana Sayyid 'Ali Naqi, *Shia Itihas ki Sanchhipt Rooprekha*, (Translated by Sayid Muhibb ut Hasan Rezvo 2nd. Edition, Imamia Mission, Aligarh, 1413AH/ 1992 AD.
6. Rizvi, Saiyid Athar Abbas, *Aadi Turk kalin Bharat*, Aligarh, 1956.
7. Rizvi, Syed Najmul Raza, *Attharahvi Sadike Zamindar*, Delhi, Peoples Publishing House, 1988.
8. Siddiqi, Mrs. Humaira (Transliterator), *Ghuzesht e Lucknow*, (Original author: Mawlana Abdul Halim Sharar.), 3rd. Edition, Bhuwan Vani Trust, Lucknow, 1999.
9. Siddiqi, Shakeel, *Purana Lucknow*, Lucknow, 2012, Bharat Book Centre.
10. Umar, Prof. Muhammad: '*Sanskritike Saat Adhyay, Qatil krit Haft Tamasha ka Hindi Anuwad*', Kitab Ghar, Aligarh, 1990.

G. English: Dictionaries, Encyclopaedias, Gazeteers and Settlement Reports

1. Eliade, Mircea (Editor in Chief), *The Encyclopedia of Religion*, MacMillan Publishers, London.
2. Hastings, James (Editor), *Encyclopaedia of Religion and Ethics*, Edinburg, 1914.
3. Hughes, Thomas Patrick, *Dictionary of Islam*, Reprint, New Delhi,1995.
4. Nevil, H.R., *District Gazetteers of the United Provinces of Agra and Oudh*':
   (1) *Volume XXXVII*: Lucknow (Allahabad, 1904.)
   (2) *Volume XXIX*: Ghazipur (Allahabad, 1909.)
   (3) *Volume XXXI*: Gorakhpur (Allahabad, 1909.)
   (4) *Volume XXVIII*: Jaunpur (Allahabad, 1908.)
   (5) *Volume XXVI*: Benaras (Allahabad, 1909.)
   (6) *Volume XXX*: Balia (Allahabad, 1907.)
   (7) *Volume XXXII*: Basti (Allahabad, 1907.)

5. Reid, J.R.: *Report on the District of Azamgarh, compiled in connection with the completion of the Sixth Settlement*, Government Press, Allahabad, 1877.
6. Taher, Mohamed: *Encyclopaedic Survey of Islamic Culture*, New Delhi,1997.
7. Thomson, J.: *Report of the Collector of Azimgurh on the Settlement of the Ceded Portion of the District, commonly called, chakla Azimgurh*, December,1837.
8. Vaughan, J.: *Report on the Settlement Operations in Parganas Sikandarpur and Bhadaon, District Azamgarh for 1874-79*, Government Press, Allahabad, 1880.
9. Yarshter, Ehsan (Editor): *Encyclopaedia Iranica*, Tehran, 1982.

H. Accounts of Foreign Travellers

1. Bernier, Francois (translated by Archibald Constable and Edited by V.A. Smith): *Travels in Mughal Empire* (1656-1668), Second Revised Edition, London.
2. Heber, Reginald: *Narrative of a Journey through the Upper Provinces of India from Calcutta to Bombay*, 1824 to 1825, 2 vols. Philadelphia: Carey, Lea and Carey, 1826.
3. Manucci, Niccolo (translated by William Irvine): *Storia Do Mogor*, Vol. II, Calcutta, 1965-66.
4. Monrique, Sebastian: *Travels of Sebastian Monrique*, published by Hakluyyt Society, London,1928.
5. Monserrate, S.J. (Commentarius translation by J.S. Hoyland and annotated by S.N. Banerjee.): *The Commentary of Father Monserrate, S.J. on his journey to the Court of Akbar*, 1992.
6. Roe, Thomas (Edited by William Foster): *The Embassy of Sir Thomas Roe (1615-1619)*, London 1926.
7. Sleeman, W.H.: *A Journey through the Kingdom of Oude in 1849-1850*, 2 volumes, London, Richard Bentley, 1858.
8. Tavernier, Baptiste Jean, *Travels in India*, (translated by B. Ball and Edited by W. Crooke), Second Revised Edition, published by MacMillan and Company, London,1925.

9. Terry Edward: *A Voyage to East India*, published by J. Wilke, London, M.D.C.C.L XXVII.
10. Valentia, George, Viscount, *Voyages and Travels to India, Ceylon, the Red Sea, Abyssinia and Egypt in the year 1802-1806*, Vol. I, London 1809.

I. Modern Works

1. Ahmad, Muhammad Taqi: *Tarikh Badshah Begam*, Allahabad, 1938. Digital Library India; Jai Gyan, item 2015.81764; Reprint, New Delhi, 1977.
2. Ahmad, Shafi: *Two Kings of Awadh*, P.C. Dwadash Shreni Aligarh,1971.
3. Alam, Muzaffar: *The Language of Political Islam in India*, c 1200-1800, Permanent Black, Rani Khet, 2004.
4. Ali, Mrs. Meer Hassan, '*Observations on the Mussulmauns of India, Descriptive of Their Manners, Customs, Habits and Religious Opinions, Made during A Twelve Years' Residence, in their Immediate Society*. (Second Edition, Edited with Notes and, An Introduction by W. Crooke, Late of the I.C.S.), Deep Publications, Delhi, 1975.
5. Ali, Syed Ameer, *The Spirit of Islam*, London, Christopher, 1946.
6. Ansari, I.H. and Qureshi, H.A. *Tohfa-i-Taza of Fakhir Khairuddin and Minutes of Charges of Warren Hastings*, New Royal Book Company, Lucknow, 2009.
7. Ansari, Mohammad Azhar, *European Travellers under the Mughals* (1580-1627), Idaarah-i-Adabiyat-i-Delhi, 1975.
8. Arjomand, Sayyid Saeed: Imām Reza (a.s.), *The Eighth Imām of the Shī'īte, Fourth Edition, Islamic Research Foundation of Astan Quds Razavi'*, Mashhad 2004.
9. Arjomand, Syed Ameer: *The Shadow of God and the Hidden Imām*, Chicago University Press, Chicago,1984.
10. Azhar, Mirza Ali, *King Wajid Ali of Awadh*, Royal Book Company, Karachi, 1982.

11. Bilgrami, S.J.R: *Husayn and Nation Building*, Imamiya, Mission, Lucknow, 1970.
12. Cole, J.R.I: *Roots of North Indian Shī'īsm in Iran and Iraq, Religion and State in Awadh, 1722-1859*. OUP. Delhi, 1989.
13. D'Souza, Diane: *Shia Women, Muslim Faith and Practice*, Zubaan, New Delhi, 2012.
14. Desai, Ziyaud-Din Abdul Hayy: *Centres of Islamic Learning in India*, Publication Division, Ministry of Information and Broadcasting, Govt. of India, New Delhi, 1978.
15. Donaldson, Dwight M: *The Shī'īte Religion: A History of Islam in Persia and Irak*, Luzac & Company, London, 1933.
16. Dudney, Arthur Dale: *A Desire for Meaning: Khan-i-Arzu's Philology and the Place of India in the Eighteenth-Century Persianate World*, Columbia University, 2013.
17. Dudney, Arthur: Dale: *Pages from a Forgotten History*, Hay House Delhi, India, 2015.
18. Elphinstone 'Hon. Mount Stuart: *An Account of the Kingdom of Caubul*, London, 1893.
19. Engineer, A. A: *Origin and Development of Islam*, Orient Longman, New Delhi,1980.
20. Faruqi, Shamsur Rahman: *A Stranger in the City: The Poetics of Sabk-I Hindi*, Department of Languages and Cultures of Asia, University of Wisconsin-Medison, 2004.
21. Fisher, Michael, H., *A Clash of Cultures: Awadh, The British, And The Mughals*, Manhor Publishers, New Delhi, 1987.
22. Fischer, Michael M.J.: *Iran, From Religious Dispute to Revolution*, Harvard University Press, London, 1980.
23. Harcourt, E.S. and Fakhir Hussain: *Lucknow, The Last Phase of an Oriental Culture*, Abdul Halim Sharar, Oxford University Press, 1999.
24. Hasan, Amir: *Palace Culture of Lucknow*, B.R. Publishing Corporation, Delhi, 1983.
25. Hasnain, Nadeem: *MohurrumAzadaari*, New Royal Company, Lucknow, 2020.

26. Hasnain, Nadeem: *Shia Muslims of India, Religion, Society and Culture,* New Royal Book Company, Lucknow, 2020.
27. Hasnain, Nadim & Husayn Abrar: *Shias & Shia Islam in India,* Harnam Publications, Ansari Road, New Delhi,1988.
28. Hitti, Philip K.; *History of the Arabs, From the Earliest Times to the Present,* Tenth Edition, Reprint, Macmillan, London, 1977.
29. Hollister, John Norman: *The Shi'a of India,* Luzac & Co. London,1953; Second Edition, Oriental Books Reprint Corporation New Delhi , 1979.
30. Husayn, S.K.: *Social Institutions of Shia Muslims,* Classical Publishing Company, New Delhi, 1998.
31. Husayn, S.M. Akbar: *Islam in the Light of Shiaism,* Lucknow, 1955.
32. Irwin, H.C: *The Garden of India; Or Chapters on Oudh History and Affairs,* Paper Back, Hance, U.S.A. 2020
33. Jafri, S. Husayn M.: *The Origins and Early Development of Shia Islam',* Second Eedition, Qum (Iran), 1989.
34. Jones, Justin: *Shi'a Islam in Colonial India,* Cambridge University Press, New Delhi, 2012.
35. Khatak, Sarfaraz Khan: *Shaykh Muhammad Ali Hazīn : His Life, Times and Works,* Lahore, Sh. Mohammad Ashraf, 1944.
36. Khurseed, M.H: *Husayn—The Leader of Entire Humanity,* Lucknow, 1941.
37. Kia, Mana: *Persianiate Selves: Memories of Place and Origin Before Nationalism,* Stanford, California, 2020.
38. Knighton, William: *The Private Life of an Eastern King,* Oxford, 1921. *The Private Life of an Eastern Queen,* London, 1865.
39. Malik, Zahirud din: *The Reign of Muhammad Shah,* Asia Publishing House, Bombay, 1977.
40. Mirza, Agha Muhammad Sultan: *The Caliphate, Its Conception And Consequence,* Idaara-e Alīa-Tableegh-o-Ishaat, Lucknow, 1988.
41. Momen, Moojan:
   –An Introduction To Shi'i Islam, The History and Doctrines of

Twelver Shī'īsm, Yale University Press, London,1985.

–*Shī'ī Islam, A Beginner's Guide*, Oneworld Publications, London, 2016.

42. Montgomery, Martin: *The History, Antiquities, Topography and Statistics of Eastern India*, Volume-2, First Edition, Reprint, Cosmo Publications, New Delhi, 1976.
43. Naqvi, Mawlana S. Ali Naqi: *History of Islam*, Imamia Mission (Hind), Aligarh, 2002.
44. Nasreen, Farhat (translator): *Kashful Baghaavat*, Gorakhpur,
45. Nizami, Khaliq Ahmad: *Royalty in Medieval India*, Munshiram Manoharlal Publishers Pvt.Ltd. New Delhi,1997.
46. Oldenburg, Veena Talwar: *The Making of Colonial Lucknow, 1856-1877*, Princeton University Press, Princeton,1984.
47. Radhey Shyam: *Despotism on Trial*, Agra, 1992.
48. Richard, Yann (Translated by Antonia Nevill): *Shī'īte Islam, Polity, Ideology, and Creed*, Blackwell, Publishers, Cambridge, Massachusetts, U.S.A.
49. Rizvi, Saiyid Athar Abbas:

    –*'Shah' Abd al- Aziz: Puritanism, Secterian Poleics and Jihad*, Ma'rifat Publishing House, Canberra, Australia, 1982,

    –*A Socio-Intellectual History of the Isnā Ashari Shī'īs in India*, vol. I, and vol. II, Ma'rifat Publishing House, Canberra, Australia, 1986.

    –*A History of Sufism in India*, vol. I, Munshiram Manoharlal Publishers, Pvt. Ltd., New Delhi,1978 & 2003 and vol. II, 2002.

    –*Muslim Revivalist Movements in Northern India'*, Agra University Press, 1965 and New Delhi, 1995, Edition.
50. Rizvi, Syed Najmul Raza:

    –*Zamindars and Revenue Farmers of Eastern Uttar Pradesh*, Anamika Publishers & Distributors (P.) Ltd. New Delhi, 2004.

    –*The Rebel World of Eastern Uttar Pradesh*, Kalpazā Publications, New Delhi, 2021.
51. Robinson, Francis: *The Ulama of Faranghi Mahall and Islamic Culture in South Asia'*, Permanent Black Delhi, 2001.

52. Saeed, Mian Muhammad: *The Sharqi Sultanate of Jaunpur: A Political &Cultural History*, University of Karachi, 1972.
53. Saxena, Babu Ram: *A Literary History of Urdu Literature, 1940*, Digital Library of India, Jai Gyan.
54. Sherwani, Haroon Khan: *The Bahamanis of the Deccan*, Reprint, New Delhi,1985.
55. Siddique, I.H: *Perso-Arabic Sources of Information on Life and Conditions in Sultanate of Delhi*, Delhi, 1992.
56. Srivastava, A.L:
    –*The First Two Nawabs of Awadh,* second edition, Shiv Lal Agarwala and Co. Agra, 1954.
    Shuja-ud-Daulah, 2 vols, Revised edition, Shiv Lal Agarwala and Co Agra, 1961.
57. Sykes, P. H.: *The Glory of the Shia World*, London,1910.
58. Tabātabāī, Allamah Sayyid Muhammad Husayn, (Translated by Sayyid Husayn Nasr in English): *SHI'A*, Ansariyan Publications, Qum (Iran), 1989.
59. TAKIM, Liyakat Nathani: *Shī'īsm in America*, New York University Press, New York, 2009.
60. Umar, Muhammad: *Islam in Northern India During the Eighteenth Century*, Munshiram Manohar Lal, New Delhi, 1993.
61. Yasin, Mohammad: *A Social History of Islamic India* (1605-1748), Lucknow,1958.

J. Thesis

1. Khan, Abu Ayman Md. Razawanul Haq: 'Contribution of Shaykh Ali Hazīn to Indo-Persian Prose (With Reference to Tazkirāt ul Mu'asirin and Tazkirāt ul Ahwāl)', Ph.D. Thesis, Persian Department, A.M.U., Aligarh 2011.
2. Kirmani, Noor Afshan: Ali Hazīn, A critical evaluation of His Poetic Writings', Ph.D. Thesis, Persian Department, A.M.U. Aligarh, 1986.

K. News papers, Journals and Magazines.

(Hindi, Urdu and English)

1. *Hamari Tauhid*, Arbaiyn/97, Asaf-ud Daulah Aur Azādāri, Special Number, Chief Editor: Naqvī, Sibte Mohammad, Tauhid Prakashan Kendra, Imāmbārah, Ghufran Ma'ab, Mawlana Kalbe Husayn Marg, Lucknow (Hindi).
2. *Islah Sadi* Number, 1999 (Urdu).
3. *Islamic Culture*, Hyderabad (English).
4. *Journal of K.R. Cama Oriental Institute'*, Bombay,1937.
5. *Khandan E-Ijtihad* Number, Editor: Sayyid Mustafa Husayn Asif Jaisi, [Noor-e-Hidayat Foundation, Imāmbārah Ghufran Ma'ab, Lucknow], December 2004; 2007; 2008 and 2009. (Urdu).
6. *Naya Daur*, Awadh-Number, Feb-March, 1994 (Urdu), Publication Divison, Lucknow, U.P.
7. *PDF.academia.edu*. [English].
8. *Shua-E-Amal*, (Monthly, Bilingual journal), Editor : Saiyyid Mustafa Husayn Naqvi, Asif Jaisi, Noor-e-Hidayat Foundation, Imāmbārah Ghufran Ma'ab, Lucknow, 16, volumes (Urdu & Hindi).
9. *Social Scientist*, 1998. (English).
10. *Tauhid-4, Madinat ul-Ilm-* Number, November, 1986, Editor: Naqvī, Sibte Mohammad, Imambarah, Ghufran Ma'ab, Mawlana Kalbe Husayn Road, Lucknow. (Hindi).
11. *The Hindustan Times*, Lucknow-Edition, February 4,1998. (English).
12. *The Noor*, An Islamic Research Journal, Editor: Dr. Sadiq Naqvī, Hyderabad (English).
13. *The Times of India*, Lucknow-Edition, August 4, 2004. (English).

Illustrations

The Muharram Commemoration-Asaf ud-Daula, Nawab of Oudh listening to maulvi reading at night from the scriptures 1795 AD.

Lord Hastings' party in an elephant Muharram procession approaching the Rumi Darwaza in Lucknow,1814 AD.

Muharram procession at Varanasi-1831

Gate of Fatimaan

Fatimaan at Varanasi

The Shia Mosque of Gorakhpur

Scene of a majlis at Khailim Qada, Gorakhpur

Reciting soz in a majlis held at Khadim Qadā, Gorakhpur

Scene of a Majlis at Shia Imāmbārah of Gorakhpur (2021 AD)

A Scene of Shia procession at Gorkahpur

Immersion of Tazias in the river on 10th Muharram

Immersion of Tazias on 10th Muharram at Gorakhpur during rainy season

A Shia Procession at Gorakhpur

A Muharram Scene of Patna 1807 AD.

Index